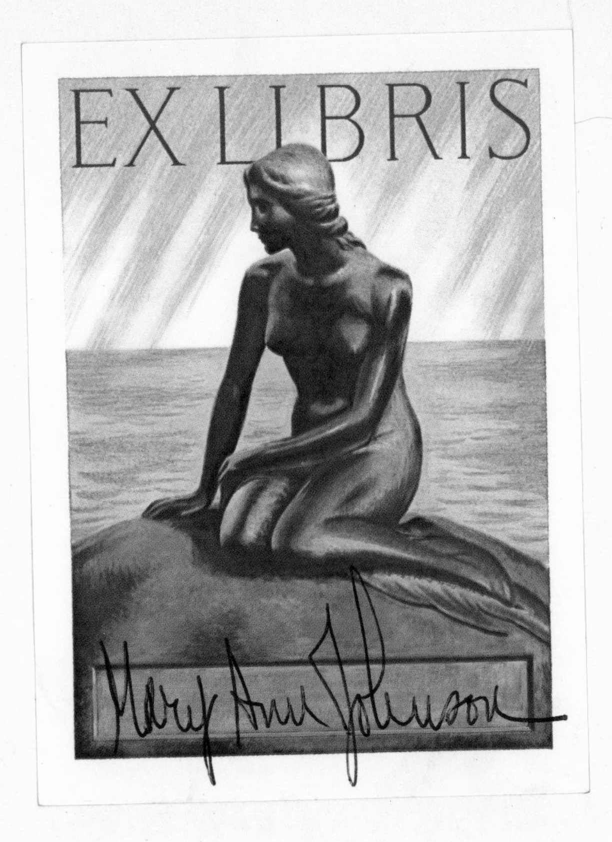
EX LIBRIS
Mary Ann Johnson

HISTORY'S 100 GREATEST COMPOSERS

HISTORY'S 100 GREATEST COMPOSERS

BIOGRAPHIES BY HELEN L. KAUFMANN

PORTRAITS BY SAMUEL NISENSON

GROSSET & DUNLAP · PUBLISHERS

New York

LIBRARY OF CONGRESS CATALOG CARD NUMBER 57-10568

PRINTED IN THE UNITED STATES OF AMERICA

A WORD FROM THE AUTHOR

"Greatness," said the pianist Godowsky. "There is no such thing as a great man. A few are less insignificant than the rest, that is all." This is one way of saying that greatness is impossible to define, even by a man who is himself great. Wherein does a composer's greatness lie? Is it in the quality of his work or in the quantity, in its originality or conformity, in its wide acceptance or in the approval of the few experts, or does greatness, as some cynics suggest, depend on how long the man has been dead? Great is a word that is freely used and abused.

Obviously it would be presumptuous for any author to make his own arbitrary selection of History's 100 Greatest Composers. It was decided, therefore, to call on the aid of America's music critics, countrywide, to make the selection. The friendly interest displayed by these busy men and women, some of whom wrote letters explaining their choices, is deeply appreciated. The selection of the subjects presented here is not the author's, although she found that it very closely paralleled the selection she would have made. Among the critics' ballots there was surprising unanimity on some composers, surprising disagreement on others, but in the American democratic tradition the majority was allowed to rule, even though it brought wistful backward glances at some names that were eliminated by the vote, especially those of some earnest and inspired living composers.

In writing biographies to complement Mr. Nisenson's perceptive portrait sketches, we have aimed to bring to life the man behind the music, to make him a fellow human being, though he does happen to be great. It has been enjoyable, while writing, to live for a time with the great composers in "the realm where magic rules."

Helen L. Kaufmann
Mackenzie Farms, Hampton, New Jersey

THE CRITICS CAST THEIR VOTES

THE AUTHOR, ARTIST AND PUBLISHER wish to thank these music critics of America's major newspapers for selecting the 100 subjects of the biographical sketches in this book.

In any culture where music is as alive as it is in America today, no one should expect those who deal with the art in the close, active way of working newspapermen to reach any sort of unanimity on a matter so many-faceted—and so fascinating—as selecting History's 100 Greatest Composers. Naturally, then, the composers treated here do not represent the selection of any one of the advisers listed below. Indeed, individually each critic may have found one or another cause for surprise if not chagrin in the results of the consensus of his colleagues.

The reader may also be astonished to find his favorite composer missing or his musical anathema honored here, but we are sure he will find as much fascination—and satisfaction—in this representation of American taste as have those who created the book.

The role of the musical experts listed here was confined to the selection of the composers to be included. They are in no way responsible for the treatment of the subjects in either picture or text.

PHIL BARNEY, *Tampa Tribune*
GEORGE KENT BELLOWS, *Baltimore Evening Sun*
CLIFFORD BLOOM, *Des Moines Register*
COL. L. R. BOALS, *Youngstown Vindicator*
ETHEL BOROS, *Cleveland News*
ED BROOKS, *New Orleans Times-Picayune*
MARTIN W. BUSH, *Omaha World-Herald*
J. DORSEY CALLAGHAN, *Detroit Free Press*
MARTIN CLARK, *Portland Oregon Journal*
EVANS CLINCHY, *Hartford Times*
ARTHUR DARACK, *Cincinnati Enquirer*
WILLIAM W. DAVENPORT, *Honolulu Advertiser*
JOSEPHINE M. DAVIDSON, *Phoenix Arizona Republic*
ROGER DETTMER, *Chicago American*
CHARLES L. DUFOUR, *New Orleans Times-Picayune-States*
CYRUS DURGIN, *Boston Globe*
RUDOLPH ELIE, *Boston Herald*
MARJORY M. FISHER, *San Francisco News*
GABRIEL FONTRIER, *Long Island Press*
CLIFFORD GESSLER, *Oakland Tribune*
ALMA GOWDY, *Los Angeles Herald-Express*
HILMAR GRONDAHL, *Portland Oregonian*
LOUIS R. GUZZO, *Seattle Times*
EDWARD P. HALLINE, *Milwaukee Sentinel*
JOHN H. HARVEY, *St. Paul Dispatch* and *Pioneer Press*
ANN HOLMES, *Houston Chronicle*
FRANK HRUBY, *Cleveland Press*
HENRY S. HUMPHREYS, *Cincinnati Times-Star*
ANNA C. HUNTER, *Savannah Morning News*
ALEX H. JOINER, JR., *Atlanta Constitution*
MYLES KASTENDIECK, *New York Journal-American*
JACK FREDERICK KILPATRICK, *Dallas Times Herald*
GEORGE H. KIMBALL, *Rochester Times-Union*
FRANCIS A. KLEIN, *St. Louis Globe-Democrat*
JOHN F. KYES, *Worcester Gazette*
RALPH LEWANDO, *Pittsburgh Press*
J. FRED LISSFELT, *Pittsburgh Sun-Telegraph*
ROBERT C. MARSH, *Chicago Sun-Times*
RAYMOND MORIN, *Worcester Telegram*
CLYDE B. NEIBARGER, *Kansas City Star*
CORBIN PATRICK, *Indianapolis Star*
DORIS RENO, *Miami Herald*
HAROLD ROGERS, *Christian Science Monitor*
IRVING SABLOSKY, *Chicago Daily News*
CHARLES SCARBOROUGH, *Richmond News Leader*
EDWIN H. SCHLOSS, *Philadelphia Inquirer*
FRANK G. SCHMIDT, *South Bend Tribune*
JULIAN SEAMAN, *Toledo Blade*
JOHN K. SHERMAN, *Minneapolis Star*
KATHERINE SKOGSTAD, *Atlanta Journal*
OSCAR SMITH, *Akron Beacon Journal*
DONALD STEINFIRST, *Pittsburgh Post-Gazette*
HARVEY TAYLOR, *Detroit Times*
ALINE JEAN TREANOR, *Daily Oklahoman*
WARNER TWYFORD, *Norfolk Virginian-Pilot*
EMMA VAN WORMER, *Syracuse Herald-Journal* and *Herald-American*
JOHN L. VOORHEES, *Seattle Post-Intelligencer*
WELDON WALLACE, *Baltimore Sun*
DOUGLAS WATT, *New York News*
E. CLYDE WHITLOCK, *Fort Worth Star-Telegram*
WALTER WHITWORTH, *Indianapolis News*
SAMUEL T. WILSON, *Columbus Dispatch*

CONTENTS

ALBENIZ, ISAAC 1
BACH, CARL PHILIPP EMANUEL . . 2
BACH, JOHANN SEBASTIAN 3
BARBER, SAMUEL 5
BARTOK, BELA 6
BEETHOVEN, LUDWIG VAN 8
BERG, ALBAN 10
BERLIOZ, HECTOR 11
BERNSTEIN, LEONARD 13
BIZET, GEORGES 14
BLOCH, ERNEST 15
BOCCHERINI, LUIGI 17
BORODIN, ALEXANDER 18
BRAHMS, JOHANNES 20
BRITTEN, BENJAMIN 22
BRUCH, MAX 23
BRUCKNER, ANTON 24
BYRD, WILLIAM 25
CHAUSSON, ERNEST 27
CHAVEZ, CARLOS 28
CHERUBINI, LUIGI 29
CHOPIN, FREDERIC 30
COPLAND, AARON 32
CORELLI, ARCANGELO 34
COUPERIN, FRANCOIS 36
DEBUSSY, CLAUDE ACHILLE . . . 37
DELIUS, FREDERICK 39
DONIZETTI, GAETANO 40
DUKAS, PAUL 41
DVORAK, ANTONIN 42
ELGAR, EDWARD 44
ENESCO, GEORGES 45
FALLA, MANUEL DE 46
FAURE, GABRIEL 48
FOSTER, STEPHEN 49
FRANCK, CESAR 50
GERSHWIN, GEORGE 52
GLINKA, MICHAEL 54
GLUCK, CHRISTOPH WILLIBALD . . 55
GOUNOD, CHARLES 57
GRANADOS, ENRIQUE 59
GRIEG, EDVARD 60
GRIFFES, CHARLES T. 62
HANDEL, GEORGE FREDERICK . . 63
HARRIS, ROY 65
HAYDN, FRANZ JOSEPH 66
HERBERT, VICTOR 68
HINDEMITH, PAUL 69
HONEGGER, ARTHUR 71
INDY, VINCENT D' 72
IVES, CHARLES 73
KHATCHATOURIAN, ARAM 74
KODALY, ZOLTAN 75
LASSUS, ORLANDUS 76
LEONCAVALLO, RUGGIERO 77
LISZT, FRANZ 78
LULLY, JEAN BAPTISTE 80
MacDOWELL, EDWARD 82
MAHLER, GUSTAV 84
MASCAGNI, PIETRO 85
MASSENET, JULES 86
MENDELSSOHN, FELIX BARTHOLDY . 87
MENOTTI, GIAN-CARLO 89
MILHAUD, DARIUS 90
MONTEVERDI, CLAUDIO 91
MOZART, WOLFGANG AMADEUS . . 93
MUSSORGSKY, MODEST 95
OFFENBACH, JACQUES 97
PALESTRINA,
GIOVANNI PIERLUIGI DA 98

PERGOLESI, GIOVANNI 100
PROKOFIEFF, SERGEI 101
PUCCINI, GIACOMO 102
PURCELL, HENRY 103
RACHMANINOFF, SERGEI 105
RAMEAU, JEAN PHILIPPE 107
RAVEL, MAURICE 108
RESPIGHI, OTTORINO 109
RIMSKY-KORSAKOFF, NIKOLAI . . . 110
ROSSINI, GIOACCHINO 112
SAINT-SAENS, CHARLES CAMILLE . 114
SCARLATTI, DOMENICO 115
SCHONBERG, ARNOLD 117
SCHUBERT, FRANZ 118
SCHUMANN, ROBERT 120
SHOSTAKOVITCH, DMITRI 122
SIBELIUS, JEAN 124
SMETANA, BEDRICH 125
SOUSA, JOHN PHILIP 127
STRAUSS, JOHANN 128
STRAUSS, RICHARD 129
STRAVINSKY, IGOR 131
SULLIVAN, SIR ARTHUR 133
TCHAIKOWSKY, PETER ILITCH . . . 134
VAUGHN WILLIAMS, RALPH 136
VERDI, GIUSEPPE 137
VILLA-LOBOS, HEITOR 139
VIVALDI, ANTONIO 140
WAGNER, RICHARD 141
WEBER, CARL MARIA VON 143
WOLF, HUGO 145

HISTORY'S
100
GREATEST COMPOSERS

ISAAC ALBENIZ

OF ALL THE five children of Senor and Senora Albéniz, none gave more trouble than Isaac. His older sister taught him to play the piano so well that he gave a concert in Barcelona when he was four, but after that he was often in mischief. Every once in a while he would run away from home and someone would have to find him and bring him back.

He was six when his father optimistically took him to Paris to enter him in the Conservatoire. His playing impressed the judges very favorably, but just as they were about to tell his father so, Isaac whirled the piano stool around, took a hard rubber ball from his blouse, and threw it with full force. It shattered the mirror in the room, and with the mirror, all hope of his being accepted as a student. "He's too young anyway," said Senor Albéniz philosophically, and sent him to study at the Conservatory of Madrid.

But when he was nine he ran away again, this time for a long absence. Eventually he drifted to Havana, and was playing the piano in one of its many night-spots, when his father found out where he was. Senor Albéniz wrote to his son, and offered him lessons with the best teacher if he would come home. This was an offer that Isaac could not resist. At twelve, he had sowed his wild oats—or most of them. He returned, studied for a year in Leipzig, and then attended the Conservatory of Brussels.

After graduation, he toured the U. S. in joint recitals with the pianist Anton Rubinstein. From then on, he led a busy life as virtuoso and composer. In the twelve years from 1880 to 1892, he composed some two hundred and fifty piano pieces for his own nimble fingers, including the swinging *Seguidillas* and *Tango in D.*

He was as prodigal with money as with music, and gave or lent to anyone who asked for it. He sold the copyright of his *Pavana* for the price of a bullfight ticket. He could always write another piece if he needed money! While he was conductor at the Prince of Wales Theater in London in 1892, he composed during rehearsals, and threw the sheets to a copyist as fast as he finished them.

The following year, he settled in Paris with his wife and three children, and worked with equal industry at composing and enjoying life. He studied French musical trends and accepted impressionism with enthusiasm. His friends were Debussy, Chausson, Fauré, d'Indy, and Dukas, and the Spanish pianist Arbós, his best friend, who lived around the corner. They all made music together.

Dukas described Albéniz as "a landscape painter with a rich palette, a generous man with his colors as with his money, the sort who, for fear five cents on a letter was not enough, would put on ten." His piano compositions are his most lasting contribution. The piano suite, *Iberia,* which consists of twelve pieces representing twelve Spanish provinces, has been called a "gallery of paintings in tone."

He died of Bright's disease, possibly as a result of hardships during his boyhood escapades. His death marked the end of the first period of the renaissance of Spanish music.

Born Camprodón, Spain, May 29, 1860
Died Cambo-les-Bains, France, May 18, 1909

CARL PHILIPP EMANUEL BACH

IF A MAN follows closely in the footsteps of an illustrious father, he is likely to become a pale imitation. If he breaks a new trail, he may get lost, and end in oblivion. Carl Philipp Emanuel, the fifth of Johann Sebastian Bach's twenty children, one of four who lived to manhood, was his father's son to the extent of preferring music to law as a career. But he was contemptuous of the "learned" music of his respected parent, and described a canon as "a dry and despicable piece of pedantry," which anyone would be capable of creating. As for counterpoint, he believed that "Many more essential things than counterpoint are wanting to constitute a good composer."

Despite his rebellious views, oblivion was not his fate. He kicked over the paternal traces, but he became the mentor of Haydn and Mozart, his art songs became the inspiration of Schubert, and appreciative keyboard performers recognize in him the father of modern piano playing.

For most of his life he was the biggest frog in a rather small puddle. When he was twenty-four, he was appointed court musician to the flute-playing Frederick the Great, King of Prussia.

While in Berlin, Carl Philipp Emanuel wrote the first methodical treatise in existence on *The True Manner of Keyboard Performance,* based on principles derived from his father and developed by himself and others. Mozart commented admiringly, "He is the father, we are the children." The historian Burney, who visited Carl in Berlin, could not praise his piano improvisations highly enough, and remarked on the "wild, careless manner in which he threw away thoughts that would have set up anyone else."

In 1767, the Seven Years' War summoned King Frederick from flute playing to fighting. Carl had been longing for more tranquility and independence than his autocratic monarch permitted, and had several times tried in vain to break away. Now the war, and the death at the same time of his godfather Philipp Telemann in Hamburg, opened the way. Carl applied for Telemann's church position and was accepted.

For the twenty-one remaining years of his life, he lived contentedly in Hamburg. He was made musical director of five large churches and was far and away the most remarkable pianist in the town. He is described as having been a rather short man, with black hair and eyes and a dark complexion. He was animated and cheerful and very witty. His home became the musical center of Hamburg and the neighboring towns. But his reputation did not extend far afield, and when Haydn, who esteemed him highly, came to Hamburg to visit him in 1795, Carl had been dead for seven years without the news having reached Vienna!

"It appears to me that it is the special province of music to move the heart," he said. In more than two hundred clavier pieces, fifty clavier concertos, eighteen symphonies for orchestra, and an immense number of chamber music and religious works, he proved his point. He was one of the first, if not the first, to use the sonata form, which emphasized melody, phrase, and figure, all of them aids to the expression of feeling. He had a genius for clear and orderly expression. And he had the good fortune to be born at a time when musical style was changing, new standards were coming to the fore, and he could participate in the change with all the power of his genius.

Born Weimar, Germany, March 8, 1714
Died Hamburg, Germany, December 14, 1788

JOHANN SEBASTIAN BACH

JOHANN SEBASTIAN BACH's son called him "Old Perruque." King Frederick of Prussia called him "Old Bach." But this serious composer was once young, even if there is no record of his having been very gay.

He was "called" to music as doctors are to medicine and preachers to the ministry. In the little German town of Eisenach where he was born, and in towns for miles around, there had been so many musical Bachs that the word "Bach" had come to mean musician. It seems strange, then, that the older brother to whom his education was entrusted should have spanked him when he found him in the attic, at the age of ten, diligently copying music by moonlight.

This did not deter young Johann from learning to play the organ and clavichord and to sing in the choir, so that by the time he was fifteen, he could assume the responsibility of supporting himself. He held several organist positions in towns which lay fairly close together, so that he could walk from one to another.

There is a story that on a long hike he passed an inn where a nobleman sat eating herring and throwing herring heads from the window. Bach, hungry like most boys, picked up a herring head and started to munch on it, whereupon the nobleman graciously stuffed a gold-piece into the next one and tossed it out. At any rate, Bach did not starve.

At twenty-two, he married his cousin, Maria Barbara Bach, and settled in Weimar under the patronage of Duke William Ernst. Here he lived for nine years, during which his fame as an organist grew. In fact, when a contest with another favorite organist, Marchand, was arranged in Dresden, Bach was there, ready to do his part, but his opponent, unwilling to challenge comparison with so renowned a performer, left town before the appointed day.

Bach was obliged to repair the organ in the church with his own hands before he could play on it the magnificent series of organ works that belong to his "Weimar period." The preludes, fugues and toccatas, the *Little Organ-Book,* and many others attest to his ambition to make music in the church an eloquent plea for the religion that was his rod and staff.

When he was invited to a more worldly post, the court of Prince Leopold, in Cothen, he found a close-knit little orchestra of eighteen excellent players awaiting him. Prince Leopold himself played in the orchestra, which Bach directed. The six *Brandenburg Concertos,* the suites and many other beautiful works for small orchestra stem from these happy days. Works for the clavichord and harpsichord also abound. Bach is credited with the present tempered system of tuning these instruments, also with discovering the value of using the thumb in playing them. For his growing family he composed in Cothen the *Little Preludes and Inventions* which are the delight of the young pianist today. *The Well-Tempered Clavier, Part I,* the *English and French Suites,* the *Chromatic Fantasy and Fugue* are clavier works which sound as well on the modern piano as on the delicate instruments for which they were written.

He enjoyed life at the court of the admiring and indulgent Prince Leopold. But his wife, Maria Barbara, died in 1721, leaving him with four small children. Soon after this, the prince took unto himself a princess who cared not a whit for "Old Bach" and his music. When Bach heard that the position of cantor in the St. Thomas School in Leipzig was open, he hastened to apply for it. To prove his fitness, he conducted his *St. John's Passion* in the church there and was subsequently rewarded with the appointment he sought. He was expected to teach singing and instrumental music, Latin, and Luther's catechism in the school on week days; to rehearse the choirs of four churches; to lead the choirs at funerals and weddings; to conduct a cantata every Sunday, and to supply new works as needed.

To this staggering assignment we owe the magnificent Passions — *St. John's, St. Matthew's* and *St. Mark's;* the great Masses; the *Christmas, Easter* and *Ascension* Oratorios; and any number of cantatas, chorales, motets, and other religious music. For the harpsichord and clavichord (he never saw a piano until he was sixty), he composed in Leipzig such well-known works as the *Goldberg Variations* (written to order to put a rich millionaire to sleep!); *Six Partitas;* the *Italian Concerto;* the second part of *The Well-Tempered Clavier,* and *The Art of the Fugue.*

Before moving to Leipzig, he took a second wife, the gentle young Anna Maddalena. Many were the happy evenings he spent in his big armchair, with his mug of ale, his pipe, and perhaps a child or two on his lap, while Anna Maddalena and the children played and sang. Sometimes he would lead them in a "quodlibet," a jam session in which they all improvised together. He was essentially a loving man, his love of family second only to his abiding love and faith in God. Of his twenty children, four sons survived, two of whom became distinguished musicians. His son Carl Philipp Emanuel became court musician to King Frederick of Prussia, in Potsdam.

"Old Bach is here," cried Frederick when Bach came to visit his son. He invited "Old Bach" to try his new Silberman piano, which the composer liked so much that he improvised a six-part fugue on a theme tossed to him by the king. When he returned to Leipzig he copied it out and sent it to Frederick with a letter of great humility, begging him to accept this "*Musical Offering.*" It is one of his most remarkable fugues.

Shortly after this visit, he was stricken with blindness. An operation aggravated his condition. For three long years he suffered, meanwhile composing from his bed songs of supplication and resignation. One of the last prophetically announced, "I stand before Thy throne, Oh Lord." A paralytic stroke was the final calamity, and with resignation he accepted the invitation extended in his chorale, "Come, sweet Death."

Born Eisenach, Germany, March 21, 1685
Died Leipzig, Germany, July 22, 1750

SAMUEL

BARBER

When Samuel Barber was about eight, he left a prophetic note on his mother's dressing-table, as follows: "To begin with, I was not meant to be an athlete, I was meant to be a composer and will be I am sure . . . don't ask me to try to forget this . . . and go and play football. – *Please*." His mother, a musician, knew that he was unusually talented and wished to keep his childhood as normal as possible. But for him, a normal childhood was one with plenty of music in it. He studied the piano, took a brief excursion with the cello, and reveled in the friendship of his aunt, the great contralto Louise Homer, and her composer-husband, Sidney Homer. Aunt Louise sang some of young Samuel's songs on her recital programs, Uncle Sidney gave him sound advice and criticism.

When the Curtis Institute of Music in Philadelphia opened its doors for the first time, in 1924, Samuel was one of the students privileged to attend. His first report card commented on his "extraordinary" gift for composition. He had been there for four years when Gian-Carlo Menotti arrived, and Samuel took Gian-Carlo under his wing. The newcomer spoke no English, and Samuel was one of the few students who could converse with him in French. The quiet, introspective Samuel enjoyed the volatility of Gian-Carlo, and soon the two teen-agers were visiting each other's homes in West Chester and in Italy. The friendship formed at the Curtis Institute has endured to this day; the two composers now share a house in Mt. Kisco, N. Y.

In 1928, Barber won the first of many prizes with a violin sonata submitted to Columbia University. He used the prize money for a summer trip to Europe, spent the summers of 1929 and 1930 with Menotti in the Italian village of Cadegliano, absorbed, composed, studied, and enjoyed life. When he was graduated from Curtis in 1933, he restated his early ambition: "Give me a quiet place to live, in the country, and a peaceful room with a piano in which to work, and I ask for nothing more." Nobody could give him this immediately, for the effects of the Depression were still felt, and the young man found work as a singer and taught for a time. But he soon went back to composing, helped by family and friends, by the unprecedented award of a Pulitzer scholarship for two successive seasons, by the interest of Toscanini, Ormandy, Reiner, and other conductors, and most of all by his own industry and serious devotion to his art.

His opera *Vanessa*, performed by the Metropolitan Opera Company, was widely acclaimed.

Many of his works have been recorded, among them the *Overture to the School for Scandal*, the *Sonata for Violoncello and Piano, Music for a Scene from Shelley, String Quartet, Adagio for Strings, Essay for Orchestra*, two symphonies, concertos for cello and violin, and so on. Since live performances, even of successful American composers, are not very frequent, it is good to know that Barber's works can be heard and studied on recordings. His biographer, Nathan Broder, says, "His work as a whole is like a living organism with a clearly stamped individuality, enriching itself as it grows."

Born West Chester, Pa., March 9, 1910
Lives Mt. Kisco, N. Y.

BELA BARTOK

THE ART of Béla Bartók was grounded in folksong, in the fine old peasant tunes rooted deep in Hungarian soil. He learned early to prefer them to the gypsy tunes commonly sung as genuine, for from the time he was a small boy, he was exposed more or less to both. His father died when he was eight, and his mother, a visiting music-teacher, took her son traveling with her from town to town and school to school. Finally, because she recognized his talent, and wished him to have an opportunity to hear and to study, she settled down in Pressburg in a steady position, and sent him to hear all the concerts and operas available. By this time, he had absorbed a great many folksongs.

He completed his education at the Royal Hungarian Music Academy in Budapest, where he remained until he was twenty-two. One day, he was visiting at a friend's country home, and followed the tempting odor of food into the kitchen. The barefooted cook stood by the stove, stirring a pot of goulash, and singing as she stirred. "Where did you learn that tune?" cried Bartók. "From my grandmother," she replied. Much excited, he begged her to repeat it, and while the goulash burned, he took down words and music.

Perhaps this incident fired his determination to make a collection of the folk music of his native land. He strapped a rucksack on his back, and with his friend Kodály, also a student at the Royal Academy, he sallied forth. For two years, at intervals, the young men went from one peasant's cottage to another, slept on floors of beaten earth, shared their hosts' black bread and cabbage soup, and collected Slovak and Rumanian, as well as native Magyar songs. Many of the melodies were based on ancient scales, and when Bartók turned to composition, he created new harmonies based on these scales. Eventually, he published a large volume of folk songs, entitled *Hungarian Folk Music,* and a number of smaller collections, giving full credit to Kodály, whose biography he later wrote.

At twenty-six, he became professor of piano at Budapest Conservatory. He and Kodály founded the progressive-minded New Hungarian Music Society, in opposition to the stand-pat Philharmonic Society. Bartók's early compositions gradually became known in France and England, though not immediately in Hungary. But a performance of his pantomime ballet, *The Wooden Prince,* in 1917, of the one-act opera, *Duke Bluebeard's Castle,* and finally of his *Second String Quartet* awakened his countrymen's interest. After the First World War, his fame spread rapidly. His works include orchestral and choral compositions, six string quartets, concerti for piano, violin and viola, the inimitable *Music for Two Pianos and Percussion,* songs, the piano suite *Mikrokosmos* and numerous other pieces for piano. *Mikrokosmos* was written for his young son Tibor and is a "must" for young pianists as well as a favorite concert number, because of its sometimes witty, sometimes philosophical, sometimes rousing commentary on the world we live in.

When the Second World War drove Bartók and his pretty young wife, a pianist, to the United States, the struggle for existence became acute. An honorary degree of Doctor of Music from Columbia University was no help in paying bills. He and his wife played two-piano recitals, but the wolf was never far from their door. Then he became very ill, and found himself unable to compose, or to play, or to plan. One day, as he lay in his hospital bed, brooding hopelessly, the conductor Serge Koussevitzky tiptoed in. After the usual greetings, Koussevitzky said, "I am permitted to stay for only a few minutes. But I want to ask you—the Koussevitzky Foundation wishes to commission a work from you in memory of my wife, Natalie. Can you, will you—?" In a spurt of energy, the sick man raised himself on his pillows, and stammered his joyful acceptance. Koussevitzky left his cheque, happy that his stratagem to help without hurting Bartók's pride had succeeded. From that day on, the composer improved. In a few weeks, he was able to travel to Florida, where he settled in a small room, with no piano. Here he composed his *Third Concerto* for Piano and Orchestra, his supreme effort, his crowning achievement, his swan song. In it are to be found the riotous rhythms, aggressive percussion, shattering dissonances, the intense dynamism and power characteristic of his works as a whole, all so strangely at variance with his shy, sensitive, withdrawn personality. After the completion of the concerto, he again took to his bed, and shortly died. His son Tibor, grown to manhood, devotes himself to the publication and recording of the compositions of this outstanding Hungarian composer of the twentieth century.

Born Nagyszentmikos, Hungary, March 25, 1881
Died New York, September 26, 1945

LUDWIG VAN BEETHOVEN

THERE IS MORE shadow than sunshine in the life of that Titan of composers, Ludwig van Beethoven. Before he was four, his father started to teach him to play the violin and piano. Ludwig could not remember the time when his father was not standing over him with a cane to rap his knuckles when he made a mistake. Johann van Beethoven was determined to force his son to become a child prodigy like Mozart, but Ludwig's genius was slower to ripen. Poverty, hard work and family responsibility robbed the boy of a happy childhood.

His mother was the only woman he ever deeply loved, and she died when he was seventeen. His father's lapse thereafter into idleness and drunkenness made Ludwig the head of the family. At twelve he had become court organist, then court pianist and violist in the orchestra of the Elector of Bonn. Soon the fame of his piano improvisations spread beyond his home town. A brief visit to Vienna in the hope of studying with Mozart came to nothing, though Mozart's verdict was, "Watch that young man, some day he will make a noise in the world."

Not until he was twenty-two and had moved to Vienna to study with Haydn, did his career as a composer get under way. In the enchanted city of Vienna he found noble patrons who exclaimed over the improvisations that poured from his blunt-fingered, hairy hands. They took lessons from him too, and paid him well for the works he composed for their private orchestras and string quartets. The Prince and Princess Lichnowsky invited him to live in their palace, gave him an annual income and four fine stringed instruments, and set the fashion of condoning the many eccentricities of his genius.

The clumsy, swarthy young country bumpkin dressed carelessly, came to meals late or not at all, left the piano in a huff if anyone talked while he played, and was quiveringly sensitive to real or fancied slights. But his music made up for all shortcomings. During those first years in Vienna, a flood of pieces for various instruments and combinations poured from his pen: the *Kreutzer Sonata* for violin, the *Moonlight* and *Pathetic* sonatas and three concertos for piano; the first six string quartets, the *First* and *Second Symphonies* for orchestra. This was music liberated from conventional trammels, free as music had seldom been — original, expressive and powerful. By the time he was thirty-one, publishers were vying for his works, in which they recognized a new and authoritative voice. His notebooks teemed with scrawled ideas and parts of ideas. He thriftily banked in them the treasure that was to bring him rich dividends when, after turning it over and over, he invested it in his compositions.

At thirty-one he became painfully aware of the most calamitous infirmity that could befall a musician. He was growing deaf. Walking in the country with his pupil, Fritz Ries, he failed to hear the sound of a nearby shepherd's pipe. He was thrown into a panic. Pills and panaceas proved of no help. A period of solitude in Heiligenstadt gave him the blues. He contemplated suicide and in his will, the famous Heiligenstadt Testament, he explained why.

He did not become totally deaf until his fiftieth year, but after 1804 the buzzing in his ears grew progressively worse. When he realized that there was nothing to be done, he vowed, "I will take Fate by the throat. My infirmity shall not get me down." He could still hear music in his mind, if not always with his ears. In a burst of creativity, he returned from Heiligenstadt to Vienna to compose the *Eroica Symphony (No. III)*, and his only opera, *Fidelio*. His *Fourth* and *Fifth Piano Concertos*, his *Fourth, Fifth, Sixth, Seventh* and *Eighth Symphonies;* the great *Rasumowsky Quartets,* and countless other works were wrung from him during the decade from 1804 to 1814, and still he poured ideas into the notebooks.

Creation with Beethoven was no easy, lighthearted process. He toiled over every measure, sitting at his untidy desk, which was littered with rusty pens, half-eaten food, and dirty socks. He lumbered through the streets of Vienna, pushing aside those who got in his way. He wandered in the beautiful countryside where he forgot to eat or sleep when he became lost in the stars. Or he raged up and down his room in the very agony of creation.

There are those who believe that it is because, not in spite of his deafness that Beethoven's genius burned so intensely and that he became the exponent of emotion and expressivity, the massive link between the classic and the romantic composers.

The years from 1815 until his death were far from happy. He never married, though he was often in love, and his household, he said wryly, "resembled a shipwreck." Most old bachelors become crotchety, and Beethoven's difficult disposition and deafness made him the more so. He adopted his nephew Karl, a source of endless worry and expense. Yet, despite his troubles, he composed two of his greatest works during these years, the mammoth *Ninth Symphony* with its choral movement, and the *Solemn Mass.*

They were performed at a concert, with Beethoven himself conducting. The mighty roar of soloists, chorus, orchestra and organ thrilled the audience, but Beethoven could not hear a sound. At the end, the listeners burst into loud applause; Beethoven was still beating the time. Not until one of the singers turned him gently to face the audience did he *see* the applause. With tears coursing down his cheeks, he bowed his acknowledgment. This was his last public appearance (1824).

He contracted pneumonia when, in December 1826, he drove with his nephew Karl in an open carriage from his brother Johann's suburban home to Vienna. His health had always been poor, despite his rugged frame. Now weakness intensified the jaundice and dropsy from which he suffered. On an afternoon in March 1827 he lay unconscious. A terrific storm was raging. There was a mighty thunderclap. Beethoven opened his eyes, lifted a clenched fist and shook it in that spirit of protest and rebellion that ended only with his death.

A revolutionist who created faster than he destroyed, a champion of the people, he "made music broadly human, he left it superhuman."

Born in Bonn, Germany, December 16, 1770
Died in Vienna, Austria, March 26, 1827

ALBAN BERG

Alban Berg grew up in a comfortable home in Vienna, where books and music were his familiar friends. His older brother and sister took music lessons from which Alban profited so much that when he was fifteen, he started to compose. He had no idea of making music his profession until, four years later, he met Arnold Schönberg, who was teaching in Vienna. This meeting changed the course of Alban's life. Schönberg's twelve-tone system, his individual style and form, were music to Berg's ears. Firmly he abandoned a conventional career as a government employe to become Schönberg's disciple. Without slavishly following his master's lead, he accepted enough of his teaching to influence the spiritual trend of his own work and to lay the foundation of his own original style.

That his idiom was as unpopular as Schönberg's in the beginning was evident at the performance in March 1913 of his first orchestral work, the *Altenberg Songs,* which Schönberg conducted. The audience so resented the strange and unfamiliar combinations of sounds, that they staged a near-riot. Nothing could be heard above the turmoil. The hall was cleared, the concert was cut short, and Berg had his taste of martyrdom.

The opera *Wozzeck,* which made him famous overnight, was an antidote to this experience. *Wozzeck* was inspired by a play he attended shortly before the outbreak of the First World War. The subject gave him no rest until he had set it to music, and he composed his opera mostly while serving in the army. The powerful appeal of the subject, the remarkable dramatic expressivity of the music, and above all, the originality of the writing brought triumphant success immediately to this difficult opera.

An amusing story is told in connection with *Wozzeck.* It appears that a zealous newspaper reporter wrote an article for a Viennese daily deploring the fact that the composer of *Wozzeck* was neglected and starving in a garret. Berg, highly amused, read the paragraph to a friend over the telephone and said, "Tonight we shall starve better than usual; come and starve with my wife and me." They went, in Berg's new car, to one of the best restaurants in Vienna for dinner. Berg paid the check.

After *Wozzeck,* he composed outstanding chamber music. When his *Lyric Suite* was performed at a concert of the International Society for Contemporary Music, the appreciative hush at the conclusion told more eloquently than applause of the profound effect on the audience.

During the last seven years of his life, he was engaged with a second opera, *Lulu.* Death overtook him before he had completed it, but the symphonic suite which he made of parts of the score is often performed.

One more work must be mentioned, the fiendishly difficult violin concerto, a requiem for a young girl who was very dear to him. It became his own requiem, for though it was completed in August 1935, it was not performed until after his death. In his final delirium, he talked of his unfinished *Lulu.* On Christmas Eve, he died, some years earlier than Schönberg.

The list of his compositions is small, but his contribution is large when measured in terms of sincerity, originality and power.

Born Vienna, Austria, February 9, 1885
Died Vienna, Austria, December 24, 1935

HECTOR BERLIOZ

NAPOLEON declared himself emperor the year that Hector Berlioz was born. The boy grew up in the strict atmosphere of a French bourgeois small town that gloried in Napoleon's victories and mourned his defeats. His father, a doctor, supervised his education at home, and his mother, an intensely religious woman, exercised rigid control over him and his sisters. Since he did not go to school until his eighteenth year, he had many solitary hours in which to develop the power and originality of thought that were to mark his music and make him a rebel against traditional rules.

He found a flageolet in a bureau drawer, and taught himself to play it so well that his father allowed him to take singing, flute and guitar lessons. There was no piano in the Berlioz home; in the early 1800's pianos were still a rarity. So, unlike most composers, Berlioz did not learn to play the piano, and later was refused a position as teacher of harmony at the Paris Conservatoire on this account!

When his father urged a medical career, his own suggestion that music was preferable went unheeded. A silver flute offered as a bribe if he would study medicine in Paris was the argument that finally induced him to bow to his father's wishes. Flute in hand, he climbed aboard the dusty stagecoach that was to take him to Paris. He began his new life in 1821, the year of Napoleon's death. He was eighteen.

"My first sight of the dissection room so filled me with horror that I jumped out of the nearest window and ran breathless all the way home," he wrote in his *Memoirs.* Yet he conscientiously attended lectures for a year, and at the same time heard every concert and opera to which he could beg, borrow or steal admission. Then, in the temporary closing of the medical school, he saw his opportunity to escape the hated dissecting-room forever. His announcement to his family that he intended to become a composer produced maternal hysterics, paternal disapproval, and united opposition from sisters, cousins and aunts. But he stood firm, became a student at the Paris Conservatoire, attended every musical performance in sight, and studied the scores carefully before and after each performance. "It's a piccolo, you wretch," he shouted when a passage scored for the piccolo was played on a flute, and "Where are the trombones?" when they failed to make their entrance on time.

Cherubini, the irascible Director of the Conservatoire, is said to have actually chased young Berlioz around the library table after the young man expounded his subversive ideas on harmony in the classroom. For three lean years after this, Cherubini voted against awarding Berlioz the Prix de Rome, and without pity, watched him struggle to keep alive on what he could earn as a chorus man while attending the Conservatoire.

The handsome Hector, with fiery blond hair and deepset, equally fiery blue eyes, was a romantic figure. But the English actress with whom he fell madly in love did not at first find him so. When he threw himself at Henrietta Smithson's feet at the entrance to the stage door and threatened to take poison if she did not marry him, she thought him quite mad.

He finally won the Prix de Rome and went to the Eternal City, only to return, homesick for Paris, before the year had expired. He was twenty-six when he gave his first concert in Paris, at which his prize-winning *Cantata* and new *Fantastic Symphony* were performed. The fair Henrietta, who had been in England, was in Paris by chance, and Berlioz invited her to the concert. The written narrative he supplied with the Symphony left no doubt that he intended the music to express his love, his disappointment, his resentment and scorn. The melodies were appealing, but the like of the stormy orchestration had never before been heard. The powerful brasses and tympani were a challenge to the ears of the public and the heart of his beloved. From his place at the tympani, Berlioz watched Henrietta, drowning in an ocean of sound. Worn down by his extraordinary wooing, she wearily consented to marry him, but the warmth of the romance cooled rapidly, and after a few years they lived apart.

The years of manhood were years of unending struggle: for bigger and better orchestras, for which he composed bigger and better works; for money to present his grandiose creations; for recognition. He was a prophet not without honor save in his own country. When he conducted his *Harold Symphony* in Paris in 1834, it was an Italian, Paganini, who rushed to congratulate him and who later sent him 20,000 francs for the magnificent viola obbligato it contained. At about the same time, the French government commissioned a *Requiem* for an official ceremony. He produced a most impressive work for soloists, chorus, organ and an enlarged orchestra which employed sixteen brasses instead of the usual four, an overwhelming volume of sound, dramatic rather than religious. It almost bankrupted him, for he paid out of his own pocket for the extra instruments.

The composer worked incessantly and augmented his income by writing brilliant musical criticism. His *Treatise on Orchestration and Instrumentation* has become a classic, though in it he advocates an orchestra of five hundred pieces! His oratorio *L'Enfance du Christ (The Infancy of Christ)* was a success in Paris, but to his operas and symphonic poems the Parisians turned a cold shoulder. His narrative symphony, the *Fantastic;* his dramatic symphony, *Romeo and Juliet,* and his "opéra de concert," *The Damnation of Faust,* fared somewhat better. In other countries, especially Germany and Russia, his compositions were hailed as works of genius, and he as an outstanding innovator. Mendelssohn, Schumann and Liszt spoke up for him in Germany. Moussorgsky, the Russian composer, said: "In music there are two giants, the thinker Beethoven and the super-thinker Berlioz."

Not only a super-thinker but a super-feeler, the composer ultimately broke down under a series of disasters. His second wife died in 1862. His opera *The Trojans in Carthage* was hissed at its first performance in Paris the following year. After later performances a friend reported to Berlioz, "People are beginning to come." "Yes," replied the ill and dispirited composer, "they are coming, but I am going."

The death of his son Louis in 1867 was the last straw. Berlioz went on a final tour to Russia, the scene of his greatest triumphs, and thence to Monaco, "to lie down among the violets and sleep in the sun." But the soft climate of southern France could not heal his broken heart, and he returned to Paris to die.

Born Côte-St.-André, France, December 11, 1803
Died Paris, France, March 8, 1869

LEONARD
BERNSTEIN

A BRIGHT, particular star in the galaxy of young American composers today is Leonard Bernstein. He refuses to become a specialist —one who knows more and more about less and less—but juggles five careers in music at once, and makes a success of all of them. He is a virtuoso pianist, a gifted conductor, a television star, a classroom teacher, and a businessman. All this and personal magnetism too!

His father Samuel, who at sixteen fled to America to escape the pogroms in Russia, is a scholarly idealist with both feet on the ground. By the time "Lennie" was born, Samuel was doing so well in the beauty-parlor business in Boston that he believed his son could do no better than to go into business with him. But when Lennie was eight and Samuel took him for the first time to the synagogue, something happened to the boy. He was so moved by the rolling organ tones and the singing of the choir that he wept. When he was ten a piano was installed in the Bernstein living room, described by Bernstein today as "a brown upright horror." Piano lessons continued through the Latin School and Harvard, and, after graduation, a course in conducting under Fritz Reiner at the Curtis Institute in Philadelphia.

But it was Serge Koussevitsky who gave "Lenyushka," as he affectionately called him, the kind of encouragement which made him a successful conductor in his twenties. He was a prodigy of twenty-five when, as assistant conductor of the New York Philharmonic, he conducted a Sunday afternoon broadcast on sixteen hours' notice because of the sudden indisposition of Arthur Rodzinski. After that, he conducted the New York City Symphony Orchestra, the Boston, Cincinnati, St. Louis, Israeli, and other orchestras.

He composed four symphonies. In the first, *Jeremiah,* completed in 1942, he turned to Hebrew liturgy, offering "along with Biblical rumblings and stylized Semitic murmurs, some beautifully sad and soaring melodies for soprano." It won the award of the Music Critics' Circle of New York as "the most outstanding orchestral work by an American composer heard in New York during 1943-44." His fourth symphony was also based on Hebrew liturgy—*Kaddish,* a prayer for the dead. Into his music, be it grave or gay, he poured his special individuality. He composed a delightful ballet, *Fancy Free,* which was the germ of a musical comedy, *On the Town.* He produced an opera, *Candide,* and though it was not a popular success, he announced confidently, "I am the logical man to write the great American opera." He continued. "I want to write symphonic music, I want to keep on trying to be, in the full sense of that wonderful word, a musician." On television he gave brilliant, musically illustrated lectures on such diverse subjects as modern music, Johann Sebastian Bach, light opera, and jazz, displaying, for the benefit of millions, the power of clear analysis, the cultural knowledge, and the enthusiasm which make teaching and learning a pleasure.

Born Lawrence, Mass., August 25, 1918
Living New York, N. Y.

GEORGES BIZET

When Georges Bizet selected as a subject for an opera a novel that had already sold many thousands, it seemed like a shrewd idea. That it backfired was no fault of his or his music. The Carmen of Prosper Mérimée's book, bad girl though she was, was good company. Bizet had no inkling, as he composed the Toreador Song which was to become as popular as "Yankee Doodle," that Carmen in an opera would rouse the bourgeoise wives of Paris to righteous indignation, while Carmen out of a yellow-backed novel had wheedled her wicked way straight into their husbands' hearts. Nor did he know that when the storm of disapproval died, his musical portrayal of the seductive cigarette girl would win worldwide acclaim as the perfect opera. His tragedy was that he died believing his greatest work to be a failure.

He was ill-prepared for disappointment, for his life had flowed smoothly, if not excitingly. His father, a singing teacher, recognized Georges' precocious talent and entered him in the Conservatoire when he was only nine. He was a good boy who did his homework diligently and came to his classes well prepared. For eleven years he remained at the Conservatoire, studying under the best teachers. Over the years he won a first prize for piano, another for organ, another for fugue. He was a thorough conformist: not for him the rebellion of a Berlioz or a Debussy.

At nineteen, the award of the Prix de Rome sent him for three contented years to the Villa Medici. Shortly after his return to Paris, he composed an opera, *The Pearl Fishers.* Only the Invocation was applauded; the rest, romantic and charming as it was, did not impress the public and the critics. But Bizet was only twenty-five. His marriage to the daughter of his composition professor, Halévy, was a happy one. Family ties now bound him to a teacher who was a helpful critic. He composed *La Jolie Fille de Perth;* a one-act opera, *Djamileh;* incidental music to a play, *L'Arlésienne;* piano works for two and four hands; two symphonies. *Carmen* was his masterpiece.

At its first performance in Paris, Bizet was in the opera-house, a quivering bundle of nerves. The applause after the first act was mild—neither approving nor disapproving, but as if judgment were being reserved. Bizet went out into the lobby, and encountered the composer d'Indy, who clapped him on the back and told him that his work was good. "You are the first who has said that, and I fancy you will be the last," said Bizet somberly. He left the house before the end of the opera and reported to his waiting family, "A deadly frost! An audience like ice! Not a single effect, nothing made a hit." The next day, the critics tore the opera limb from shapely limb. The music was condemned as—of all things—too Wagnerian on the one hand, not gypsy enough on the other. There was no mention of its clarity, its warm melodies, its lilting rhythm and general charm. The opera continued to run; it enjoyed thirty-seven performances the first season, a good record. But Bizet was inconsolable. For some time he had suffered from a heart ailment. Three months after the première, on the day of the twenty-third performance, he died.

Born Paris, France, October 25, 1838
Died Bougival, near Paris, France, June 3, 1875

ERNEST BLOCH

A LARGE AUDIENCE had assembled to hear Ernest Bloch's new piano quintet, and he was asked to make a few remarks explaining the work. "When a chicken comes to your table, do you ask whether it is fresh killed or cold storage?" he said. "You do not. You eat it. I ask you to do the same with my music. If it is good, you will like it without explanation; if not, no word of mine will make you enjoy it." He took his place at the piano and motioned the other artists to begin. The independent spirit of that speech is characteristic of Bloch the composer. His exuberant talent is magnificently free.

Bloch's parents were not musicians, but they permitted him to study the violin and he did the rest. He commuted from his home in Geneva to Brussels for lessons with the great Ysaye. In Geneva, he studied with Jacques Dalcroze. Later he went to Berlin to take composition with Iwan Knorr, who, he said, "taught me the greatest thing of all, to teach myself." For a while he found himself traveling in Switzerland and Germany, selling the cuckoo clocks his father manufactured, but he became known as a composer while still selling clocks. When his opera *Macbeth* was performed in Paris, he was thirty. Romain Rolland pronounced it one of the most important works of the modern school. It did not make Bloch's fortune, though it did confirm him in his decision to compose as a profession.

Maud Allan, the English dancer, met him in Paris and invited him to lead the orchestra going with her on a tour of American cities. Bloch, then thirty-six, regarded this as the opportunity that knocks only once. He accepted and was not a little dismayed when the tour failed and the manager left him stranded without funds in the middle of the U. S. A. But he worked and played his way back to New York, took a hall bedroom, and waited for a lucky break. It came soon. His *Suite for Viola and Piano* won the Coolidge prize at the Berkshire Festival of 1919. The Flonzaley Quartet performed his *Second String quartet in B minor* to a cheering audience. Soon after this, he was invited to conduct the Boston Symphony Orchestra in his *Trois Poèmes Juifs* (Three Jewish Poems). And finally, an all-Bloch program was given under the auspices of the Society of the Friends of Music. All this within one year of his coming to America! And it was not because his music was simple. The quarter-tones and dissonances caused one New England lady to remark of his quartet played by the Friends of Music, "Well, I don't call that being *friendly* to music."

For two years, he taught at the Mannes School in New York, then he directed the Cleveland Institute of Music. His main difficulty there was due to his habit of staying after classes in his office at the school to compose, forgetting the time, and being confronted at nightfall by an irate janitor who wanted to go home. Those hours were used to good purpose, for after four years in Cleveland and five more as director of the San Francisco Conservatory, he was able to devote himself entirely to composition.

He is best known for his compositions on Jewish themes, which are unique. In *Schelomo,* a Hebrew Rhapsody for violoncello and orchestra, he expresses the "magnificence, the pomp and sumptuousness of a king enthroned, along with the pessimistic despairing philosophy of the ruler." In the poignant *Israel Symphony,* the Wailing Wall of Jerusalem is the backdrop, dancers mime the drama of the Day of Atonement and other holy days, voices and orchestra complete the effective work.

Bloch wrote, "It is the Jewish soul that interests me, the complex, glowing, agitated soul that I feel vibrating throughout the Bible; the freshness and naiveté of the Patriarchs, the violence that is evident in the prophetic books; the Jew's savage love of justice; the despair of the Preacher in Jerusalem; the sorrow and the immensity of the Book of Job; the sensuality of the Song of Songs. All this is in me, and it is the better part of me. It is all this that I endeavor to hear in myself and to transcribe in my music; the venerable emotion of the race that slumbers way down in my soul."

At the nationwide celebration of Bloch's seventieth birthday there was no dearth of material for the all-Bloch programs presented in his honor. Until his death, at seventy-nine, he lived in semi-retirement in Oregon. But he continued to compose, and his works still glowed with their old youthful fire.

Born Geneva, Switzerland, July 24, 1880
Died Portland, Oregon, July 15, 1959

LUIGI

BOCCHERINI

Suppose a chamber music aficionado were asked on a quiz show to name the composer of a given string quartet. If it happened to be Luigi Boccherini, he should be forgiven if he named Haydn. There was such a strong affinity between these two contemporaries that their quartets are often mistaken. Haydn's many symphonies and oratorios are as famous as his quartets. Boccherini's fame, on the other hand, rests primarily on his chamber music, which comprises two octets, sixteen sextets, one hundred and twenty-five string quintets, twelve piano quintets, eighteen quintets for strings with wind, ninety-one string quartets, fifty-four string trios, and miscellaneous works galore. Whew! Besides these, there are four cello concertos, symphonies and other large works. The charming minuet always referred to as *the* Boccherini minuet, as though it were the only one he had ever written, is known all over the world.

Luigi's father, a double-bass player, taught him the elements of music, then sent him to Rome to study violin, cello and composition with the Abbé Vanucci. His education completed, Luigi formed a working partnership with the violinist Filippo Manfredi, and the two young men went gaily on a tour, giving joint violin and cello recitals. They landed in Paris and lingered there, tasting success, and enjoying the taste. The Spanish ambassador to France became one of a growing circle of their admirers and invited them to Madrid where, he assured them, the Prince of the Asturias would give them a royal welcome. Filled with pleasurable anticipation, they set out for Spain.

The Ambassador had reckoned without the whims of royalty. At first neither the prince nor the reigning king took any notice of their arrival in Madrid. But the king's brother, the Infante Don Luis, took Luigi under his wing and paid him a fat salary. Soon the king too became his patron; for his music was irresistible. Luigi settled down in the luxurious Spanish court, with nothing to do but write chamber music, play the cello and enjoy himself. He did all three in the grand manner until one day the king reproved him for a certain passage which he considered trite and hackneyed. Luigi promised to change it, but saucily repeated it, thinking His Majesty would not know the difference. His Majesty did – and Luigi was dismissed from the court. He transferred his activities to the court of Friedrich Wilhelm II of Prussia for a ten-year interim, during which Friedrich Wilhelm paid him a modest salary and monopolized his services.

When the Prussian king died, Luigi returned confidently to the scene of his former triumphs. Gone were the friends of yesteryear. In all Madrid, no patron came forward to bid for the services formerly so highly prized. A serious illness weakened Luigi, and his finances went from bad to worse. He could no longer play the cello, even found it difficult to compose. Prince Lucien Bonaparte was appointed French ambassador to Madrid and came to the rescue with a small salary. There was a brief flare-up of the old fire in Luigi. But Bonaparte was recalled, and now there was nobody for the tired man, old at sixty, to turn to. His last years present a sordid picture of poverty. He made guitar arrangements for amateurs and sold what he still could write for practically nothing. His death at sixty-two was a release.

Born Lucca, Italy, February 19, 1743
Died Madrid, Spain, March 28, 1805

ALEXANDER BORODIN

ALEXANDER BORODIN was the illegitimate son of a Russian prince, who indulged him in his desire to serve two exacting mistresses, music and medicine, during his early years as a student. Medicine became his profession, music his professional hobby. While doing a chemical experiment in the laboratory, he would hum or sing the original melodies that occurred to him, and in the midst of writing a treatise on chemistry, he would jot down the germs of his musical ideas. Music was ever present in his mind. He looked forward to summers, for it was then that he found the leisure for composition. During the winters, his musical friends jested with him. "I hope you are ill today," was their preferred greeting, for they knew that a bad cold which kept him indoors meant that he would add a few new pages to the quartet or symphony he was writing, or to his opera, *Prince Igor*.

Borodin was the youngest of "the Five" Russian nationalist composers, the others being César Cui, Mily Balakireff, Modest Mussorgsky, and Nicolai Rimsky-Korsakoff. All were amateurs in that they gained their livelihood partly in professions other than music. All believed passionately in their self-imposed mission to hold up a mirror that would reflect in music, their music, the complex Russian soul. Balakireff, the leader and mentor of the group, never allowed them to lose sight of this object.

Balakireff urged Borodin to write his first symphony, and Borodin's wife, a charming concert pianist, also encouraged him to an undertaking he had been too modest to attempt. No one was more surprised than he when the first symphony was well received. He promptly started to compose a second. Though the second, in B minor, took six years to complete, what with Borodin's busy life of practicing medicine and lecturing, he persevered. When the first performance was imminent, he could not find the first and last movements of the symphony, though he and his wife searched high and low. If he had not opportunely fallen ill, the music might have been lost forever, but a bad cold saved the day.

With a high temperature and a raging headache, he penciled the score of the vanished movements in bed, and had them ready in time for the performance in January 1876. "Never has a professor of the Academy of Medicine and Surgery been found in such a position," he declared. The following year, he visited Liszt in Weimar and played with him a four-handed transcription of the score. "It is vain to say there is nothing new under the sun," exclaimed Liszt. "This is quite new. . . . You have a quick and vital spring within you; the future belongs to you." Beautiful songs; two quartets; three symphonies; a symphonic poem, *On the Steppes of Central Asia;* and his unfinished opera, *Prince Igor,* complete the list of his compositions, brief but of great significance. The ferocity of the twelfth-century *Prince Igor* is well expressed in the splendid savage ballet of *Polovetzian Dances,* a feast for the eye and the ear.

The tall dark doctor with drooping moustaches lived in a rambling apartment on the ground floor of the St. Petersburg School of Medicine. He and his wife adopted a number of orphans and brought them up as their own. Because of his belief in women's rights, he founded the first School of Medicine for Women in Russia and taught there. He was a pioneer in scientific discoveries. He spent himself freely, perhaps too freely.

At a party in his home one evening, he sang and played parts of his new Third Symphony. He was in high spirits. He had written to his wife, who was in Moscow, "Tomorrow we have a musical party here. It will be very grand — but I must not unveil the mysteries." While talking with a friend at the party, he grew deathly pale and toppled forward. He was dead. Two wreaths mark his tomb. On one are inscribed chemical formulas and the titles of his scientific books, on the other musical themes and the titles of his compositions.

Born St. Petersburg, Russia, November 12, 1833
Died St. Petersburg, Russia, February 28, 1887

JOHANNES BRAHMS

"BRAHMS to see me – a genius" is the notation in Robert Schumann's diary when the twenty-year-old Johann paid his senior the first of many visits. It required less courage in 1853 to pronounce a man a genius than it does today and when Schumann voiced his opinion publicly, it was respected, as it had been in the case of Chopin.

Johann's father, an impecunious double-bass player in the Hamburg theater, educated the boy in music from his earliest years. Johann learned everything his father could teach him about the violin and cello, took piano lessons from one teacher and composition from another, practiced diligently, read every book he could lay hands on, covered reams of paper with exercises in harmony and counterpoint, and thus acquired an adequate education.

Bach and Beethoven were the composers on whom he modeled his style, but his classical leanings did not interfere when he was sent, at the age of nine, to play the piano for the entertainment of carousing patrons in the waterfront cafés of Hamburg. When he was fourteen, he appeared at a public concert, where he played pieces by Bach and Beethoven, and also a set of variations of his own.

There was a touch of the jolly gypsy in Brahms, which came to the surface when he went on tour as accompanist to Eduard Remenyi, a Hungarian violinist. With Remenyi, he wandered from town to town in Germany, and Remenyi took him along when he went to visit the famous violinist Joachim in Hanover. Joachim so strongly approved Johann's compositions that, unasked, he gave him letters of introduction to Liszt in Weimar and Schumann in Düsseldorf.

The visit to Liszt was not a success. Brahms listened attentively while Liszt played the composition he had brought to show him. But he fell sound asleep when Liszt followed it with a lengthy sonata of his (Liszt's) own. This could hardly be construed as a compliment. In later life, Liszt recalled the incident when, having generously applauded a Brahms work, he said to him, "As you do not like my compositions, I must give a double measure of admiration to yours."

The visit to Schumann, on the other hand, was a conspicuous success. It marked the foundation of a three-way mutual admiration society, consisting of Robert Schumann, his wife Clara, and Brahms. Schumann hailed Brahms as "a musical prophet, the like of whom he had never heard before." Clara, the finest pianist of the day in Europe, played Brahms' piano works better than he did himself and carried them to the public of the many cities she visited on her extensive tours. When Schumann died, in July 1856, it was to the twenty-three-year-old Brahms that Clara turned for comfort. They remained life-long friends. So close was the relationship between the mature Clara and the young man fourteen years her junior, that certain biographers believe that he remained a bachelor because of it.

It seems more in accord with his disposition to have remained a bachelor because all his life he resented any ties that deprived him of his freedom. "It is as hard to marry as to write an opera," he said, and so he never did either one. He worked best when there were no entangling alliances to hamper him, no deadline to be met, no sponsor to be consulted.

From 1854 to 1858 he lived in Detmold as conductor of the orchestra and teacher of the Princess Frederike. This left him plenty of time to wander about in the Teutoburger Forest, meditating on music, and plenty of time to read. During these years, he became a walking encyclopedia.

At twenty-nine, he went to Vienna to conduct the Singakademie. He wrote some fine choral works for this group, but resigned after a year, preferring to go his own way. Another engagement with the Gesellschaft der Musikfreunde (Society of Friends of Music) in Vienna ended the same way after three years.

He knew that he was at his best when he was working at a leisurely pace in his simple bachelor's quarters, alone. He rose every day at 5 A.M., prepared his own coffee because nobody else brewed it strong enough to suit him, and set to work. For recreation, there were walking trips, or gatherings of his friends and admirers, who called themselves "the Brahmins."

Although his works were on the whole well received, he had his moments of discouragement. On his fiftieth birthday, he stood at his writing-desk with blank paper before him, determined to start a symphony. No ideas came. "I am too old to compose any more," he mourned. "At fifty, a man is through." He laid down his pencil, pinned his plaid shawl over his shoulders, and went off to visit friends who had invited him to a birthday dinner in the country. Their affection, coupled with fresh asparagus and champagne, produced a better mood. After dinner, he went for a stroll and suddenly found himself singing a melody – F, A, F – to the words, "Frisch und frei." He hurried home and wrote it down at once. It became the main theme of his *Third Symphony in F major.*

Brahms was a painstaking composer, who worked over and over his pieces before he pronounced them finished. It was ten years from the time he started to write his *First Symphony* to the day when he allowed it to be published. The years in Vienna from 1874 to 1897 were uneventful in every way except in so far as they were punctuated by great works. His output comprises four symphonies; other works for orchestra including the *Academic Festival Overture* and the *Tragic Overture;* choral works such as the *German Requiem* and *Marienlieder;* numerous motets, canons and vocal ensembles; two hundred and thirty songs of unique beauty; two concertos for piano, one concerto for violin and one for cello; much chamber music; and pieces for a variety of instruments, especially the piano. His works have been compared to a gypsy woman dancing in a tight corset, "Latent heat beneath a formal exterior."

He caught a chill as he stood, bareheaded and grief-stricken at the funeral of his dear friend Clara Schumann, and it was only a few months until he followed her to the grave.

Born Hamburg, Germany, May 7, 1833
Died Vienna, Austria, April 3, 1897

BENJAMIN BRITTEN

BENJAMIN BRITTEN, a twentieth-century boy wonder, remained at fifty a wonder in respect to the quality and quantity and variety of his output, and the energy with which he engineered publication and performance. There was no Papa Mozart to keep his nose to the grindstone when he started composing at five, playing the piano at seven and so on. His father was a dental surgeon, and Benjamin was the youngest of four children. His mother was a singer, from whom he may have inherited his talent. At school in his early teens, he said he wrote "symphony after symphony, song after song, and a tone poem called *Chaos and Cosmos,* although I fear I was not sure what these terms really meant." He went on to the Royal College of Music in London, developed an enthusiasm for Mozart, Schubert, Mahler, Stravinsky, Schönberg and Berg, surely a catholic taste. And at twenty-one, he started to earn his living by composing, producing compositions in profusion and to order. The poet W. H. Auden became his collaborator. Auden's friendship awakened Britten to a "fuller sense of an artist's political responsibility, a deeper appreciation of the beauties of English poetry, and a growing awareness of the esthetic problems involved in the alliance of words and music."

Young Benjamin spent three of the war years, from 1939 to 1942, in the United States, continually composing and giving concerts of his works with Peter Pears, his preferred song interpreter. He became homesick, however, and returned to England, with a commission for an opera from the Koussevitzky Foundation safely in his pocket. He sailed on a small Swedish freighter, which took a month to cross the Atlantic, during which time he kept busy in his tiny cabin next to the refrigerating plant, and emerged with a *Hymn to St. Cecilia* (his birthday was on St. Cecilia's Day) and *A Ceremony of Carols,* both of which have become well-known and well liked.

The opera he composed for the Koussevitzky Foundation was *Peter Grimes*, with which his name is indissolubly linked. He loved the sea passionately, for his childhood home was directly on the North Sea. From Crabbe's poem, *The Borough,* he asked his librettist to extract the story of the seaman, Peter Grimes. The opera opened the Sadler's Wells Theater shortly after the final defeat of Germany and attracted world-wide interest. The list of performances reads like a tour of Europe and America. It has the kind of originality which apparently appeals to many different types of people. Another opera, *The Rape of Lucretia,* followed, then the lyrical comedy, *Albert Herring.* At age fifty, Britten had composed three successful operas, besides any amount of chamber music, choral music, incidental music to plays, and film scores. Where could he go from there?

Always the delight of music festivals, he organized a festival of his own in the small city of Aldeburgh. *Let's Make an Opera* was performed there the following year, and in fact every year thereafter saw the performance of a new Britten work or the repetition of an old one there. He was, in 1964, unquestionably the brightest light in contemporary English music.

Born Lowestoft, England, November 22, 1913
Living in England

MAX

BRUCH

Max Bruch is not a one-work composer, although the popularity of his *Violin Concerto in G minor* and the frequency with which it is performed might lead to that conclusion. He composed many other successful works, both instrumental and choral. Their flowing Rhenish melodies and typically German feeling give them great appeal.

In the land of his birth, his choral works—*Odysseus, Das Feuerkreuz, Schön Ellen, Frithjof-Scenen*—have attracted fully as much attention as the *G minor Concerto,* but in London, Paris and New York his instrumental works were preferred. Of these, there are violin and cello concertos; the *Romance* for violin and orchestra; the *Scottish Fantasy;* and the *Kol Nidre Variations* and *Concertstück,* both of the latter for cello with orchestra.

Bruch was well prepared for his career in music. His mother, a famous singer, guided his early training carefully. Much of it he received in Bonn, Beethoven's birthplace, just a few miles up the River Rhine from Cologne. Between his ninth and his fourteenth years he composed seventy pieces of music and climaxed this youthful achievement by winning a four-year scholarship from the Mozart Foundation in Frankfurt. Study under the best teachers followed; there was no question of his becoming anything but a composer. He visited Leipzig, Munich, Mannheim and other German music centers, studying, composing, and meeting musicians, simultaneously giving and taking. Then, after a few years of teaching, and a taste of playing as concertmaster in an orchestra, he gave himself over to composing and conducting, and some teaching.

Ten years elapsed between the first tentative sketches of the G minor Violin Concerto and the completed score. After it had been performed, he was not satisfied with it. He made some changes and sent it to the celebrated violinist Joseph Joachim for his opinion. Joachim's many suggestions for its improvement were taken in good part; Bruch changed the concerto accordingly and finally published it with a dedication to Joachim, who was the first artist to play the revised version in public.

Twelve years later, the famous Sarasate played it in England, and so great was the enthusiasm that Bruch, who was at the performance, was invited to remain to conduct the Liverpool Philharmonic Orchestra. He did so for three years, from 1880 to 1883. But there was much murmuring in the orchestral ranks against his German efficiency and strict drill-master methods. The men did not like his German accent, his professorial beard and spectacles, and his blunt manner. There was a sigh of relief when he resigned.

But from Bruch's standpoint the years in England were not wasted. He found happiness in his marriage to a singer, Clara Tuczek. When he left Liverpool, he was invited to conduct in many other cities, received many honorary degrees, and continued to compose.

For the last ten years of his life, he lived in retirement, and died serenely at eighty-two, having outlived his wife by a year.

Born Cologne, Germany, January 6, 1838
Died Friedenau, Germany, October 2, 1920

ANTON BRUCKNER

It is difficult to think of Bruckner as the center of a controversy, for a milder, quieter, simpler, more pious peasant could not have been found in all Austria. He was born in a tiny village, the son of a poor schoolteacher. His father died when he was three, and he was sent to the monastery of St. Florian's to learn music as soon as he was old enough. His piety probably stems from this early teaching, as does his love of music. At seventeen, he became the schoolmaster of his little village, at a salary, we are told, of about eighty cents a month. He continued his study of the elements of music and became a first-class organist. After twelve years of application to composition, harmony and counterpoint, he asked to be examined. When he displayed his knowledge before a group of learned judges, one of them exclaimed, "He should have examined us!"

At thirty-two, he was appointed organist in the Cathedral of Linz and began to compose in earnest. Twelve years later, he was summoned to Vienna as court organist and professor of composition at the Vienna Academy of Music. With many misgivings, he left the peace and seclusion of Linz; in Vienna he felt like Daniel in the lions' den. It was not long before the lions showed their teeth.

In 1863, he had been completely overwhelmed by hearing a performance of Wagner's Tannhäuser. In one blinding flash, he recognized the prophet he was to follow for the rest of his days. He became the perfect Wagnerite, the uncritical worshiper. It was his object in life to find a place for the Master's operatic theories in the symphony. He had already composed two symphonies, which had been reasonably well received. The Third he reverently dedicated to Wagner. The great man loftily pronounced him the greatest symphonic writer after Beethoven. This was the kiss of death. The storm that broke about Bruckner's head was out of all proportion to his offense. Hanslick, the staunch supporter of Brahms and opponent of Wagner, was so unrelenting in his attack that, when the emperor asked Bruckner what reward he wished for his services, the composer is said to have replied, "Make Hanslick keep quiet."

The result of the hullabaloo was that no conductor was willing to direct a Bruckner symphony, and for years his works went unheard. Not until seven years after he had completed his Fourth, the *Romantic Symphony*, did Hans Richter courageously elect to perform it (1881). Bruckner was at the rehearsal. Richter told how Bruckner came to him after the symphony, his face shining, and pressed something into his hand. "Take it, and drink a mug of beer to my health," said Bruckner. It was a thaler (about fifty cents)! The conductor kept the tip and had it fastened to his watch-chain as a souvenir. The concert was a fiasco.

Bruckner's nine symphonies are unduly long, with dreary stretches between the moments of inspiration, "inlaid with gold and weighted with lead," according to one critic. But the conductor Felix Weingartner said, "I confess that scarcely anything in the new symphonic music can weave itself about me with such wonderful magic as can a simple theme or a few measures of Bruckner."

The composer died at seventy-two, leaving his ninth symphony unfinished. But he had the satisfaction, in his later years, of receiving the recognition so long denied him. A Bruckner Society of his admirers perpetuates his memory and has his works performed.

Born Ansfelder, Austria, September 4, 1824
Died Vienna, Austria, October 11, 1896

WILLIAM BYRD

WILLIAM BYRD was born in Robin Hood's county of Eincolnshire, during the reign of Queen Elizabeth, a glamorous period in Merrie England. It is true that in those days heads were frequently lopped off from bodies for what today may seem trivial reasons. A Catholic, for example, had to be clever to keep his head in every sense, for dissent from Protestantism was not the least of the reasons for summary execution when the country became Protestant under Elizabeth. But somehow, Byrd lived through changing rulers to be eighty years old and died all in one piece. His "musicke" probably saved his life, for he wisely composed for both the Protestant and the Catholic churches. He paid homage to the former in a *Great Service* and a *Short Service,* and to the latter in masses, madrigals and hymns, which greatly enriched the church music of their time.

Not much is known of William's youth, for the records of that day are incomplete. He was probably one of the Children of the Chapel Royal in London, for he is known to have been "bred up to musicke under Thomas Tallis," who was the organist and choir director of the Chapel Royal. At twenty, he was appointed organist of Lincoln Cathedral in his home town. Five years later he took to wife one Juliana Birley, and was at that time elected a Gentleman – no longer a Child – of the Chapel Royal. Here he shared with his senior, Thomas Tallis, the post of organist. Queen Elizabeth graciously granted to him and Tallis the exclusive right to print and sell music in her domain. Though between them they composed a great deal that was fit to print, they found that the high-sounding grant brought them honor but little income. Byrd respectfully requested a raise, and the Queen responded by presenting him with a lease on a comfortable manor in Gloucestershire. Byrd settled his family there and commuted daily on horseback between Gloucestershire and London to discharge his duties at the Chapel Royal.

He is described as a man "of himselfe naturally disposed to Gravitie and Pietie," and the description applies to his compositions. His three *Great Masses* earned him the title in England of Father of Musick; he ranks with Palestrina in the purity of his church writings. Volume I of his *Cantiones Sacrae,* dedicated to Queen Elizabeth, was the first collection of Latin motets ever to be printed in England. They were remarkable in other respects, more especially in the contrapuntal skill displayed by Byrd, even before the great contrapuntist, J. S. Bach, was born. Byrd impartially composed two volumes of *Cantiones Sacrae* for the Protestant church, and two collections of *Gradualia* for the Catholic church. There are three large books of madrigals, too, in which he states his aim "to perswade every one to learne to sing," concluding, "Since singing is so good a thing, I wish all men would learn to sing." Vocal solos with string accompaniment were new to England's "nest of singing birds," accustomed only to part singing without instruments. Among the many solos written by Byrd is one, *My Little Sweet Darling,* with an instrumental accompaniment described as "of entrancing beauty, and well ahead of its time." His chamber music for strings without voice may be described in the same terms.

Byrd wrote for the old-fashioned "chest of viols" with its six sweet but small voices. He chose musical forms which clearly foreshadow those of the following century. As for his keyboard pieces, contained in the *Parthenia* collection, they admittedly set a new high in form and style. During his life, he was recognized as the foremost composer of keyboard music in all of Europe, his reputation having traveled far beyond the boundaries of the island on which he dwelt.

It is odd that this consecrated man and composer should have left trailing clouds of lawsuits as well as immortal music. But it seems he was often in legal hot water – those records *have* survived. He seems, in fact, to have spent almost as much time in the law-courts as at his music-desk or in the organ-loft. He planned to move to a new home, Stondon Place in Essex, for which he paid hard cash. Because of some obscurity in the title, his ownership was disputed, and he fought tooth and nail for his rights. He seems rather to have enjoyed that sort of fight, especially when he won. Having won, he lived at ease in Stondon Place until his death, and willed it, free and clear, to his children.

A richer heritage was the reputation he left them. An English musicologist, Edward Lockspeiser, exclaims in print that "there was no branch of composition, sacred or secular, vocal or instrumental, which this marvelous musician did not attempt, and in which he did not excel." He was in truth as his epitaph said, "Mr. W. Birde, homo memorabilis," a man to remember.

Born Lincoln, England, about 1543
Died Essex, England, July 4, 1623

ERNEST
CHAUSSON

Ernest Chausson was the logical, though not the biological, descendant of César Franck, for whom he had a strong affinity. During his three years of study with the seraphic Père Franck, he learned to channel his emotions into music of solid structure and simplicity.

In terms of quantity, his output was small. This is not wholly because of his untimely death at forty-four. Mozart and Schubert, who died even younger, at thirty-five and thirty-one respectively, poured out masterpieces in a torrent during their brief lives. Chausson, hesitant, diffident, and fearful that his best was not good enough, produced only a trickle, but a trickle possessed of clarity, beauty and significance. The *B flat major Symphony*, and the *Poème* for violin and orchestra are the best known of his works. The Symphony entered the concert repertoire via the conductor Arthur Nikisch. Although it had been heard in Paris, it did not catch the French ear until Berlin set the seal of approval on it at a concert conducted by a Hungarian! The *Poème* appears on concert and recital programs and is one of the standard pieces used to test the violinistic ability of students graduating from conservatories. Its combination of soaring melody, brilliant technique, and spontaneous emotion presents many hazards; when the hazards are surmounted, the piece is highly rewarding. It is intensely expressive – an uncontrollable cry of pain. The *Concerto for Violin, String Quartet and Piano;* the piano trio, piano quartet, and unfinished string quartet; the symphonic poem *Viviane* and a handful of exquisite songs help to keep green the memory of this sensitive, rather melancholy young man.

After his student days at the Conservatoire, he served for ten years as secretary of the Société Nationale de la Musique and was one of its most active members. The composers Gabriel Fauré, Henri Duparc, Vincent d'Indy, Pierre de Bréville, and Charles Bordes were his friends and fellow-members. They joined him in his valiant attempts to preserve "musical righteousness as they saw it." They wished to purify French music as Palestrina, years earlier, had purified the music of the church. To the young composers who drifted in and out of his office, Chausson preached Franck's ideals. When the neophytes were receptive, he helped them to publication and performance by every means in his power. "If he met with ingratitude, he did not mind it, for kindness was natural to him, and he was generous because he was in love with generosity," said his friend Pierre de Bréville. When he entered a publisher's office to show his own manuscripts, he usually managed to slip in a few by some young unknown. He was more interested in helping them than himself.

His sudden death came as a shock. He was riding a bicycle on his own estate. Perhaps he was buried in his thoughts and didn't notice the gathering speed as he coasted down a hill. He lost control of the machine and crashed head-on into a stone wall. He died of a fractured skull.

Born Paris, France, January 21, 1855
Died Limay, France, June 10, 1899

CARLOS CHAVEZ

While Chavez was growing up in Mexico, there were no serious composers, no organized orchestra, no musical season there. He started from scratch. His first sketchy piano lessons were with his older brother Manuel; later he worked under the Mexican folklorist, Ponce, and still later went briefly to Berlin.

As the youngest of six children of an Indian mother and a Spanish father, he represented a fusion of the two strains that people Mexico, and so he considered himself a true Mexican, envisaged himself as a composer of genuine Mexican music. He refused to accept conventional teaching of theory and harmony, but read the books himself, analyzed in his own terms the writings of the classical composers, and evolved his own style. Before he was twenty-one he had produced a number of works, based partly on the Indian folk melodies his mother had sung to him in his childhood, partly on those he learned when he went to live among the Indians as one of them.

He first came to New York in 1923, an unknown young man with a ballet under his arm. It was *El Fuego Nuevo (The New Fire)* which had been commissioned by the Secretary of Education in Mexico. While waiting around for the ballet to be produced, he lectured in halting English on Mexican folk song, illustrating his talks with his collection of Indian instruments, some of which he later employed in the *Sinfonia India.* At twenty-four, the dark-skinned, earnest young man with straight black Indian hair and graceful Indian walk gave an impression of tremendous latent power and primitive force.

After his return to Mexico, he took his place not only as its leading national composer, but as conductor of the Mexican Symphony Orchestra. He organized this semi-amateur body in 1928 and built it into a national institution. The same year, he became Director of the National Conservatory of Music, and under government auspices initiated exhaustive researches into folk music and ancient instruments. A small orchestra using only these instruments was a by-product of the researches.

Finally in 1933 he became Chief of the National Department of Fine Arts and composed a piece, *Llamadas,* for orchestra and voices, for the dedication of the fine new Palace of Fine Arts.

After resigning, he devoted himself to composing, teaching, and guest-conducting. He became a familiar figure in the United States, where he conducted most of the large orchestras, often in performances of his own works. The list of his compositions lengthened with the years, the latest an opera, entitled *Panfilo and Lauretta,* produced in the Brander Matthews Theater in New York in May, 1957.

In a discussion of some of Chavez' compositions, the *Sinfonia India,* the *Sinfonia di Antigona,* the ballet *H. P.* (Horse Power), and the *Piano Sonatina,* Aaron Copland concluded that "Chavez' music caught the spirit of Mexico—its naive, stolid *mestizo* soul . . . that he succeeded in using folk material in its pure form while at the same time solving the problem of its complete amalgamation into an art form, and that, singlehanded, he created a style, part Indian, part Spanish, part modernist, that no future Mexican composer can afford to ignore."

Born outside Mexico City, June 13, 1899
Lives Chapultepec, Mexico

LUIGI

CHERUBINI

HE WAS a strange phenomenon—this boy born in sunny Italy, with so little sunshine in his soul, but with music there in abundance. He taught himself to play the violin on a wretched instrument that he found lying around at home (his father was a harpsichordist), and one day slipped into the chair of an absent violinist in the theater orchestra and played, at sight, the part on the music-rack. He was then ten years old. He had already written his first compositions, having been taught the rudiments by his father and local teachers. The instruction was dry, with no emphasis on the joy of music, but it left him with habits of industry and a substantial backlog of knowledge. When he went to Bologna to continue his studies he took to counterpoint like a duck to water and mastered its difficulties with an ease that put others to shame. His book, *Cours de Contrepoint (Course in Counterpoint),* written many years later, is evidence of the thoroughness of these early studies. "As a contrapuntist, he was worthy to walk arm-in-arm with Bach," said one of his biographers.

From his twenty-eighth year, he made Paris his home. The years of the French Revolution, when, as his wife remarked, "in the morning the guillotine was kept busy and in the evening one could not get a seat at the theater," did not disturb Cherubini. For the crowded theater, he composed an opera, *Lodoiska,* which, written during a revolution, revolutionized the French stage and provided a model for later French opera composers, though today it is never played.

When Napoleon came to power, he had a run-in with Cherubini which ruined any possibility of imperial patronage for the composer. "You have great talent, Citoyen Cherubini, but your music is too loud; let us talk of Paisiello's which lulls me gently," said Napoleon. "I understand perfectly, Citoyen Consul," retorted Cherubini, "you prefer music that does not prevent you from dreaming of affairs of state." Cherubini refused to conduct at Napoleon's court soirées in Schönbrunn, and when the French Conservatoire was founded, Napoleon appointed him to a low-salaried post—tit for tat. Always reserved and severe, now he was bitter and unsmiling. His marriage, in 1795, apparently did nothing to sweeten his disposition.

After Napoleon's downfall, he achieved recognition at last. In 1821, he became Director of the Conservatoire, and at different times was made superintendent of the king's chapel (Louis XVIII), a chevalier of the Legion of Honor, and a member of the Institut Français. For twenty years he ruled the Conservatoire with a rod of iron. The fiery eyes under beetling brows darted their lightning impartially on the gentle César Franck and the fiery Berlioz. He resigned at eighty-one, leaving his neat little office in apple-pie order for his successor. He was a potent force, remarkable pedagogue and organizer, and an influential composer. Though of the vast quantity of music he wrote, little is heard today except the overtures to the operas *Lodoiska, Médée, The Water-Carrier,* and *Anacreon,* he was a really great artist, as uncompromising in his ideals as in his life.

Born Florence, Italy, September 14, 1760
Died Paris, France, March 15, 1842

FREDERIC CHOPIN

FRÉDÉRIC CHOPIN was a hot-house flower from his earliest youth, an exotic plant that required protection from adverse elements. Unfavorable criticism, unrequited love, the struggle for existence, were not for him. He played dolls happily in the garden of their home with his older sister Louise and two younger sisters Isabel and Emily, while his parents did their best to maintain the spiritual hot-house in which they lived at the proper temperature.

At an early age, Frédéric took part in amateur dramatics and musicales; he was an excellent mimic and could have been an actor.

But he started to play the piano when he was four, and by the time he was eight, he was known as a child prodigy. He was taken to Warsaw, whirled in a golden coach from one great house to another, caressed by noble ladies and presented with gifts by noble gentlemen, much as the boy Mozart had been. Like Mozart, he loved to improvise, and when he was twelve, and Joseph Elsner, Director of the Warsaw Conservatory, took his musical education in hand, he started to compose in earnest. His *Rondo in C minor,* published when he was fifteen, is by no means his first composition, though marked Opus I.

At this time he worked so hard that he broke down and was ordered to the country for a long rest. When he recovered, he returned to his music more zealously than ever. He visited Berlin and Vienna and, like every other musician, fell in love with Vienna and determined to settle there. At the same time, he decided that the life of the virtuoso was the life for him.

His farewell concert in Warsaw was crowded with tearful well-wishers. His friends serenaded him, and his teacher Joseph Elsner presented him with a silver cup filled with Polish soil. Did Elsner have a presentiment that his favorite pupil was never to return to Poland?

Hardly had Chopin set foot on Austrian soil than Warsaw was seized and occupied by its historic enemy, Russia — not for the first nor the last time in its history. This depressed the patriotic Chopin terribly. The failure of his first public concert in Vienna, and the immediate need for money depressed him still further. No help from home was now possible. The hothouse plant drooped. Yet before going on to Paris, he chronicled in a great composition his defiance of Russia and his hopes for the liberation of his beloved homeland. This was the thunderous *Revolutionary Etude,* Opus 10, No. 12.

In Paris, his spirits revived. His slim, pale elegance, his exquisite manners, his unhealthy charm, and most of all, his wonderful piano playing aroused the interest of sophisticated Paris. A new-found patron, Prince Radziwill, invited him to a musicale where his piano playing — intimate, delicate, and unique — brought him the promise of pupils in sufficient number to provide him with the white kid gloves and fitted frock coats he had to have if he was to take his place in the *haut monde* of Paris.

Soon the most distinguished musicians, artists and poets became the friends of this "poet of the piano." He wrote home, "I move in the highest circles and don't know how I got there." The composers Cherubini and Bellini, Mendelssohn and Liszt, Meyerbeer and Berlioz; the painter Delacroix; the poet Heinrich Heine; the singers Pauline Viardot-Garcia and Maria Malibran sat enthralled in his candle-lit salon while his incredibly fleet fingers and inspired pedaling infused new meaning into the music he played.

At twenty-five, Chopin visited Schumann, who promptly headed an article about his young visitor in the *Neue Zeitschrift für Musik,* "Hats off, gentlemen! A genius!" Clara Wieck, soon to be married to Schumann, played and approved Chopin's pieces too. His latent resolve to devote more effort to composition than to concertizing was strengthened by their encouragement. This year he was desperately in love with Maria Wodzinska, a friend of his youth. He proposed, she refused, he was desolate. But he found consolation in composing a waltz, *Les Adieux,* which he dedicated to their lovers' parting.

On the rebound, he was engulfed in the powerful masculine personality of the novelist George Sand (Mme. Dudevant). The curious attachment to this cigar-smoking matron which altered his whole life he described as "an episode without beginning and with a sad end." While in Majorca with her and her two children, he completed the marvelous *Twenty-four Preludes* which are among his best-loved works. For ten years, he and Mme. Dudevant lived in neighboring apartments in Paris in the winter and spent summers together at her home in Nohant. He was often ill, and she nursed him devotedly. But in 1846, her daughter Solange maliciously created a quarrel which broke their liaison. Chopin left George Sand, never to return. He even refused to see her on his deathbed. After their parting, he composed no more.

Now his health failed noticeably. He summoned all his energies for a concert in the Salle Pleyel in Paris in February 1848. Though it cost him dear in health and energy, it was successful and he planned another. But the Revolution of 1848 canceled the second concert and forced him to flee Paris. He went to Scotland, the worst possible climate for his tubercular larynx, and after a few wretched, foggy months, he crept home to Paris to die. The cherished Polish soil Elsner had given him was buried with him.

No lover wooed his lass more tenderly and persistently than Chopin the piano, and it responded to his wooing as it did to none other's. The reason Chopin played his own pieces so much better than those of other men was because of the perfect understanding that existed between him and the instrument. He worked painstakingly over his two hundred and three piano pieces before bringing them to the keyboard. He created a whole vocabulary, a romantic idiom which raised piano music to a more expressive plane than it had ever occupied.

Born Zelazowa-Wola, Poland, March 1, 1809
Died Paris, France, October 17, 1849

AARON COPLAND

AFTER LISTENING to Aaron Copland's taut, tense, brilliant music, it was a surprise to find its composer to be a loose-limbed, relaxed, quiet-spoken gentleman. The Copland dynamo must have been buried deep, for at first glance there was no evidence of the electricity which charges his compositions.

When young Aaron left his home in Brooklyn, he went to France, rejecting the accepted routine of a couple of years in Munich, Berlin or Vienna. He sought out Nadia Boulanger at the American School in Fontainebleau, and became her prize pupil. He was already a competent pianist, having studied with his sister and with Victor Wittgenstein and Clarence Adler. His study of theory with Rubin Goldmark had stimulated his interest in composition, and his selection of his career was as calm and reasoned as though music were a business like any other. But in his student days he gave evidence of not being the perfect business man. The French music publisher, Durand, offered him twenty-five dollars outright for a short piano piece, *The Cat and the Mouse,* which the teenager played at a students' recital. Without hesitation, Aaron accepted the offer. Twenty-five dollars looked like a lot of money. He asked for no royalties, and though many thousand copies were sold, only the publisher benefited. Aaron did not make that mistake again!

He returned to New York, a shy, slim youth with an engaging smile, bringing in his trunk the now well-known *Symphony for Organ and Orchestra.* At Nadia Boulanger's insistence, and with her at the organ, it was performed under the baton of Dr. Walter Damrosch. At the conclusion, Dr. Damrosch turned to the audience and boomed, "If a young man at the age of twenty-three can write a symphony like that, at the end of five years he will be ready to commit murder." But Aaron was introduced to the League of Composers, many of his works were played there, he soon took his place in the forefront of young American composers, and he did not commit murder. He became a director of the Copland-Sessions concerts, where he helped audiences through the first shock of dissonant music by his helpful comments. He became director of the League of Composers, of Yaddo, of the International Society for Contemporary Music, and of the Berkshire School of Music in Tanglewood, Mass., successor to Serge Koussevitzky. Having been obliged to move from several New York apartments because of his habit of composing at night with the collaboration of a noisy piano, he made his home in Ossining, New York.

His large work, for orchestra, *Lincoln Portrait,* with a text taken from the Gettysburg Address, has appealing dignity and power. *Appalachian Spring,* a ballet which was first danced by Martha Graham and thereafter appeared as a suite on numerous programs, won a Pulitzer Prize and an award from the Critics' Circle of New York. This is but one of the many prizes and awards bestowed upon him.

His *Connotations for Orchestra,* commissioned by Lincoln Center for the Performing Arts in New York City, was premièred at the gala opening concert of its new Philharmonic Hall in 1963.

He composed for the theater, for the orchestra, for chorus, and for chamber music groups, music of the here and now, music expressive of changing currents of life in these United States. He was one of the first serious composers commissioned to write a piece for radio broadcasting. His scores for the films *Of Mice and Men, The City, Our Town,* and *The Heiress* have that much-desired combination of ear and eye appeal on which television also depends. Copland's scores, eminently suitable for these pictures, are musically strong enough to be played in the concert hall.

Laurels rested lightly upon his receding brow. He displayed no envy, but an unusual appreciation of his colleagues at home and abroad. With quiet impersonality and tolerant humor, he raised his voice in classrooms and lecture halls, in books and articles, in support of the contemporary composer. In his works, as well as his words, he did all that one man could to interpret the modern world in music that can be understood. Aware of the vast new public created by radio, recordings, and television, he rejoiced that, "For the first time, democracy has entered the realm of serious music."

Born Brooklyn, N. Y., November 14, 1900
Living Ossining, N. Y.

ARCANGELO CORELLI

AT A TIME when the great Italian violin-maker Anton Stradivarius was bringing the instrument to perfection, the advent of a Corelli who would play upon it to equal perfection appears nothing short of a miracle. Performers are usually soon forgotten, for their music dies upon the air as it is born. Corelli is an exception. He has retained his stature as one of the finest violinists that ever lived, father of all fiddlers, and this although he never played above the third position. He is represented here as a composer, for his ability to write beautiful music equalled his ability to perform it.

Tranquility is the keynote of his character. In his youth, of which few records exist, he is known to have studied counterpoint with Simonelli and violin with Bassini. He traveled in Germany and remained for some months at the court of the Elector of Bavaria in Munich. Possibly he spent some time in Paris after this, where Lully then ruled the world of music. Lully's jealousy of this potential rival resulted in unfriendly acts and is said to have contributed to the decision of the sensitive youth to return to his fatherland. At thirty-two he settled down pleasantly in Rome, in the palace of his patron, the wealthy and art-loving Cardinal Ottoboni. Here he remained until his death.

Every Monday, there was a concert in the Cardinal's palace which was the great event of the week in aristocratic circles. Corelli conducted these concerts and played the violin at them too. He composed solo violin sonatas and performed them to the admiration of his audiences. He composed dances and church music with equal felicity and facility. He composed chamber sonatas and concerti grossi which were models of stylistic purity. They foreshadowed the style of orchestral writing which was later to be developed by Haydn, Mozart, and Beethoven. Because he was himself a violinist, he wrote with the lucidity, economy and dignity which befit that instrument, and excluded whatever he considered contrary to its nature. Six large volumes contain the twelve *Concerti Grossi* and the sixty *Sonatas* which he composed.

His fame as a violinist spread beyond Italy, and students from every country flocked to Rome to study with him. They all loved the maestro. He was amiable, gentle, and modest, and simple in his tastes. He ate and drank sparingly at tables groaning with food, dressed plainly, and went afoot while others rode in sedan chairs or carriages. This appears to have been asceticism rather than excessive thrift, for he spent money freely on occasion.

His one extravagance was his collection of paintings, over which he brooded like a mother hen over her chicks. Many artists came to visit Cardinal Ottoboni in his Palace. Corelli met them all and asked their advice before he bought a picture. Thus over the years he assembled an unusually fine collection. Handel said, maliciously, "Corelli likes nothing better than seeing pictures without paying for it, and saving money." Corelli invested money in art when he considered it worthwhile and died a comparatively rich man.

He very seldom left the favorable surroundings of the palace to travel. But musicians came to visit him in Rome. When Handel came, he brought one of his own cantatas. They were written in a fiery, dramatic style; Handel wrote operas without scenery and costumes and called them cantatas or oratorios, since, as they were "sacred music," the church would produce them. Corelli played the solo violin part. Handel explained to him how he wished a certain brilliant passage to be performed. Corelli did not follow Handel's instructions, but rendered it in his usual serene style. Handel lost his temper, snatched the violin from Corelli's hand and played the passage himself. Corelli's only rebuke for this rudeness was to remark, with the utmost politeness, "But, my dear Saxon, this music is in the French style, with which I have had no experience."

The king of Naples tried often to induce Corelli to visit his court. But Corelli was content to stay in Rome. Finally, when he was fifty-five and had won general recognition of his playing and his compositions, he accepted an invitation to give a concert in Naples. The orchestra, under its conductor Alessandro Scarlatti, played the introduction to Corelli's concerto so well that he remarked approvingly, "They play well in Naples." But while Corelli was playing his own concerto, the king, bored by the length of the Adagio, walked out during the performance.

Corelli was hurt. But worse was to come. At another concert, he was to play a piece by Alessandro Scarlatti with Scarlatti conducting. He made a conspicuous error; in the very beginning, he started to play in C major instead of C minor. "Let us begin again," said Scarlatti courteously. Corelli was flustered. He made the same error a second time. Scarlatti had to stop the orchestra, and point it out to him. Corelli was deeply humiliated. He returned to Rome immediately after the concert.

In Rome he found everyone talking about a new young violinist. People had not forgotten Corelli; they still loved him as much as ever. He believed, however, that he had been superseded. He brooded over this to such an extent that he became ill. And in 1713, he died because he could no longer bear to live. His grave in the Pantheon, near the painter Raphael's, is marked by a marble monument erected by Cardinal Ottoboni.

Born Fusignano, Italy, February 12, 1653
Died Rome, Italy, January 10, 1713

FRANCOIS COUPERIN

THE CHOICEST fruit that grew on the Couperin family tree was François, last of his line, justly called The Great. He was a hot-house fruit, which mellowed in the artificial heat of the court of Louis XIV. When Louis, the Sun-King, smiled, his rays warmed and encouraged the object on which they rested. He smiled often and affectionately upon François. The coat of arms he bestowed upon him depicts the sun, shining brightly from a cloudless blue sky studded with silver stars, upon a golden lyre which reflects its rays. The design is pleasantly emblematic of Couperin's life.

He was born in Paris, and Paris was his home from the cradle to the grave. Maître Thomelin, the court organist, a close family friend, gave him such a thorough musical training that, when the master was gathered to his fathers, the pupil inherited his position. Louis himself supervised the competition, and chose young François from many applicants to be his court organist.

François was married at twenty-one, and a few years later, he added the title "Maître de Clavecin des Enfants de France," not because he had so many children of his own, but because he was the royal family's preferred harpsichord teacher. He played and composed for Louis' gorgeous court spectacles, and was in every way a satisfactory court musician. He was nothing loath to teach the harpsichord, which he preferred to all other instruments. In his original works it is obvious that he realized that the sweet but brief tone could be made expressive only if it was given music especially written, and especially suited to it, not the same music given to the voice or the organ. This was a vital discovery.

After hearing some trios by the Italian composer Arcangelo Corelli, Couperin decided that the Italian had the right idea. He noticed that the audience was as enthusiastic as he was. So he wrote his next compositions in the Italian style and signed them Pernucio, an Italian version of his own name. He did not own up to having written them until they had sailed to success under Italian colors.

In 1726, he published a large folio volume of sonatas for two violins and harpsichord, *Les Nations,* and followed it later with four more volumes of music for harpsichord alone. There were no music-publishers in his day, but these precious books, preserved on copperplate, contain some of his most delectable writing. The pieces are entitled *La Voluptueuse, La Seduisante, La Sultane, La Belle Nanette,* etc. Couperin loved the ladies, and celebrated their charms in these poetic character pieces.

"I love that which stimulates more than that which overwhelms me," he said. And so his pieces have taste and refinement, and a kind of airy grace. In his textbook, *L'art de toucher le clavecin, (The Art of Playing the Harpsichord)* he gave valuable hints about touch, about the proper way to play ornaments and embellishments, about finger technique and expressivity.

When François' health failed, the younger of his two daughters was appointed to his place. It was the first time a woman had been allowed to perform on the royal harpsichord, but there was no son, and there had to be a Couperin at the court of France!

Born Paris, France, November 10, 1668
Died Paris, France, September 12, 1733

CLAUDE ACHILLE DEBUSSY

A THIRTY YEARS' WAR against adverse criticism culminated in victory for that strange, singular and solitary Frenchman, Claude Achille Debussy, otherwise known as "Claude of France." It was his expressed intention to convey in sound the impressions produced within individuals by events and sights outside of themselves. The painter Monet was attempting to do something similar in form and color. They called themselves impressionists. Their impressionism called for an unusually sensitive and perceptive audience if it was to be understood. No wonder many critics derided their early efforts. Yet they succeeded in making their point and became originators of a whole new school of art and music.

Debussy's music is purest shimmering sound. It is usually based on a whole-tone scale, woven into a gossamer tissue of iridescent harmonies. He broke many rules to achieve his impressionistic effects. His great symphonic works, *Iberia, La Mer* (The Sea), *L'Après-Midi d'un Faune* (The Afternoon of a Faun), *Nuages, Fêtes, Sirènes;* his seventy-five piano pieces which bear such intriguing titles as *La Cathédrale Engloutie* (The Sunken Cathedral), *Jardins dans la Pluie* (Gardens in the Rain), *Reflets dans l'Eau* (Reflections in the Water); his piano *Preludes;* his one superb string quartet; his songs and sonatas all are marked with the unmistakable imprint of his unique personality.

Debussy was a Frenchman first, last, and all

the time. Born within view of Paris, in Saint-Germain-en-Laye, he was destined by his father, proprietor of a small china shop, for a career in the French navy. Perhaps from this paternal ambition stem the sounds of water in much of his music; he himself never went to sea. Thanks to the interest of his musical godmother, Mme. Roustan, he started to take piano lessons when he was seven and progressed so well that he entered the Conservatoire when he was eleven. He remained at the Conservatoire for eleven contentious years, studied improvisation with César Franck, and learned to play the piano with a glancing touch that produced an unearthly beauty of sound.

Like Berlioz, Debussy had ideas of his own which he expressed fearlessly. Thus, he was denied the Prix de Rome for two successive years—1882 and 1883—because of his obstinate adherence to his musical beliefs. When the prize was finally awarded to his cantata, *L'Enfant Prodigue* (The Prodigal Son), he became "a Roman against his will." So strong was his longing to be again under the rooftops of his beloved Paris that he remained in the Villa Medici for only two of the allotted three years, in what he shudderingly described as "a barracks, a veritable prison!" He met Liszt, Verdi, Leoncavallo, and Boito in Rome. He went on summer trips as accompanist to Mme. von Meck, Tchaikowsky's friend, who called him her "little Bussy" and introduced him to Russian music. But he still preferred Paris.

At twenty-five, Debussy became friendly with a group of poets led by the symbolist Mallarmé. Partly under their influence, partly because of a visit to Bayreuth, he became for a while a Wagner enthusiast. But his Gallic delicacy had little in common with the thunderings of the Teutonic Titan, and he passed through that phase unscathed. He responded actively to the five-tone scale of Russian liturgical music and to the Javanese Gamelang which he heard with delight at the World's Fair in Paris in 1889.

For ten years, from 1882 to 1902, he toiled at his one exquisite opera, *Pelléas et Mélisande.* "Gaby of the Green Eyes," his loyal mistress, was succeeded by Rosalie Texier, whom he subsequently married. Both women shared his hopes and fears, his triumphs and failures during these years. He completed *L'Après-Midi d'un Faune* and his three Nocturnes for orchestra, *Nuages, Fêtes,* and *Sirènes.* On the side, he wrote caustic music criticism with which he made money, if not friends. He composed at night, slept in the morning, and issued forth for a constitutional in the afternoon, a striking figure, blackbearded, with a black slouch hat and black cloak, carrying a cane to ward off his pet hates—ugly people, crying children, and undesirable acquaintances. When *Pelléas et Mélisande* was produced at the Opéra Comique, in 1902, with Mary Garden as Mélisande, Maurice Maeterlinck, author of the play, pronounced the opera "strange and hostile" to him, adding fervently, "I can only hope for its immediate and emphatic failure." But to his chagrin, the opera was an immediate and emphatic success. The composer was decorated by the French government and took his coveted place as "musicien français." The opera was taken into the repertoire of every opera company of importance.

All his life he crusaded for what he called French music — that is, music in the style of Rameau and Couperin, rather than Weber and Wagner. His plastic rhythmic patterns and his disregard of conventional structure are today admitted to be the proper means to the end he had in view.

His private life was far from serene. He presently left his wife Rosalie, known as Lily-Lilo. She despairingly attempted suicide and he felt sorry for her, but this did not prevent him from marrying Mme. Emma Bardac, who bore him a daughter, Chou-Chou. When Chou-Chou was a little girl, he wrote for her the *Children's Corner Suite,* with its delightful *Golliwog's Cakewalk.* He loved Chou-Chou better than anyone in the world and she became his solace during the last nine years of his life, when he was suffering from cancer.

Two operations failed to arrest his illness, and on March 26, 1918, he breathed his last. German long-range cannon, bombarding Paris, sounded an overstated death-knell for that master of musical understatement, of the pregnant silence, the whispered mood, and the silver tone, Claude Debussy.

Born St. Germain-en-Laye, France, August 22, 1862
Died Paris, France, March 26, 1918

FREDERICK

DELIUS

WHEN Delius's father urged that he join him in the woolen business, the young man romantically suggested that an orange grove in Florida would be more to his liking. His father bought him the grove, but with the assistance of an organist, "Freddy" soon learned to forget oranges and memorize music. He did stay around long enough to remark with interest how haunting were the songs of the Negroes working on the plantation; later he embodied them in a piano concerto.

Leaving the oranges to ripen in their own way, he went to Danville to ripen in his. He taught music there until his father, seeing that there was no help for it, sold the orange grove and told his son to come home. Edvard Grieg, Freddy's good friend, pleaded with Delius Senior to let Freddy study music in Leipzig and won the father's reluctant permission. But neither parent would ever listen to Freddy's compositions.

In Germany, his music was fairly well liked. In England, the land of his birth, his unfamiliar idiom seemed to puzzle the public. A listener complained about a piece that it didn't seem to get anywhere, and the English seemed to feel that this was true not only of that particular piece, but of his others and of the composer also. This mattered little to him. In 1897, he married a painter, Jelka Roszen, and with money inherited from his father, bought a villa in France, near Fontainebleau. For forty-five years, this was their home. She painted, he composed, and except for the visits of friends, they lived a retired life. In France, Delius's music was almost wholly unknown until near the end of his life.

At intervals, the Deliuses took trips. They spent many summers in Norway with the Griegs. The second theme of Delius's tone-poem *On Hearing the First Cuckoo in Spring* is a Norwegian folk tune. In 1914, they went to England to escape the German invasion of France. Now it began to be noised about that the fifty-two-year-old Delius was worth listening to, that his music was impressionistic like Debussy's and romantic as well, that the conductor Thomas Beecham thought well of it, and "after all, *he* ought to know." Fifteen years later, when Delius, a sick man, again came to London it was to attend a Festival in his honor. At a series of six concerts, all of his writings except his stage works were performed. Seated in his wheel-chair, he received a decoration from the hand of King George V.

He had wonderful stamina, this Englishman. For ten years he was blind and paralyzed. Yet up to the very end he continued to dictate music, note by note, to his wife and his secretary. "He would wriggle about in his chair, gesticulate wildly with his hands until he could go on no longer and would be carried away, exhausted," said his secretary.

"It is only that which cannot be expressed otherwise that is worth expressing in music," was Delius's belief. He lived as he composed, "Not to be understood, but for those who understand."

Born Bradford, England, January 29, 1862
Died Grez-sur-Loing, France, June 10, 1934

GAETANO

DONIZETTI

In the days when singers displayed their tonsils with the double object of revealing both the natural charm and the acquired technique of the human voice, Donizetti was in his element. Rossini had created an enormous audience for the flowing melody, vocal gymnastics, and expressivity which brought fame to him and his operas. Donizetti and his friend Bellini, younger than Rossini, cashed in on the latter's success, adhered faithfully to his formula, and profited by doing so.

It is impossible to discuss Donizetti without Bellini, for their two careers were parallel until separated by death. Both were as dolphins sporting in the wake of the whale, Rossini, but Donizetti was the plumper and better fed.

He studied at the Conservatory in Naples and at the Philharmonic Academy in Bologna. When his father began mumbling in his beard about the uncertainty of music as a career, Gaetano enlisted in the Austrian army, knowing full well that this would permit leisure to compose. After three tentative and forgotten operas, he hit his stride in *Zoraïde di Granata,* composed in the barracks. He was twenty-one when it was produced in Rome, and following its première he was carried all aglow through the streets on the shoulders of the applauding people. Emboldened by its success, he determined to resign his military commission, and to become a full-time composer. From this time on he scattered operas broadcast in the many theaters of Italy. With *Anna Bolena,* performed in Milan, Paris, and London, Donizetti became a figure to be reckoned with.

He wrote *Il campanella di notte* in nine days, and is said to have remarked that Rossini was "lazy" for having taken thirteen to compose *The Barber of Seville.* Donizetti's audiences "wanted tunes and thrills, and these he gave them, for he had a Midas gift of turning everything into the kind of melody which people could remember and sing, or at least recognize when they heard it sung next day in the streets," says Donald Grout.

The best-known of his sixty-five operas are *Elisir d' Amore, (Elixir of Love), Lucia di Lammermoor, La Fille du Regiment (Daughter of the Regiment),* immortalized in the United States by Lily Pons, *Linda di Chamonix,* and *Don Pasquale.* Like Rossini, Donizetti was God's gift to prima donnas, who reveled in the bel canto trills and legato, the daredevil vocal leaps of his arias. The Mad Scene in *Lucia di Lammermoor* has been the making, as well as the undoing, of many a coloratura soprano, and has become well worn in the process. *Lucia* is Donizetti's masterpiece.

He was professor of counterpoint at the Royal College of Music in Naples and later its director. He traveled occasionally to witness performances of his operas in Vienna, Paris, Rome and Milan, and was well liked in Europe. Although he lacked the dramatic sense, the power and originality and brilliance of Rossini, he played an admirable second fiddle to the great man, and was humble enough to rejoice in doing so. He ceased to compose only when a paralytic stroke intervened and compelled him to return to his home in Bergamo where he died.

Born Bergamo, Italy, November 25, 1797
Died Bergamo, Italy, April 8, 1845

PAUL
DUKAS

There is a kind of delicate reserve which is peculiar to the highly cultured Frenchman, a barrier of aloofness which is gently maintained and which cannot be surmounted. Paul Dukas, loved by his students and friends and even by the composers whose works he criticized, was never really close to any of them. His hard-working childhood may have accentuated his tendency to withdraw.

His parents recognized his talent but could not afford to give him music lessons, and a neighbor's piano on which he taught himself to play was his only music teacher until he entered the Conservatoire at seventeen. There he studied and practiced night and day for seven years to make up for lost time.

It was really the orchestral scherzo *L'Apprenti Sorcier* (The Sorcerer's Apprentice) that brought him the most unstinted and widespread recognition. He composed this delightful musical satire to a poem by Goethe. Goethe had taken the mocking tale of a spindle-shanked magician and his fake magic from *The Lie Fancier,* a dialogue dating from the second century before Christ. Thus the story was ancient, but the subject was still timely, and the music Dukas composed was strictly up-to-date. The animated rhythms and brilliant orchestration, the dramatic excitement, and above all the humor which Dukas imparted to it, made his program piece pictorial long before Walt Disney gilded the lily by adding pictures to the music.

Dukas' reputation does not rest solely on *L'Apprenti Sorcier,* though this is the most generally familiar of his works. *Ariane et Barbe Bleue,* an opera, deserves to be better known. Maurice Maeterlinck wrote the text with one eye on his friend Dukas, hoping that an opera would come of it. It did. Dukas created a strong and beautiful work, which bears comparison with Debussy's *Pelléas et Mélisande.* The heroine Ariane, who symbolizes "the liberating pity that struggles against the enslavement and feebleness of humanity," appealed strongly to the high-minded Dukas, and he wrote for her his most inspired arias.

In his busy life as a teacher of composition and as one of the steering committee at the Conservatoire, as a member of the Société Nationale de la Musique, of the Légion d'honneur, and of other honorary societies, as a contributor to newspapers and periodicals, he always found leisure for composition. Yet, in his forties he stopped going to publishers with his works, and a short while before his death, at seventy, he tried all his unpublished manuscripts in the heat of self-criticism and found them wanting. He ruthlessly destroyed them in a "Burning of the Books" which seems truly deplorable in view of the excellence of the few surviving compositions. His quiet influence in the direction of classic simplicity and refinement took effect on many composers of his generation in France and in Spain.

Born Paris, France, October 1, 1865
Died Paris, France, May 17, 1935

ANTONIN DVORAK

THE COMPOSER of the *American Quartet* and the *New World Symphony*, Dvořák, was not an American but a Bohemian, who also created a large body of national music expressive of the individuality of his own country. His American pieces, which made him particularly well-loved here, were composed while he was in America, bitterly homesick for his native land. The famous theme of the New World Symphony, based on the Negro spiritual "Goin' home," expresses his personal nostalgia.

Any musician would be homesick for the village in which Anton passed his boyhood. Here people sang as naturally as they breathed. Anton's earliest recollections were of the village green, where his jolly young father, the innkeeper, tinkled a zither as boys and girls danced. Anton learned to play folksongs on the violin before he started to study music seriously. They appealed to him more than the three R's he learned from the village schoolmaster, or the kitchen and the butcher's block where he helped his father. There were eight young mouths to feed in the Dvořák family and not much food to put into them.

By the time Anton was sixteen, he had learned to play the piano, violin and organ so well that his parents permitted him to enter the Organ School in Prague. During the next years, he often had to tighten his belt, for his only income while studying came from occasional engagements with a band, and he was always hungry.

The year after his graduation, 1860, was a turning-point in his life. His country had been freed from Austrian rule. Smetana had come back from Sweden aflame with the ambition to create a Bohemian national music for a free nation. Dvořák was fired by the idea, but it was some time before he saw his way clear to acting upon it.

For twelve years he had to support himself any way he could. He played in a theater orchestra. In his humble lodgings, he studied borrowed scores and worked on compositions modeled on those of the great composers of the past. Schubert and Beethoven were his gods. A near-Wagnerian grand opera, *Alfred,* and a would-be comic opera, *King and Collier,* were failures. But he persevered, and with a cantata, *Hymnus,* and a popular hymn, *The Heirs of the White Mountain,* he struck his stride. Both were patriotic works which brought him recognition. He resigned his theater job to play the organ in a church, and this left him more time for composition.

During these years, he married the younger sister of the girl he loved and lived happily with her. When their little daughter died, he composed a *Piano Trio* (G minor) and a *Stabat Mater* in mournful tribute. But a few months later, he submitted a set of gay and rhythmic dances, the *Moravian Duets* for 2 voices and piano, and won a State prize. Brahms was one of the judges, and became Anton's great friend and protector.

The *Moravian Duets* brought him money, which he sorely needed. They became immensely popular and so did the *Slavonic Rhapsodies* and *Slavonic Dances,* which followed. In them Dvořák recaptured the Bohemian folksong feeling of the village green without employing actual folksong melodies. The melodies were his own. Overnight he became famous. He went to bed at night unknown and awoke to find himself headlined in the newspapers. Bewildered as he was by the sudden rise to fame and fortune, it did not turn his head. He never learned to huff and puff and behave like a great man. A peasant he was, a peasant he remained all his life.

He went to London to conduct his *Stabat Mater* in 1884. His concerts attracted large audiences, and he returned to Prague with pockets well-lined. He invested his English pound notes in a house on his brother's estate in southern Bohemia, Vysoka. Here he spent six months of the year. For the rest of his life, Vysoka was home to him and his family. Though he became director of the Prague Conservatory, visited other countries, and was everywhere honored as composer, conductor and teacher, he returned like a homing pigeon to Vysoka.

After a general celebration of his fiftieth birthday, which he passed up to walk in the woods of Vysoka with his family, he reluctantly traveled to New York to direct the National Conservatory of Music there, taking with him his wife and six children. Even in the nineties he found the bustling city hard to get accustomed to. The rapid tempo took his breath away. He took long walks. Twice a week he went to the zoo in Central Park, pretending he was in the country. He worked hard and reorganized the Conservatory into a splendid school. His students loved him. He composed big works. But he was wistful when he watched the big steamers leaving their docks and pointing toward Europe.

The happiest hours of his exile were spent in Spillville, Iowa, where some of his countrymen, homesick like himself, had created a Bohemian village. Dvořák played national hymns on the church organ there and talked his own language in the village inn. Spillville was to him an oasis in the desert of America. Part of the *New World Symphony,* which he orchestrated in Spillville, was inspired by the Negro tunes that his student Harry Burleigh (later a distinguished singer) sang for him. At the first performance of the symphony in Carnegie Hall in 1893, Dvořák received a tremendous ovation. He found love and admiration wherever he went in America. Because of his childlike simplicity, his dark lively eyes, his crushing handshake, Americans took to this Bohemian.

Yet it was with heartfelt relief that he returned to his homeland. It meant more to him than Niagara Falls, which amazed him, or Negro songs, or success, or his devoted friends and pupils in America, much as he loved them all.

During his later years he acquired a fine collection of honorary degrees and gold medals. He was the first musician to be granted a seat in the upper house of the governing body of Austria. His friend Brahms died in 1897 and this was a great loss, but on the whole, life was sweet. By this time, Dvořák was known worldwide as the outstanding composer of his country, second only to Smetana. His musical speech had simplicity and directness, beauty of sound and perfection of form, and a folksy flavor which was universally appealing.

Death came to him as suddenly as fame had. He was sixty-three when an apoplectic stroke brought to an end a career full of the joy of living.

Born Nelahozeves, Bohemia, September 8, 1841
Died Prague, Bohemia, May 1, 1904

EDWARD ELGAR

On June 2, 1957, the English nation celebrated the centennial of the birth of Edward Elgar, its most British of British composers. Not only are Elgar's ancestors pure Saxon, but he was born, grew up, and returned to die in a picture-book English village, set among the hills of Malvern. Over these hills he wandered in his boyhood; he never tired of them.

In the intervals of caring for seven children, his mother read aloud to them, selecting the best English literature for her family, but Edward received little formal instruction, and left school at fifteen. He helped his father sell musical instruments, and from his father he learned to play the organ. He picked up the violin, cello and double-bass, the bassoon, trombone and piano on his own. "A stream of music flowed through our house and the shop, and I was all the time bathing in it," he explained. He plunged into such musical activities as there were in the neighboring town of Worcester, where the Three-Choir Festivals were sometimes held. When he was twenty-three, a salon piece he composed, *Salut d'Amour,* attracted interest. A series of cantatas and oratorios which followed caused his name to become locally known.

But it was with the *Enigma Variations* that he made his first real dent in the hard shell of the listening public. By this time he was forty-two and had been married for ten years. His wife's encouragement meant so much to him that his success as a composer may be said to have begun and ended with his marriage. After Lady Elgar's death, in 1920, he composed very little. The *Enigma Variations,* dedicated to "my friends pictured herein" is a brilliant orchestral piece in which thirteen friends and the composer himself are characterized, one variation to a person. Guessing which friend was which variation must have been an agreeable game at Victorian dinner-parties.

A huge oratorio, *The Dream of Gerontius,* did not stir American audiences as it did the English, though it was highly praised by Richard Strauss in Germany. But the six *Pomp and Circumstance Marches,* the *Cockaigne Overture* and the *Enigma Variations* appear often on American programs. On the strength of the *Pomp and Circumstance Marches,* written for the coronation of Edward VII, Elgar was knighted in 1904. Some years later he received a baronetcy.

In the two symphonies and other works of Elgar's maturity the English critic Ernest Newman says that the British heard "the swan song of a dying civilization, the bleeding to death of their world." Elgar did take the First World War very much to heart and expressed his feelings in sundry patriotic compositions. But he never surpassed "Land of Hope and Glory," a march from *Pomp and Circumstance,* which became as popular as "God Save the King." During his later years he guest-conducted in Europe and America and was everywhere well liked.

With a "laugh like a minor second which is never resolved," conversation "presto scherzando" (fast and joking), and a gracious lady at his side, Sir Edward had many and sufficient claims to popularity. He believed in musical education to create listeners, not merely performers, and he believed in radio and recordings, new in his generation, as aids to music education. After Lady Elgar's death, he gradually withdrew from public life and died in a nursing home after a long illness.

Born Broadhurst, England, June 2, 1857
Died Worcester, England, February 23, 1934

GEORGES ENESCO

An all-around musician, who played violin, viola, cello and piano with equal ease, Enesco liked nothing better than to play every part in a string quartet in the course of an evening. His musical memory was phenomenal; he conducted without a score. He thought of music in broad symphonic terms, his sparkling blue eyes seeming to look beyond the small phrase into music of grand proportions.

As a student at the Conservatory of Vienna and the Conservatoire in Paris, he carried off all the first prizes in violin and in his teens went on a triumphant concert tour. He was only nineteen when he composed the *Rumanian Rhapsodies for Orchestra.* The folksong melodies, frenzied rhythms, and gypsy flavor made these pieces so popular that whenever he laid down the violin bow for the conductor's baton, he was requested, willy-nilly, to place one of the two *Rhapsodies* on his program. In a patriotic gesture, he had presented them to the Rumanian government, and in consequence, he could not collect royalties on the many performances. But he was court violinist to Queen Carmen Sylva, eventually married one of her ladies-in-waiting, the Princess Marie-Tuscano, and was decorated and honored by his queen. His humility, simplicity, humor and tolerance, added to good looks, made him extremely well loved. On his large estate in Cordaremi, Enesco exercised a benevolent paternalism over the peasants, much as Verdi had done in Busseto. He tried to avoid politics, but when his estates were confiscated by the enemy at the end of the Second World War, he followed young King Michael into exile. Although he would have liked nothing better than to live quietly and devote himself to composition, he was obliged, late in life, to return to the concert stage in order to support himself and his wife.

He had composed chamber music, music for orchestra, songs, and miscellaneous works. His great dream was to see his opera *Oedipe* performed. He conducted it in Paris in 1936, and hoped for further performances in other capitals of the world. He brought the score to New York on one of his trips, and played it on the piano for a group of friends, singing the voice parts, and translating from French into English as he went along. He said that when he first read the text written by the poet, Edmond Fleg, he "felt the music rushing toward me like a road." The music was dynamic, urgent, masculine, and overwhelming, well suited to the tragic epic of Oedipus, but the opera was not performed in New York during his lifetime.

He was a frequent visitor to the United States until ill-health forced him to remain at his home in Paris. In one of his last letters he wrote, "I am proud to think that Americans take an interest in my work, and I have profound fellow-feeling and enormous admiration for the United States." The United States felt the same toward Enesco, foremost Rumanian composer and musician of his century.

Born Dorohoiu, Rumania, August 19, 1881
Died Paris, France, May 4, 1955

MANUEL DE FALLA

The shining white city of Cádiz was the birthplace of this son of Spain. His mother, a concert pianist, gave him his start, and when he was in his teens, he entered the Royal Conservatory of Music in Madrid, where Felipe Pedrell taught him composition. Pedrell was then about sixty, an embittered man, disgruntled that his research into Spanish folksong and his aim to make it the basis of a national Spanish music had not been realized. He inspired the receptive Falla with his enthusiasm for "root music," as, a few years earlier, he had inspired Granados.

Falla, trained to be a concert pianist, was far too shy for that career. But he was so thrilled by the first symphony concert he attended that he determined to become a composer. He was then seventeen.

His lyric drama, *La Vida Breve (Life is Short)* won first prize in a competition of the Academy of Fine Arts in 1905, and shortly after this he carried off the first prize for piano in a contest open to all the pianists in Spain. Now he was established in a dual career, but the struggle to support himself was just beginning. He was very poor. He scrimped and saved for an excursion ticket to Paris, fell in love with the city, and remained there one year for each day of the ticket, seven in all. Poor as he was, he found himself rich in the friendship of such men as Debussy, Dukas, and Charpentier, who shared his burning enthusiasm for Spanish rhythm and melody.

Except with such friends as these, he was shy to the point of agony. He once presented himself at the door of a wealthy amateur in Paris to whom he had been recommended as a teacher. He picked up his laundry on the way and had it with him in a brown paper parcel. The footman who opened the door saw the parcel, and told him haughtily to use the tradesmen's entrance. Too shy to protest, he allowed the door to be shut in his face and never went back. He was so shrinking that his friends once presented him with a vase inscribed, "I am the palpable ghost of Don Manuel de Falla."

There is nothing ghostly about his music, which pulsates with flaming vigor. In Paris, he began the composition of his "symphonic impressions" for piano and orchestra, *Nights in the Gardens of Spain,* which he completed after his return to the nights and the gardens. He wrote, "The themes are based on rhythms, modes, cadences and ornamental figures which are peculiar in Andalusia, although they are seldom employed in their original form". . . Something more than the sounds of festivals and dances inspired these "evocations in sound," which immediately placed Falla as the foremost living Spanish composer. His ballet-pantomime, *El Amor Brujo (Love the Sorcerer)* enhanced his reputation. He continued to gather folksongs, and assembled a great deal of thematic material before he went to live, in solitude, silence and seclusion, in Granada. Here, at the foot of the snow-capped Sierra Nevada Mountains, only the murmur of tumbling waterfalls and perhaps the tolling of a distant church bell broke the silence. Mme. Wanda Landowska was one of the few friends whom he admitted to his monastic retreat. To her he dedicated a beautiful *Sonata for the Harpsichord.*

Among other things, he wrote here a score for a ballet, *El Sombrero de Tres Picos (The Three-Cornered Hat).* He played parts of it on the piano for Diaghileff, the ballet impresario, who commissioned him to make a ballet of it. One evening, Falla, Diaghileff, and the choreographer Massine went together to a primitive little town in search of local color. They met a blind man in the street, singing and accompanying himself on a broken guitar. Falla incorporated the plaintive haunting melody into his score. Compounded of brisk action, uproarious comedy and typically Spanish humor, as well as song and dance, *The Three-Cornered Hat* is one of the most popular works in the ballet repertoire. The *Fantasia Boetica (Andalusian Fantasy)* is more scholarly, and less picturesque, but it captures, without employing the actual tunes, the warmth and individuality, the Oriental quality and true spirit of Spanish folksong.

When Franco became Dictator of Spain, after the Spanish Civil War, Falla was living quietly in Granada. He became president of the Institute of Spain in 1938, and that year visited Argentina. After the outbreak of the Second World War, he went, with a devoted sister, to make his home in Argentina. There was nothing warlike about Falla, described at this time as "a tiny man with large eyes burned into his bald skull . . . his features elongated as if by a combination of spiritual discipline and disease. He had the fanatic, suppressed asceticism of St. Francis as imagined by El Greco." He worked in Argentina on an oratorio, *Atlantida,* on which he had already spent ten years. But his health was poor, his means modest, and he was homesick. He sank into a state of lassitude, weakness and depression, and died suddenly in 1946, leaving his most ambitious composition, *Atlantida,* unfinished.

Born Cádiz, Spain, November 23, 1876
Died Alta Gracia, Argentina, November 14, 1946

GABRIEL

FAURE

Gabriel Fauré is inevitably compared with César Franck. He was as gifted, lovable and pious a man as the older man and in his way as creative a composer.

Since he excelled in the writing of songs and wrote a great many, his name is generally linked with that form of art. They are characterized in the main by exquisite clarity, impeccable taste, and rare poetic sensitivity, projected in a manner that is wholly French. Those who enjoy chamber music rejoice in the two sonatas for piano and violin, two piano quartets, two piano quintets, and other works for cello, violin or flute with piano. Beautiful balance of the parts, unobtrusive harmonic innovations, and a flowing limpid quality delight the ear in this "living-room music."

Of his larger works, the *D minor Symphony* yields first place to César Franck's in the same key, but the *Violin Concerto,* the *Pavane,* and the *Requiem* are frequently heard. His suite, *Pelléas et Mélisande,* suffered by comparison with the opera on the same subject by his admired friend and contemporary, Claude Debussy. Impressionistic music, tenuous though its texture, cast a substantial shadow on contemporary composition, especially if, like Fauré's, it leaned to the romantic.

The biography of this cultured Frenchman is largely the story of a series of uneventful positions as organist in various French churches. He studied music at the Niedermeyer School of Religious Music in Paris, where Saint-Saens was one of his favorite teachers. Then he in turn taught at the Conservatoire, where such leading younger figures in music as Maurice Ravel, Nadia Boulanger, Florent Schmitt, Roger Ducasse, Charles Koechlin, and Georges Enesco were proud to call themselves his students. For fifteen years, from 1905 to 1920, he was director of the Conservatoire, where, unlike the tight-lipped Cherubini, he ruled "with malice toward none."

During the last twenty-five years of his life, he was made a member of the French Academy, a Commander of the Legion of Honor, and president of the Paris Section of the International Society for Contemporary Music. These honors were accorded him with hardly a dissenting voice, for he earned them during his later years when he did his best work. He was more than fifty years old when he came into his own as a composer.

Aaron Copland wrote, "It is not difficult to see why Fauré's example was inspiring to a generation of composers who were quickly tiring of impressionism. They easily overlooked the fact that Fauré had his roots in the romantic movement, because his was a pre-Wagnerian brand of romanticism—delicate, reserved, and aristocratic. Moreover, no matter what its derivation may have been, it possessed all the earmarks of the French temperament: harmonic sensitivity, impeccable taste, classic restraint, and a love of clear lines and well-made proportions." Paul Dukas wrote that Fauré's music is proof that "an original mind can avail itself of traditional musical forms, and without doing them violence, use them to convey contemporary ideas." Since Fauré's death in 1924, his reputation has been growing steadily without fanfare, but with a quiet deliberateness that he would have been the first to approve.

Born Pamiers, France, May 12, 1845
Died Paris, France, November 4, 1924

STEPHEN

FOSTER

"STEVIE" liked to moon around by himself instead of playing with the other boys, he loved to go to church with the Negro maid and join there in the singing of spirituals, and he spent hours playing the flute, bought with his own hard-earned pennies. Still, his adoring mother did not recognize his talent for music and raised no objections when he was "sold down the river" to his brother Dunning in Cincinnati to be a bookkeeper. He was then twenty and had had practically no instruction in music.

But he was always scribbling tunes. At thirteen he had composed a quartet for flutes. Before going to Cincinnati, he had written *Old Uncle Ned, Oh Susannah, Open Thy Lattice, Love, Louisiana Belle,* and other songs. He sold some of them in Cincinnati and managed to convince his family that his talent for songs might be worth more in dollars and cents than his meager equipment as a bookkeeper. So the top floor of the Foster house was done over, and "Stevie" returned home to occupy it. For the next few years, he lived there in a state of pleasant irresponsibility. Twice a week, he went to try his songs with a group of friends. In 1850, he married Jane MacDowell, who had mingled her soprano with his tenor at these meetings.

Songs came bubbling and found a ready sale with the Christy Minstrels. The most famous of the songs that he handed to his friend, E. P. Christy, was *Old Folks at Home.* The name of Christy appeared on the title-page as composer, and not until *Old Folks at Home* had been sung in every country, translated into every language, did Foster publicly acknowledge his authorship. *Old Folks at Home* had the universal touch, which, in Foster's songs, made up for his lack of technical skill and for his other limitations. Because of this universal appeal, the two-hundred-odd songs he produced in his thirty-eight years have gained lasting importance in the music of America. *Camptown Races, Massa's in de cold, cold ground, Come where my Love lies dreaming, Old Dog Tray, Old Black Joe, Jeanie with the light brown hair* —these are a few of the best-loved ones.

When his mother died, in 1860, the fountain of his inspiration ceased to flow. He missed her terribly. He took his wife and child to New York, hoping to sell more songs at a better price. But he had started to drink, and the habit became uncontrollable. He would write a song in the morning, sell it in the afternoon, and drink the proceeds in the evening. His wife and child left him, and in a dingy hall bedroom he lived sordidly alone. One day, he got out of bed, fell against the old-fashioned pitcher and basin, and was badly cut. A few days later, he died in the charity ward of Bellevue Hospital. In his wallet, there was no money but a scrap of torn paper with the line, "Dear friends and gentle hearts." Was it to be a line of a song, an appeal for money, or the beginning of a letter? Nobody knows.

Born Lawrenceville, Pa., July 4, 1826
Died, New York, N. Y., January 13, 1864

CESAR FRANCK

A WELL-KNOWN picture of Père Franck, Pater Seraphicus, seated at the organ with a halo above his head, has established him in our minds as a saint. Certainly there was something unusually pure and good in the man and his music.

He was sixty-seven when the orchestra of the Paris Conservatoire gave the first performance of his only symphony. It is now recognized as the first important symphony composed by a Frenchman. But at this performance, the public, frankly puzzled by the novel cyclic form, failed to appreciate what Louis Biancolli terms the "angelic whirrings" of the symphony. "We don't understand it," they shrugged, and left it at that. The professors said, "Who ever heard of using an English horn in a symphony?" Charles Gounod, composer of the opera *Faust*, left before the performance was over, growling that the symphony was "the affirmation of incompetence pushed to dogmatic lengths." Franck himself paid no attention to the apathetic orchestra, and the unkind criticism, and when he returned home, and his family questioned, "How did it go?" he replied, "Oh, it sounded well, just as I thought it would."

What was Franck doing during the years before the symphony was played? He was busy most of the time earning a living. He was a teacher at the Conservatoire, an organist at the Church of Sainte-Clothilde, and a composer from five to seven A.M. His sire was determined that he should become a concert pianist, and took him on a tour of the provinces when he was eleven. Two years later, the family moved to Paris, and after a year of study with Anton Reicha, César entered the Conservatoire where he was first to study, then to teach, for the remainder of his life. As a Belgian, he could not compete for the Prix de Rome, but he won an extraordinary prize for sight-reading, and studied composition.

The year 1848, marked by a political upheaval in Paris, marked a revolution in Franck's life also. He married an actress, cut loose from his father's leading strings, and set up housekeeping for himself in a frugal home. This was his one known revolt. Symbolically, on the day of his wedding, he and his bride had to climb over the barricades erected in the street by the revolutionaries, to get to the church.

Mme. Franck was a thrifty housewife, to whom he handed his pay envelope every month without a murmur. There is a story of a brief flare-up of spirit, when he held out a few francs and concealed them to pay for a ticket to Bayreuth, where he longed to hear Wagner's operas in their native habitat. But his wife discovered the cache (or cash) in his bureau-drawer, and triumphantly confiscated it for household expenses. César never went to Bayreuth, nor any farther away than the bus-ride to the church, the Conservatoire, and the homes of his students.

He improvised so beautifully on the organ at St. Clothilde that those who came to pray remained to listen. Never did he touch the keys without first falling on his knees in prayer. At fifty he became professor of organ at the Conservatoire, where his organ classes were actually classes in composition. D'Indy, Chausson, Chabrier, and Fauré thankfully waited while Père Franck, with his good smile, drew a well-worn notebook from his pocket and dictated one of his own themes on which they were to improvise. He was an insignificant figure of a man, whose coatsleeves were threadbare and trouser-legs too short, but these students appreciated his soaring spirit and profound knowledge.

All the time, he was writing music systematically, day after day, with little prospect of publication or performance. The *Prelude, Chorale and Fugue,* the *Prelude, Aria and Finale,* and other stunning works for the piano; three operas; choice chamber music, including the *Sonata for Violin and Piano;* the *Piano Quintet,* the *Piano Quartet,* the *String Quartet;* oratorios and symphonic poems such as *Ruth, Redemption, Psyché* and *Les Béatitudes;* religious works for voice with organ and for organ alone; and the monumental symphony swelled his output to large proportions. Yet he might have died unwept, unhonored and unsung, had it not been for the friends and students who believed in him. They arranged a concert in 1887, where Franck at last experienced the delight of hearing his works come alive. When there was carping at the quality of the performers, Franck said quietly, "You expect too much, *mes enfants.* For my part, I was very well pleased." Three years later, Eugen Ysaye's magnificent string quartet played the Franck Quartet at a concert of the Société Nationale de la Musique, which Franck had helped to found and to direct. It was heartily applauded, and Franck remarked serenely, "You see, the public is beginning to understand me." It was none too soon.

A few months later, he was struck by an omnibus while crossing the street. He continued on his way to the home of a student, where he had promised to take part in a two-piano performance of his *Variations Symphoniques.* He tried to conduct "business as usual," until an attack of pleurisy resulting from his injury prevented him. He paid a last, feeble visit to his organ at St. Clothilde, and played his *Three Chorales* before taking to his bed. A copy of the score was beside him when he died.

Franck's mystical, ecstatic music, his insistence on delicacy, symmetry and purity, exercised an influence on the young French composers of his time, many of whom came to him at the Conservatoire and at the Société Nationale de la Musique. His seriousness, piety and idealism were a salutary contribution to French music.

Born Liège, Belgium, December 10, 1822
Died Paris, France, November 8, 1890

GEORGE GERSHWIN

A Brooklyn youngster who prided himself on being the roller-skating champion of his block, George Gershwin skated into music with only a gentle push from another Brooklyn boy. Max Rosen, who was to become a concert violinist, played a little number in public school assembly one day, and George decided right off that "this music stuff" was for him. He started fooling around on a friend's piano and taught himself quite a bit. When an upright was installed in the Gershwin living-room for the benefit of brother Ira, who was permitted to take lessons at fifty cents an hour from a "professor," George shoved Ira gently but firmly off the piano bench and took over the piano, the professor, and the fifty-cent lessons. In the end, Ira was none the worse off, for he was the Gilbert to George's Sullivan, the supplier of witty lyrics to George's tunes.

At sixteen George was introduced to Tin Pan Alley when he became a song plugger for the music publishing house of Remick. All day long, he played other men's song hits on the piano in order to boost sales. He rang in a few of his own, too, but at first nobody paid any attention to them. Soon after he changed jobs, to work as rehearsal pianist in a Ziegfeld production, he wrote his first musical comedy, *La La Lucille.* He was twenty-one. It was a hit! He turned out Broadway hits in rapid succession—*George White's Scandals, Lady Be Good, Oh Kay, Strike Up the Band, Funny Face, Girl Crazy, Of Thee I Sing,* and each one contained tunes that swept the country. Through myriad fads in popular music, including rock 'n roll, the rhythm of those Gershwin songs remains irresistible.

The famous *Rhapsody in Blue* was the product of the time, the place, and the Whiteman all together. Paul Whiteman, the most popular orchestra leader of his day, commissioned it in 1924. George wrote it in ten days, but refused to deliver it, insisting that it wasn't good enough. Whiteman stationed himself in an armchair in George's study and announced that he was staying until he had the score. George finally admitted defeat and gave him the manuscript. "The damn fool, did he think he could improve it!" exclaimed Whiteman after a quick read-through. He gave it to Ferde Grofé to orchestrate (George knew little of orchestration), and on February 12 it was given a grand performance, with Whiteman conducting and George playing the solo. With Gershwin, jazz was not a trick, it was a quality, as one critic remarked. Jazz as art music was something really new. The *Rhapsody in Blue* aroused audiences to hysterical demonstrations. Concert performances, radio broadcasts and recordings made it a familiar friend in countries all over the world.

After this success, George decided that he ought to study composition. He went to Paris and approached Igor Stravinsky to ask him for lessons. Stravinsky asked quizzically, "Monsieur, excuse me, but what was your income last year?" "About $100,000," replied George. "And from you," exclaimed Stravinsky. But George did study before composing the *Concerto for Piano and Orchestra in F Major.* Dr. Walter Damrosch, who conducted the première, acclaimed the composer as "the Prince who has taken Cinderella (jazz) by the hand and openly proclaimed her a princess to an astonished world."

The semi-operatic *An American in Paris* paved the way for his last important work, *Porgy and Bess.* In this grand-opera folk-opera with a libretto by DuBose Heyward, George did with Negro material what he had previously done with jazz: he raised it to a higher level, dignifying it into opera as he had wrought jazz into symphony. A member of the all-Negro cast refused to believe that the composer was not at least part Negro, so well did he reproduce the spirit of the Southern Negro in his melodies. In 1935 the consensus of opinion was, "Here is the first completely successful and completely American opera." Twenty years later, a company was sent to Europe to play *Porgy and Bess* in all the important capitals. In the Soviet Union, the cast was showered with attention, as the composer would have been had he been present.

George was taken ill at the end of the opera's first season, before he could realize that for a second time he had led the way in a new direction. When the news that he was dying of a brain tumor was flashed from Hollywood, nobody could believe it. He was only thirty-nine, it couldn't be true. But it was all too true, and his career came to an untimely end on July 11, 1937.

Born Brooklyn, New York, September 26, 1898
Died Hollywood, California, July 11, 1937

MICHAEL GLINKA

BECAUSE HE WAS one of the first to recognize that Russian serfs and peasants had minds and hearts, parts of the anatomy supposedly reserved for aristocrats; because he was actually the first to express their disregarded thoughts and feelings in music; and because he fathered the school of Russian "national" composers, Glinka became, in Liszt's words, the Prophet-Patriarch of Russian music, the first to give his country music of a definitely national character.

He was brought up as an aristocrat, in a hothouse atmosphere at variance with his latent sympathies. His education was that of a wealthy dilettante, and though at ten he averred "Music is my very soul," the statement went unheeded except for lessons in violin, piano and voice as part of his general education. He heard much folk song while growing up on his father's estate, and apparently kept his eyes open. When he was sent to Italy for his health, the Italian operas and the study of composition did more for him than the climate. He wound up with a few months of music in Vienna and Berlin, then returned to St. Petersburg. At thirty-two, he was married and ready to begin work on his great patriotic opera, *A Life for the Tsar*. The opera had a typical Russian folk-hero, who sacrificed himself to prevent the seventeenth century Tsar Michael Romanoff from falling into the hands of the Poles who were invading his country. Some aristocrats in the audience pronounced it "coachman's music," to which Glinka heatedly replied, "What matter, since the coachmen are superior to their masters?" But the reigning Tsar liked the warm melodic music with the tangy folk flavor, and he liked the idea of a Tsar being rescued, even by a peasant. He gave Glinka a valuable ring, and appointed him choirmaster of his chapel.

Six years later, Glinka brought forth another opera, *Russlan and Ludmilla,* in quite another style. It was based on a poem by Pushkin, and was a rambling fairy tale which left the audience cold. Furthermore, the sounds were strange, with daring harmonies and rhythms, not smoothly flowing like those in *A Life for the Tsar*. A grand duke said jestingly that his preferred punishment for offenders was to condemn them to listen to a complete performance of *Russlan and Ludmilla.* On the other hand, the writer Dostoievsky called it "a Slavic *Magic Flute*." Although it was not a success at its première in St. Petersburg, and although only the Overture is now heard in other countries, it is credited with having laid the foundations of the national Russian style, having been the starting-point of the oriental element apparent in later Russian music, having that "unmistakable, highly colored idiom that obviously differentiates Russian from other types of music."

Glinka was depressed, the more so as he had been separated from his wife. His health worsened and he left Russia in search of a cure. He set out for Spain but stopped in Paris en route, and made the acquaintance of Berlioz and Meyerbeer before going on to Spain. The *Jota Aragonesa* and *Summer Night in Madrid,* some chamber music and songs did not greatly enhance his fame, which rests on his operas. On his last trip abroad he visited Berlin, where Meyerbeer arranged a concert in his honor. He died in Berlin of a cold, contracted at the concert.

Born Smolensk, Russia, June 2, 1803
Died Berlin, Germany, February 15, 1857

CHRISTOPH WILLIBALD GLUCK

TWENTY OPERAS written before his fortieth year, were the trial balloons that Christoph Willibald Gluck sent up before he had the big idea which brought him honor and distinction. Although he was the son of a Bavarian gamekeeper, not a member of the privileged classes, he learned very early how to behave in the salons of the nobility. Wherever his father's occupation called him the son went too and picked up quite a respectable education here and there. He studied philosophy, history, science, and music in a Jesuit school. In Prague, where they spent some time, he sang in church and studied the violin and cello. He also listened to German light opera, and dreamed of composing it. At twenty-two, he stayed some months in the palace of Beethoven's patron, Prince Lobkowitz, in Vienna, and studied harmony there with Sammartini. He seems to have developed at a leisurely tempo and to have taken plenty of time for his own musical experiments.

He spent ten years in Italy, where his compositions, in no way remarkable, were successful enough. In 1745, he was invited to London to compose an opera for the Haymarket Theatre. But the concert he gave on the musical glasses, with orchestra, was more acclaimed than his opera, for in London, Handel ruled the opera with an iron baton forged in Italy. There was no chance for the young Gluck. Handel was polite to him, but when his back was turned, he remarked that "Gluck knows no more counterpoint than mine cook." This may very well have been true, for Handel's cook, an excellent singer, knew a great deal of counterpoint!

Gluck had become interested in Greek classic art, possibly because of a casual meeting with an archaeologist. He began to wonder if Italian-style opera might be improved by the application of classic Greek principles. He tucked the notion away in the back of his mind but took it out occasionally to look at it. He had little opportunity to test it for some years. In 1749, he married the wealthy Marianne Pergin. It was a romantic marriage, for her father opposed Gluck's suit and Marianne resisted her suitor's wooing for a long time. Marianne was Viennese, and five years after their marriage Gluck became musical director at the Austrian court in Vienna. But the Empress Maria Theresa preferred French and Italian pastorals to heavier works, and Gluck learned to temper his talent to her shorn taste. There was still no chance to write according to his new ideas. When finally he resigned his position at court, he continued to give singing lessons to the Princess Marie Antoinette, who loved the gruff German, never gruff with her.

In 1756, the Pope conferred on Gluck the Order of the Golden Fleece for his opera *Antigone*. After this, Christoph called himself Ritter Gluck and displayed the order proudly on his broad chest. It was in the opera *Orfeo ed Euridice*, produced in Vienna the following year, that there is the first evidence of Gluck's "reformed" style. This opera holds within it, clad in Grecian simplicity, the elements of the modern music-drama. It is difficult to write dispassionately of its touchingly lovely music, so pure, so rarefied, yet so tender and dramatic. In *Alceste*, his second opera in his new style, we find noble melodies and arias, vigorous and dramatic choruses, a genuine orchestral accompaniment, and an expressive overture. In the preface to *Alceste* he explained earnestly: "My purpose was to restrict music to its true office, that of administering to the expression of the poetry and the situations of the plot, without interrupting the action or weakening it by superfluous ornament." He developed these ideas in *Paris and Helen*, but the pleasure-loving Viennese preferred something lighter.

Rameau, whose classic style had influenced Gluck, had paved the way for him in Paris. When an invitation to Paris was extended, Gluck willingly accepted. He composed *Iphigenia in Aulis* for the French market, and in 1773, he and Marianne went to Paris to supervise rehearsals. His old pupil, Marie Antoinette, was now the wife of the French Dauphin. She was on Gluck's side whatever happened, and plenty happened. An Italian composer, Piccinni, was egged on to compose an opera on the same subject as Gluck's. The Italian opera fans, led by the King, confronted the French opera fans, led by the Queen. From opposite corners of the opera house, the factions glared at each other. Voltaire, Rousseau, and other intellectuals also took sides. Mozart, trying to make his way in Paris, was lost in the excitement. Gluck retired to Vienna to await developments and to compose *Armide*. The controversy, fomented for the sake of excitement, died at last. Needless to say, Gluck won. *Iphigenia* made Rameau and Lully seem "old hat." It was the modern music of its day, hailed for innovations which were little short of revolutionary. And this in a city where a visit to the opera had been regarded in court circles by the men as an excuse to drink wine, play cards, shoot dice, and discuss politics, while the women giggled and flirted and talked audibly. Only when some special feat of vocalism on the stage called them to attention, did the occupants of the loges deign to watch the performance. For Gluck to induce them to do so was truly an achievement.

"If the Greeks had had a musician, they would have had Gluck," said one critic. The seven great operas on which his fame rests are classics. But he did not live with the simplicity he advocated in music. In their palatial home in Vienna he and Marianne entertained royally, ate and drank and made merry without stint. Mozart and his wife dined with them there and were impressed by their lavish hospitality. How could a composer be so rich, they wondered. But Gluck paid a high price for his fun. He grew too stout and his blood pressure went up. He was warned to watch his step. Marianne, alarmed, watched it for him. One day, however, he eluded her loving care and drank a glass of the wine that he craved, then went for a drive. That evening he suffered a final stroke. He died at seventy-three, a bon vivant to the end.

Born Weidenwang, Germany, July 2, 1714
Died Vienna, Austria, November 15, 1787

CHARLES GOUNOD

ASKED to name the most popular French opera in the repertory, the Director of the Opera in Paris replied, "Gounod's *Faust,* unquestionably." Performed for the first time in 1859, for the two thousandth time in 1934, and goodness knows how often since then, *Faust* established Gounod as a French composer. There was some unfavorable publicity when a critic stated, after the première, "I don't believe that Gounod wrote the opera himself, it's so much better than anything he's done before, and so different in style." The critic's words produced an uproar, he was challenged to a duel, and had to retract or fight. He retracted. But a half-century later, the remark was repeated, with a sequel to the effect that Gounod had stolen the score from an unknown genius. To make it more dramatic, the genius had died in a mental hospital. But the charge was never proved, and in no way affected the popularity of opera or composer.

Gounod was a gentleman, to start with. His mother was a fine pianist, his father a distinguished painter, and between them they gave their son every possible educational advantage. Charles attended the Conservatoire, and was sufficiently gifted, industrious and charming to please his teachers, and to win the Prix de Rome. During his prescribed sojourn in the Eternal City, he "got religion," became particularly interested in composing for the church, and studied Palestrina's writings assiduously. At twenty-three, he heard his own mass performed in Rome. He returned to Paris, became organist and choirmaster in one of the churches, and was fully decided to study for the priesthood. For five years, he was known as the Abbé Gounod.

But he took no orders after all, excepting those issued by his worldly young friends, Fanny Mendelssohn, the talented sister of the composer Felix, and Pauline Viardot-Garcia, prima donna at the Opéra Comique. They re-routed him from pulpit to stage, and only a few months after composing a *Solemn Mass* which brought his name before the public, he came out with his first opera, *Sapho.* He was thirty-four, and must have enjoyed the mild scandal occasioned by his return to the fleshpots. He brought out *La Nonne Sanglante (The Bleeding Nun)* and incidental music to Molière's play, *Le Medécin Malgré Lui.* The attractive bachelor was a well-liked figure on the Parisian boulevards at the time that he composed *Faust.* A sentimental story, not quite "comme il faut," melodies that could be carried away and sung from memory, are the ingredients of *Faust* that gave the greatest pleasure to the French bourgeoisie. The matrons clasped the erring Marguerite to their ample bosoms in defiance of middle-class morality, and would not be gainsaid. But only after *Faust* had been accepted in other countries were they permitted to do so, and this was not until ten years after the first performance in Paris!

None of Gounod's other operas achieved the popularity of *Faust. Romeo et Juliette* was mildly successful, so was *Mireille.* Some smaller works, such as *The Funeral March of a Marionette* and *Ave Maria* (Meditation on Bach's Prelude in C) are affectionately cherished by the public. His oratorios *The Redemption* and *Death in Life* were acclaimed. When he visited London, the ladies there who had been brought up on oratorios, clustered about him as devotedly as did their opera-loving sisters in Paris.

At the end of his life, the priest in him triumphed over the pagan after all. Blind and paralyzed at seventy-five, the erstwhile gay bachelor's last composition was a solemn *Requiem.* After a private hearing in his study, he reached over to take the music and place it in his cabinet. As he reached, he fell unconscious to the floor, and his death followed shortly. Hosts of admirers and disciples followed him to his last resting-place in the cemetery at St. Cloud.

Born Paris, France, June 17, 1818
Died Paris, France, October 13, 1893

ENRIQUE

GRANADOS

SENSITIVE, intuitive, languorous, passionate, Granados was described as "one of the most delicious visionaries among the artists." He recreated Spain in music. His was not the Spain of the tourist, however. Not for him the clicking castanets of the cabaret and the pseudo-gypsy song and dance. What concerned him was the primitive peasant life of the Spanish people. Like his friend Isaac Albéniz, who preceded him by seven years, and Manuel de Falla who followed him, he was able to fix in music the individuality of the people of the differing provinces of Spain. His countryman, Pablo Casals, told him wryly, "Granados, every form you employ has been employed before, and yet from them you have evolved something never heard in the world before."

In his youth, he was somewhat delicate and was unable to undergo the rigorous course of musical training prescribed for composers. But he studied in Spain with Pedrell, teacher also of Albéniz and Falla. Pedrell was a folksong specialist whose enthusiasm fired all three to the creation of a genuine national music. When Granados went to Paris to continue his studies, his ill health prevented his regular attendance at the Conservatoire, but he studied privately with Charles de Bériot and other teachers and became a brilliant concert pianist. He played his own pieces so eloquently when he went on tour that he convinced audiences and critics that they were the most wonderful works of their kind—as many of them indeed were.

His first opera, *Maria del Carmèn*, appeared when he was thirty-one; it was mildly successful. Some chamber music, a few orchestral and stage works, lovely songs in the style of the eighteenth century "tonadillas" punctuated his life of teaching and concertizing. But like Chopin, he was in love with the piano and concentrated upon it the full force of his talent. The four volumes of *Spanish Dances* which are familiar to audiences represent but a small part of the eloquent works with fascinating titles which he composed for his instrument.

In his home in Barcelona the white plaster walls of the study were hung with paintings and tapestries by Goya, the people's artist. *Goyescas* is a reinterpretation for the piano of Goya's interpretation in art of the life of the Spanish people. There is not a weak or colorless line in the paintings and tapestries of Goya, nor in the two large volumes of Granados' *Goyescas*. With *Goyescas* he broke definitely with the past to create modern Spanish piano music.

He was much pleased when he was invited to make an opera of *Goyescas*, and looked forward to its production in Paris in 1914. The outbreak of the First World War prevented this, but two years later the opera was gorgeously produced at the Metropolitan Opera House in New York. He wrote an orchestral intermezzo for the performance, which became a favorite concert piece. When Senor and Senora Granados waved good-by to their six children and sailed to attend the performance, they little thought that they would never again see their family. They had taken return passage on the Sussex, an English ship. It was torpedoed in mid-Atlantic by a German submarine. Granados escaped to a lifeboat, but when he saw his wife struggling in the water he jumped overboard to rescue her. The last that was seen of them, they were sinking, clasped in each other's arms. They died as they had lived—together.

Born Lérida, Spain, July 29, 1867
Died at sea, March 24, 1916

EDVARD GRIEG

Edvard Grieg was fifteen, when, as he recalled it, "on a beautiful summer day, a man on horseback in full gallop reined up his fiery Arab steed" and dismounted to pass the time of day. The rider was Ole Bull, the famous Norwegian violinist, a good friend of Edvard's parents. Edvard worshiped him. At dinner that day the Griegs showed Ole some of their son's attempts at composition. "You must go to Leipzig and become a musician," said Ole positively. At this time, Edvard was planning to become a minister. Mathematics was not required for the ministry, and he disliked that branch of learning so thoroughly that, when he was a small boy, if it rained he would get his clothes soaking wet on the way to school so that he would be sent home to change them and would miss the mathematics period. But the ministry was forgotten when Ole Bull pronounced him worthy to enter the magic realm of music, to which his mother had already introduced him.

He went to the Conservatory in Leipzig and worked so hard that he suffered a nervous breakdown, complicated by pleurisy which left him with only one usable lung. But he graduated and shortly afterward made friends of the composers Nils Gade and Richard Nordraak. The latter friendship is important in his life, for from Nordraak, Grieg learned to think in terms of national music based on folksongs. With Nordraak, Grieg founded the Euterpe Society, whose members were pledged to the promotion of Norwegian music.

His marriage with his cousin, Nina Hagerup,

who sang his songs enchantingly, was a singularly happy one which further advanced his musical career. With Nina, Edvard gave concerts throughout Europe, featuring his piano music and his songs, which brought the cooling breeze of the Norwegian fjords to stuffy concert halls. The song, *I love you,* which he wrote for Nina and which she introduced, was a favorite of the Norwegian soprano, Kirsten Flagstad, when she visited this country.

The *Piano Concerto in A minor* and the *Peer Gynt Suite* are his strongest works. The *Piano Concerto* was composed when he was twenty-five, in the flush of ardor of the first year of marriage. It is full of "a joy of life, amorous longing, and youthful fire," to quote Grieg's German biographer. Another commentator found much to remind him of Liszt in the fiery concerto. It is no wonder, then, that Liszt enjoyed reading it at sight from the manuscript when Grieg visited him in Weimar, nor that he urged the young composer, "Keep it up, don't let them intimidate you." There is a great deal of sticky sentimentality in the comments on the concerto, but it is really a stunning piece, which every virtuoso delights in performing.

Some time after the concerto was written, the playwright Ibsen asked Grieg to compose incidental music for his play, *Peer Gynt.* Edvard hesitated. He did not care for Ibsen's satirical treatment of his beloved countrymen, as symbolized in the shiftless, bragging dreamer, Peer. Only the fact that he needed money at the time induced him to accept the offer. Ironically, the play with his music and the orchestral suite he later made from it established his fame solidly both in and outside of Norway. He received honors and degrees from every country and a pension from his government in recognition of his contribution to Norway's culture.

He built a charming villa among the hills, and here he and Nina lived. From Troldhaugen they went to give concerts together, to Troldhaugen they returned for long periods of rest and recreation. The English composer Delius, the Australian Percy Grainger, and many other figures well-known in the musical world visited them there.

When Grieg was invited to Paris during the Dreyfus trial, he refused to go, because he disapproved of the way it was being conducted. He was a man of strong convictions in a weak body. Small, frail, with legs so short they barely reached the pedals when he was seated, he looked his best at the piano, for his head with its mass of wavy hair was magnificent. He was dearly loved and deeply mourned when he died in his sleep at sixty-four, peacefully, as he had lived.

Born Bergen, Norway, June 15, 1843
Died Bergen, Norway, September 4, 1907

CHARLES T. GRIFFES

"GRIFFES FACED AND SOLVED the problem of bread versus creation which confronts every artist—he tried to do both, and lost . . . Long hours of teaching small boys their musical A B C's, and long nights of composing or writing out parts which he was too poor to have copied by a professional at last wore down his frail body." That, in a nutshell, is the saga of Charles Tomlinson Griffes as seen by R. F. L. McCombs. To Marion Bauer, his fellow-composer, he was "a vital part of the American tradition," although he died at the age of thirty-six.

This gifted composer was talented in fields other than music. He drew well, etched on copper, and painted in water colors. But he preferred music, and after graduating from high school went to Berlin to study for a career as a concert pianist. It was Humperdinck, of *Hansel and Gretel* fame, whose teaching and whose example made Charles decide to become a composer, not a performer. When he returned to America with high ideals and a low bank-balance, he took a position as music teacher at the Hackley School in Tarrytown-on-the-Hudson and stayed there until his untimely death.

His *Poem* for flute and orchestra is the most mature of his works.

For a time French impressionism interested him; three tone-pictures for the piano, including *The Lake at Evening*, emerged from this interest. His best-known work for the piano is the *Roman Sketches*, of which there are four. The first, *The White Peacock*, is chromatic, in languorous mood, with none of the harshness associated with the cry of a peacock, or with the modernist school either. The other movements have descriptive titles, *Nightfall*, *The Fountain of the Acqua Paola*, and *Clouds*. A *Piano Sonata* and *Fantasy Pieces* for piano, and some lovely songs are often played; so is his string quartet, *Two Sketches based on Indian Themes*.

In *The Pleasure-Dome of Kubla Khan*, a tone-poem for orchestra, he found a subject over which he could labor with love. The poem, "The Pleasure-Dome of Kubla Khan," by Samuel Taylor Coleridge, is the darling of students of elocution, who zestfully declaim:

"In Xanadu did Kubla Khan
A stately pleasure-dome decree;
Where Alph, the sacred river, ran
Through caverns measureless to man,
Down to a sunless sea."

With no less zest did the young composer let his imagination run free in describing the pleasure-dome in sound. The vague, foggy beginning suggests the sacred river; the outlines of the palace rise into view, then gardens, with fountain and green lawn. Sounds of revelry are heard, which rise to a wild climax, and then suddenly break off, allowing the music to return to its gray beginning.

Griffes overworked while composing it, and when he was told that it would be performed by the Boston Symphony Orchestra, his effort to finish copying the parts by hand in time for the performance brought on the pneumonia which caused his death. He lived just long enough to be told that his work had been a success. Griffes is one of the few American composers whose claim to recognition is unchallenged, despite the meagerness of his output.

Born Elmira, New York, September 17, 1884
Died New York, N. Y., April 8, 1920

Peter Tchaikowsky

Born: Votkinsk, Russia, May 7, 1840.
Died: Moscow, Russia, November 6, 1893

His first governess described Tchaikowsky as a "porcelain child," sensitive, charming, but fragile. His youth was in no way remarkable. He studied law, and at nineteen he became a clerk in the Ministry of Justice in St. Petersburg. He was a popular young man, for he played the piano nicely, danced well, and was always ready to attend an opera or a ballet performance. When he was twenty-one, a cousin showed him how to modulate from one key to another on the piano, and he became greatly interested. He persuaded his father to allow him to take courses at the Conservatory of St. Petersburg. After a couple of years, he resigned his boring job in the ministry and gave himself completely to the study of music. In Anton Rubinstein's class in orchestration, the young man was transformed into a threadbare, hard-working student. After his graduation in June, 1866, he accepted a poorly paid job with Nikolai Rubinstein, Anton's brother, in the newly-formed Conservatory of Moscow. He suffered the first of many nervous breakdowns when the performance in Moscow of his First Symphony, was denied.

During Tchiakowsky's first ten years in Moscow, he made the acquaintance of the writers Turgenev and Tolstoi, the composers Liszt, Wagner and Saint-Saens. His unhappy marriage to Antonia Milyukova, ended in divorce, followed by his own breakdown. Living quietly in Switzerland,

Peter Ilyich Tchaikovsky

Born: Votkinsk, Russia, May 7, 1840
Died [illegible], Russia, November 6, 1893

[illegible]

he finished the works interrupted by his marriage, the opera Eugen Onegin (ER-JAN) (O-NA-GIN) and the Fourth Symphony. He composed the beautiful Violin Concerto, a long piano sonata, and other smaller works. In his relief at his refuge, he produced masterpieces.

Fortunately, he was not obliged to compose with one eye on the dollar, for a "beloved friend and patroness," Madame von Meck, was making him an annual allowance which supported him comfortably. When, without explanation, she abruptly withdrew her support after fourteen years, Tschiakowsky experienced another nervous breakdown. Tchaikowsky missed her letters more than her money, for by this time, in 1890, he was so famous that he could support himself.

In 1891 he was invited to New York to conduct the gala concert at the opening of Carnegie Hall. He was homesick before he ever started. But his music was received with enthusiasm, and so was he, and there were happy moments before he returned to Russia. Nevertheless, black depression settled on him after his return, and in that mood, he finished his sixth and last symphony, aptly titled the Pathetic. Its first performance in Moscow in 1893 was coolly received.

Nine days after the concert he complained of feeling ill. Saying he was thirsty, he gulped a drink of water from a tap. A cholera (COLLAR-A) epidemic was raging in Moscow at the time. Tchaikowsky's reckless disregard of the simple sanitary precaution of boiling the water he drank brought death.

He was possibly the greatest symphonist after Beethoven,

and certainly the most popular. And he was by far the most expressive ~~Romantic~~ composer that Russia produced.

GEORGE FREDERICK HANDEL

When Beethoven lay on his deathbed an English friend sent him Handel's works, complete in forty giant volumes.

"Handel was the greatest, the most skilled composer who ever lived. I can still learn from him," said Beethoven.

Handel was born in the same year as Johann Sebastian Bach. But while there were so many musical Bachs that the word came to mean "musician" in Bach's part of Germany, Handel's parents were totally unmusical. His father was indeed opposed to his becoming a musician, and like a dutiful German son, Frederick hearkened to the paternal command and prepared to become a lawyer. But at seven, he had taught himself to play the harpsichord, practicing on an instrument smuggled into the attic, and when his father took him on a visit to a neighboring duke, the boy's playing so delighted the duke that the father was persuaded to seek a music-teacher for his son. Frederick then learned to play the violin, oboe, harpsichord and organ and studied harmony, counterpoint and composition with Friedrich Zachau, the best teacher in Halle.

When his father died, Frederick was barely eighteen. But without hesitation, he dropped the detested law and accepted a position as organist in the Dom church.

He served several years' musical apprenticeship in Hamburg, capital of German opera, where he played the violin in the orchestra and composed his first opera, *Almira*. In Hamburg he fought his famous duel with a rival harpsichordist. A coat-button, which deflected his adversary's sword, supposedly saved Handel's life. But for the button, we might never have had the *Messiah,* or the *Largo,* or the *Water Music,* or the *Harmonious Blacksmith,* to say nothing of the magnificent operas and oratorios of his later years.

His first opera was a success, and he followed it immediately with a second, *Nero.* This too was a success, too much so for Handel's good. For jealous rivals conspired to make life in Hamburg unpleasant for him, and in 1706, at the age of twenty-one, he shook the dust of Germany from his feet and went to Italy. As Mozart did later, he fell in love with all things Italian, especially Italian opera. In Florence, Rome, Venice and Naples he felt thoroughly at home. The opera he composed, *Rodrigo,* was Italian in text, in musical style, and in feeling. Its warm, flowing lyricism brought its composer to the attention of such wealthy sponsors as Prince Raspoli and Cardinal Ottoboni, and he was much sought after.

At a costume ball in Rome, Domenico Scarlatti heard a guest, masked and disguised, improvise on the harpsichord. Before Handel could throw off his mask, Scarlatti cried with delight, "That must either be the famous Saxon or the Devil!" (The two men became friends.)

In 1710, Handel returned to Germany, to become director of the opera in Hanover. But almost his first act was to request a leave of absence to go to London, where his opera *Rinaldo* was to be given.

Rinaldo was a hit. The English preferred Italian opera to all others, and there was at that moment no composer in London to supply it. This international German, who wrote like an Italian with a German accent, suited the English taste perfectly. He settled in London for life in 1712. He changed his German name to the English equivalent and became a naturalized citizen in 1726.

During the ten years from 1720 to 1730, Handel was to London what Lully had been to Paris. At the Royal Academy of Music, dedicated to Italian opera, he directed the productions, engaged the singers, and composed and produced fifteen successful operas.

But he did not continue to rule unchallenged. In 1728, the *Beggar's Opera,* an English ballad opera, light, spicy and satirical, raised its siren voice. The public hearkened and with one accord succumbed to the siren's spell. Handel's operas now played to empty houses, and finally he was obliged to close the Royal Academy. The reason—no funds.

At fifty-two, he suffered an apoplectic stroke and was ill for some months. When he returned from taking the cure in Aix-la-Chapelle, he was bankrupt but restored in body and undaunted in spirit. He decided to regain his lost prestige by way of the oratorio. Every year from 1738 to 1751, he produced an oratorio, sometimes two, and the English loved his oratorios as they had loved his operas.

The greatest of them all is *The Messiah.* At the rousing *Hallelujah Chorus,* audiences rise spontaneously to their feet today as they did at the first performance. "I did think I did see all Heaven before me, and the great God himself," said Handel of this Chorus.

For the last seven years of his life the composer was blind. His oratorio about the blind Samson was prophetic of his own fate. But he continued to play the organ and conduct to the last.

When he died, he was buried in Westminster Abbey with all the pomp and ceremony that England bestows upon her favorite sons.

Born in Halle, Germany, February 23, 1685
Died in London, England, April 14, 1759

ROY

HARRIS

Recent performances of Roy Harris' *Seventh Symphony* have released a flood of laudatory comment on this climactic composition, and an appraisal of his highly significant contribution as an American composer.

His ancestors were of pioneer stock, and he was born in a log cabin in Lincoln County on Lincoln's birthday, surely an ideal beginning for an American composer. He spent his boyhood in the San Gabriel Valley of Southern California, where his environment was one of profound silences and open spaces, in which the spirit could expand. He was a farmer until the First World War called him to the colors.

When he returned from the War at twenty, a long-limbed, rangy, muscular young man with abundant energy and swarming ideas, he took desultory piano lessons with his mother and studied music alone in the evenings. Then he won a Guggenheim Fellowship and submitted to the formal discipline of Nadia Boulanger in Paris. "I finally decided to choose music as a life work because it was the only language which I found to be constant," he says. "I made my choice late in life. I was twenty-eight years old." He returned to the United States in 1929, bringing his first major work, a concerto for piano, clarinet and string quartet.

His life has been punctuated with more than the usual mishaps. An accident to his spine compelled him to lie on his back for six months. While staring at the ceiling he composed a string quartet, and discovered he could capture musical thoughts best without benefit of piano. In 1955 he was nearly killed in an automobile accident. Fortunately he recovered fully.

He now has five children, the older of whom share his interest in music and baseball, a wife who turns from caring for the newest baby to play his brilliant *Fantasy for Piano and Orchestra,* or to take part in a concert or recording session. They live in a rambling house in Pittsburgh, from which he exits periodically as visiting lecturer at the university in Carbondale, Illinois, and other nearby centers of culture.

"I hate the little tiny nervous pieces," says Roy Harris, and his works show it. They are virile, energetic, well-made, and above all, large in concept and execution. Besides his seven symphonies, many of his works have been recorded, including several piano concertos, *Symphony for Voices, Johnny Comes Marching Home* for orchestra, *Song for Occupations,* and a great deal of chamber music. When Leonard Bernstein, as a stripling, heard Harris' Third Symphony premièred in 1939, he found it "mature in every sense, beautifully proportioned, eloquent, restrained and affecting," and said that he experienced "a strong desire to hear the Harris [symphony] again, because it greatly excited me." He not only heard it, he conducted it.

Roy Harris' is a creative talent of large dimensions. His is the music of a "young, an eager, a wholesomely optimistic spirit. For Harris, there is no musical Waste Land."

Born Lincoln County, Oklahoma, February 12, 1898
Living Pittsburgh, Penn.

FRANZ JOSEPH HAYDN

THE LITTLE Austrian peasant, Joseph Haydn, slept on straw before he landed in a feather-bed at the court of Prince Esterhazy. He was one of twelve children of a humble wheelwright and a cook in the tiny village of Rohrau and learned about the struggle for existence in his own family, where there was never enough to feed all the hungry mouths.

When he was a spindly boy of six, a cousin, attracted by his "weak but pleasing voice," took him to Vienna to study in the choir school. The cousin was not a good provider, neither was the choir school, and he continued to be hungry. He received excellent musical training. But in a restless moment, he cut off the pigtail of the man on the bench in front of him. This boyish prank gave the director an excuse to expel him from the school. His voice had started to change, and his usefulness as a choir-boy was at an end. An older boy, Spangler, befriended him, allowed him to share his attic, and gave him the music paper he was too poor to buy for himself. Haydn was always scribbling music, which consumed reams of paper.

In his early twenties, he found a patron, Count Fürnberg, with whom he played string quartets. For the count he composed his first eighteen quartets. He went next as music director to Count Morzin, where he directed a small orchestra. He composed his *Symphony No. 1* for this group, the first of the hundred and four he was to compose during his life. When Count Morzin could no longer afford the luxury of a resident composer, Haydn thankfully accepted the invitation of Prince Paul Anton Esterhazy to be his musical director. Later he was transferred to the retinue of Prince Nicholas Esterhazy and remained with the Esterhazy family for thirty idyllic years.

"This is the life," he might have said. The spring and summer months were spent in the country, in Hungary but close to Vienna. When the weather began to grow bleak, the establishment was moved bag and baggage to Vienna for the winter. Haydn loved Vienna. He loved the ladies, loved them the more because he had married a nagging wife who gave him no peace. He loved the bustle and gaiety in the city's streets. He adored Wolfgang and Constanze Mozart and took part in string quartets at their Sunday morning musicales.

One year the Prince took longer than Haydn thought fair to give the signal to depart for the city. Chuckling to himself, Haydn invited his patron to hear a new symphony. When the court had assembled in the white and gold salon, Haydn bowed respectfully and started the symphony. When they came to the last movement, the players rose one by one, blew out their candles, and tiptoed from the stage. Finally the last musician departed; the stage was dark and silent. This was the famous *Farewell Symphony.* The Prince saw the point, laughed indulgently, and gave the long-awaited signal for departure.

In the beautiful but solitary country, "there was no one to confuse and torment me, and so I was obliged to become original," said Haydn. During his Esterhazy years, he composed five masses, eleven operas, sixty symphonies, forty string quartets, about one hundred and twenty-five cello trios, thirty clavier pieces, besides all sorts of occasional works for birthdays, weddings, funerals, etc. This is the composer who naively stated, "I was never a quick writer, and always composed with care and diligence."

When Prince Nicholas, the most generous and genuinely musical of the Esterhazys died, Haydn was almost sixty. It may have been at this time that he was called upon to compose his *Minuet of the Ox.* He was in Vienna, seated at his desk, when a neighboring butcher entered hat in hand. He stammered out his request that the great Herr Haydn should write a minuet for the wedding of his daughter, offering to pay any price. With a twinkle of the eye, Haydn promised him the minuet in twenty-four hours. A few days later, he heard the sound of music, and stepped out of his balcony to see the wedding procession approaching. His minuet was being played, and at the head of the procession was a milk-white ox, decked with garlands of flowers. "For you," said the happy butcher, halting the ox at the doorstep.

Having nothing more to do for the Esterhazys, Haydn now turned a willing ear to the proposal of a London manager, J. P. Salomon, that he visit London. Salomon had already vainly tried to induce him to cross the Channel. It seems that a set of fine English razors, sent by Salomon after he had watched Haydn's struggles to shave himself one morning, cast the deciding vote. Moreover, they inspired Haydn to write his *Rasierquartet* (Shaving Quartet). He visited the British Isles in 1791-2, and again in 1794-5. The twelve London Symphonies that he composed for Salomon's concerts are among his finest. He was idolized in London and received the degree of Doctor of Music from the University of Oxford and many other honors. He was inspired to write his oratorios, *The Creation* and *The Seasons,* by the Handel Festival which he attended while in England. "It is England that has made me famous in Germany," he said.

During his later years he returned to the service of the third generation of Esterhazys. Things were different now. Napoleon's armies kept coming around to harass Vienna. When the French bombarded the city in 1809, Haydn lay on his deathbed. His terrified servants clustered about him. "Do not be afraid, my children, Papa Haydn is with you," he whispered. But he knew that his end was near. He asked them to sing for him the melody of his *Kaiserquartett* (Emperor Quartet), to which he had written a remarkable series of variations. Sung to the words "Gott erhalte Franz den Kaiser" (God save Emperor Francis), it became the Austrian national hymn. On the wings of that song his soul took flight.

Papa Haydn is one of the great greats. He added to musical literature an enormous number of works in many forms. He was the father of the string quartet. "From Papa Haydn I learned all I know about string quartets," said Mozart. He developed the elementary sonata form of Carl Phillip Emanuel Bach, adding a second theme to relieve the monotony of but one. He added the murmur of muted strings, and the clear song of the clarinet to the voices of the orchestra, which he further enriched by writing the parts in such a way as to bring out the individual tone-color of each voice. And he sang into his music his bubbling joy of living, his peasant heartiness, his love of nature and of his fellow-man, his innate nobility of character. Teacher of Mozart and Beethoven, "Papa Haydn" to a musical generation, he could boast with truth, "My language is understood by the whole world."

Born Rohrau, Austria, March 31, 1732
Died Vienna, Austria, May 31, 1809

VICTOR HERBERT

IT WAS no potato famine that drove the genial Victor Herbert from Ireland to these shores. His wife, a prima donna of the Court Opera in Vienna, was invited in 1886 to the Metropolitan Opera in New York and he came along for the ride. He had previously toured Germany, France and Italy as a cello soloist, had been first cellist of the court orchestra in Stuttgart, and had composed a few serious works. As first cellist of the Metropolitan Opera Orchestra he settled down in New York contentedly and soon became an active and agreeable fixture of the musical scene. He succeeded the popular Pat Gilmore as bandmaster of the Twenty-second Regiment Band in 1893, and, resplendent in a red and gold uniform, led the band on parade up Fifth Avenue. The next year he produced his first light opera, *Prince Ananias.* The public liked it and clamored for more, which Herbert was only too happy to supply.

When he returned to New York, after six years as conductor of the Pittsburgh Orchestra, he had a soundproof apartment built. This was one of the first experiments in that praiseworthy direction, and as such it came in for a great deal of humorous comment from the newspapers. Unfortunately, it did not succeed in shutting out the sounds from the street. But Herbert was able to write operettas under any condition, or so it appeared. From 1895 on, he produced steadily until more than forty titles stood to his credit.

He had hard luck with librettists, and some of his texts came in for severe criticism, but not a voice was raised against the fresh, melodious, singable music. Someone said of him that he could set the telephone book to music failing any other libretto, and certainly his facility was amazing. Ragtime and jazz, the rock 'n roll of his time, did not appeal to him. He wrote from a sound classical knowledge and traditional taste, and if much of his appeal is sentimental, it was also lasting. Americans like his music, sentimental or not.

Naughty Marietta, Babes in Toyland, The Red Mill, Mlle. Modiste, The Viceroy, The Only Girl, The Madcap Duchess—the titles alone conjure up carefree, happy, romantic melodies. Who that heard them has forgotten "The March of the Toys" and "I Can't Do That Sum" from *Babes in Toyland,* or "Kiss Me Again" from *Naughty Marietta?* Who would deny that, with a librettist like Gilbert, Herbert might have become the American half of a team comparable to Gilbert and Sullivan?

He was personally very well liked, his two hundred and fifty pound bulk was a familiar figure wherever good food and drink were to be had, his talent as a raconteur always on tap, his good nature unfailing. The generation that knew him is disappearing, but thanks to movies, recordings and radio, he holds his own with the new generation, not as an antique, but because of the lasting appeal of his songs.

Like Frank Loesser, George Gershwin, and some others with the light touch, he tried his hand at serious music. Unlike them, he was not successful. He worked hard over his two grand operas, *Natoma* and *Madeleine,* which failed. But as the composer of light operas, this Irishman educated in Germany is claimed by America as her own.

Born Dublin, Ireland, February 1, 1859
Died New York, N. Y., May 26, 1924

PAUL HINDEMITH

In 1939, Paul Hindemith landed in New York, a small man, heavy-laden. A viola case dangled from his hand, other instruments and bulging brief-cases were piled behind him. A customs inspector approached him. "Do you play the fiddle?" he asked, curiously. "A little," was the modest reply. "Are you a musician?" "Yes." "Do you know Jascha Heifetz?" "Yes." "Do you know Rudolf Serkin, Artur Rubinstein, Mischa Elman?" Hindemith nodded, smiling. "Well, I have a collection of their recordings," said the inspector proudly. "Good," said Hindemith. "Let him in, he's all right," cried the music-loving inspector, as he marked the viola-case with the chalked symbol of admission. And in came Hindemith.

Shortly before leaving Europe, he had completed an opera, *Mathis der Maler (Mathias the Painter)*, the outcome of six months of solitary contemplation of the life of an interesting medieval character. Hitler had pronounced the opera degenerate, unfit for Nazi ears. Hindemith decided to leave Germany, blond Aryan though he was. He wished to live in a democracy.

Hindemith was forty-four when he arrived in New York. At eleven, he had played the fiddle in cafés, theaters and movie-houses. Then, for a few years, he was the concert master in the opera house in Frankfurt. With the violinist Licco Amar he helped to organize the Amar String Quartet, and toured as violist with them until 1929. He was never without his instrument and writing materials. On jogging trains, he composed string quartets, sonatas for violin and piano, cello and piano, and for various string and wind combinations. When the Amar group played his works, one critic complained that too much of the rhythmic interest was supplied by the turning wheels of the train, but it was generally recognized that his was a new talent worth watching.

"A composer should write today only if he knows for what purpose he is writing. The days of composing for the sake of composing are perhaps gone forever. The demand for music is so great that composer and consumer ought most emphatically . . . to come to an understanding," he stated forthrightly. He tried, himself, to be practical. He studied people's musical needs, accepted commissions whatever they were, wrote music of all kinds for all kinds of people. He coined the term "Gebrauchsmusik" (utility music) to describe the "practical" compositions he supplied in great number. Short piano pieces for elementary, intermediate and advanced students, scores for films and radio, pieces for a brass band, for marionettes, for children, amateurs, and dilettantes, for a mechanical organ, a mechanical piano or harmonica or any other odd instrument—the range is a wide one.

The writing of "Gebrauchsmusik" was one use to which he turned his talent. But a long list of chamber music works, several of them presented at the annual festivals of the International Society for Contemporary Music, and larger works like the ballet, *Nobilissima Visione, Concerto for Orchestra, Mathis der Maler* and *Symphonic Metamorphosis on Themes by Weber*, provide a solid foundation on which his reputation rests.

In 1942, he became head of the music department at Yale. His students adored him, not only because of the youthful and stimulating freedom of his ideas, but because of the wit which survived two World Wars and the accompanying hard knocks. One evening, he was conducting the Yale student orchestra in the open courtyard of the Cloisters in New York. It was a program of ancient music, and valuable ancient instruments had been borrowed from the Metropolitan Museum of Art. The occasion was a gala one, and the huge open courtyard was packed with people in summer evening clothes. Hardly had the concert started, when a growl of thunder was heard, the heavens opened and a deluge descended. Hindemith faced the audience, smiling. "For the sake of the instruments, we will go inside," he announced. The dripping audience adjourned to an indoor auditorium which was much too small to accommodate them. But soaking wet and uncomfortable as they were, nobody went home, and nobody who was there is likely to forget the extra special quality of magic in the music that evening.

Besides many compositions in various styles, Hindemith wrote three illuminating textbooks: *Groundwork of Musical Composition, The Craft of Musical Composition,* and *Traditional Harmony*. In 1951, a professorship in the University of Zurich was offered, with leisure to compose. He accepted, and remained there. He died suddenly after a concert in Mainz, West Germany.

Born Hanau, Germany, November 16, 1895
Died Frankfurt, West Germany, December 28, 1963

ARTHUR HONEGGER

HONEGGER'S CAREER is a fine example of success rapidly attained in all fields. His pleasant, jovial manner won him friends, and his compositions, both serious and frivolous, were immensely successful. He was born of Swiss parents but grew up in France. He was thoroughly trained in music, first in Zurich, then at the Paris Conservatoire, to which he commuted from Le Havre. In 1913 he settled in Paris and made his first determined effort as a composer with a group of songs.

The performance of his huge "dramatic psalm," *Le Roi David,* brought him into a most becoming limelight. The large oratorio handled its biblical subject sympathetically, and although Olin Downes dismissed it as "junk of all kinds from the scrap-heap of Debussy, Stravinsky, Bach," the public was all for it. It was simply enough written to be sung by the Swiss mountaineers for whom Honegger composed it, and the Parisians who heard it felt that they had at last grasped the secret of modern music. *Judith,* also an oratorio, was equally acclaimed.

A more generally performed work, in this country at least, is *Pacific 231,* composed a short time after *Le Roi David.* Honegger was fascinated by the steam-engines chugging in and out of the railway station in Paris. This was before the emergence of the electric engine, and he found the sight of the monstrous steam-engines and the noises they made highly exciting. The new streamline model, designed to draw heavy loads at high speed, Pacific 231, inspired him to a musical tour de force. He pictures the engine rushing through the night with shrieking whistle and grinding brakes, and then, in a crescendo which reaches a terrific climax in the brasses, arriving at its destination. The music of *Pacific 231* is harsh, dissonant, and tremendously effective.

Honegger started out as a member of the group of composers known as Les Six, but he did not slavishly follow the satiric lead of Erik Satie nor the jazzy, entertaining preference of other members of the group. "I do not profess the cult of the Music Hall and the Street Fair," he said, "but on the contrary that of chamber and symphonic music in their more serious and austere aspects."

He was closer in spirit to his good friend Milhaud than to the others of the Six, for like Milhaud he could write in many fields and many forms; he could be profound or he could skim surfaces. An operetta, *Le Roi Pausole,* with music as gay as the risqué French text, was a rollicking success. It ran over a thousand performances. A mimed symphony, *Horace Victorieux;* an opera, *Antigone;* the great piece for orchestra, choirs, and solo recitative, *Jeanne d'Arc au Bûcher* (Joan of Arc at the Stake) are memorable among his serious works. Honegger composed for the films, wrote chamber music, songs—in fact, he was busy in every form until his death in Paris of a heart attack.

Born Le Havre, France, March 10, 1892
Died Paris, France, November 28, 1955

VINCENT
D'INDY

THE BIBLICAL injunction to "lift up thine eyes unto the hills" was one which young Vincent d'Indy was happy to heed. As a motherless boy he spent his youth on the estate of his grandmother in the mountainous country of Ardèche. He began the study of the piano when he was eleven, but long before that he had listened eagerly to the songs of the mountaineers whom he met on his walks and climbs. As he breathed the rarefied air and heard the rarefied songs, his spirit expanded, and he developed a strain of mysticism which was to endear him to César Franck, and Franck to him. According to the French critic Julien Tiersot, the mountain songs bore "something of the purity of their atmosphere . . . something fluid, ethereal, a gentleness that is not found in the folk song of the plains."

D'Indy had studied music with various teachers, had served with the army of Paris for a year during the Franco-Prussian War, and was apathetically studying law in deference to his father's wishes when he was introduced to César Franck. He was then twenty-two. He showed Franck a piano-quartet which he had composed. "It's all right, but you still have an awful lot to learn," said Franck. This was enough for d'Indy. He enrolled in Franck's organ class at the Conservatoire and announced to his family his intention of becoming a composer. From Franck he learned much more than the technique of composing, for he emerged from the Conservatoire with the same devotion to his art, the same lofty conception of its ideals as his teacher.

He traveled and came in contact with Liszt in Weimar and Brahms in Vienna. He heard the first performance of Wagner's *Ring* in Bayreuth. He learned something from each one but preserved intact the purity of his own utterance. "The creative flame finds its true nourishment only in love and in a fervent enthusiasm for beauty, truth, and the pure ideal," he said.

The works which are most often played are the *Istar Variations, Jours d'été à la Montagne (Summer days on a Mountain)*, and *Symphonie sur un chant montagnard français (Symphony on a French Mountain Song)*, all for orchestra. Says the critic Dumesnil: "He seeks inspiration in folklore. . . . The material is preserved, marked by his personality, his free rhythms, his hardy melodic lines, and his supple inflections." The opera *Fervaal* and his chamber music have been highly praised by thoughtful musicians.

As an educator, d'Indy served his country well. His *Cours de Contrepoint* (Course in Counterpoint) is a valuable textbook, his critical essays and biographies are scholarly, his biographies of *Beethoven* and of *César Franck* penetrating. Six years after Franck's death, d'Indy helped to organize the Schola Cantorum, a school of music with religious aims, its ideals those of Franck. He acted as its principal and also as its chief teacher of composition. Previously he had been active, with Franck, in the Société Nationale de la Musique, which was devoted to the performance and publication of new or neglected works. As conductor he appeared in many cities and had the courage to perform Debussy's *Nuages* and *Fêtes* in Rome before a hostile audience, who booed and shouted. D'Indy repeated both pieces at once, whereupon the audience changed its tune and applauded. He died of a heart attack at eighty.

Born Paris, France, March 27, 1851
Died Paris, France, December 3, 1931

CHARLES IVES

DANBURY, Connecticut, was a small town when Ives was born. It has since then grown into a sizable city. The period of its growth coincided with that of young Charles. Ives Senior taught his son a great deal of music in what time he could spare from his labors as leader of the town band and researcher in acoustics. If the boy decided to invent his own musical alphabet instead of using the established one, it was not because he didn't know any better. He studied with Harry Rowe Shelley and Dudley Buck, topping off with a course under Horatio Parker at Yale. When he brought his compositions to show to the conservative Parker, "Ives, must you hog *all* the keys?" was Parker's reaction to the shock of their polytonality.

Ives was a creative businessman, active as a partner in a successful insurance business from 1906 until he retired in 1930 to devote himself to music. Though he avoided the concert halls and opera houses of big cities, he never missed a musical event in Danbury if he could help it. He played the organ in church, attended performances by the town band, never missed solos by fiddler, harmonium player, or local prima donna. He assimilated them, faults and all, and when he came to write music nothing was omitted. The wheeze of the harmonium, the squeaky and out-of-tune violin playing, the off-key singing are all included in his New England pieces.

An Ives score is Sanskrit to the uninitiated and bewildering even to initiates, to read it is a labor of love, to perform it a labor of passionate devotion. Notes dotted cryptically all over the page, a dizzy maze of strange chords, quarter tones and ejaculatory rhythms, the absence of bar separations, hit the eye dismayingly. When they hit the ear the effect is not so much confused as challenging. The strongly accented off-beat resembles jazz in being syncopated, but as Ives uses it in a complicated maze of cross rhythms it is quite unlike ordinary jazz. His songs, of which he wrote many, he often gave away to singers hardy enough to attempt them.

His Second Sonata for the piano, *Concord, Massachusetts, 1840-1860,* has four movements, entitled *Emerson, Hawthorne, The Alcotts, Thoreau.* A sympathetic performance by John Kirkpatrick in 1939 brought out the spirit of transcendentalism of Concord in mid-century. Olin Downes not only praised the sonata, but also recalled appreciatively the "kick" in Ives' previously performed *Symphony for Orchestra and Piano,* "music . . . characterized by a vitality, humor, pathos, and audacity which took the audience by storm."

As he grew older, his devotion to his art grew ever more fierce and lonely. When he died of a heart attack, at the age of eighty, he left eleven volumes of chamber music and six volumes of orchestral scores, most of them never performed. His musical thinking was far in advance of his time, but the world caught up with him thirty-five years too late, and today there is a growing appreciation of his importance as a prophet and innovator.

Born Danbury, Conn., October 20, 1874
Died New York, N. Y., May 19, 1954

ARAM KHATCHATOURIAN

ARAM KHATCHATOURIAN was awarded the order of Lenin in 1939 "for outstanding merit in promoting the development of Armenian art," and after this, he skipped from one honor to another until he came to be ranked with those two giants of Soviet music, Serge Prokofieff and Dmitri Shostakovitch.

The son of an Armenian bookbinder, he did not begin to study music until his nineteenth year, but he did his best then to make up for lost time. He enrolled in the Conservatory of Moscow and chose as his instrument the cello. He was deeply interested in the folk music of his native Armenia and did not lose sight of its importance even when his teachers introduced him to the classics of Russian musical literature. It was not long before the study of composition took precedence over the pleasure of performing on an instrument, and at twenty-four, he threw himself wholeheartedly into a composing career. He proceeded from dances and small works to the composition of his *First Symphony,* in 1933, which commemorated the fifteenth anniversary of the admission of Armenia to the Soviet Union.

In 1939, his *Poem about Stalin,* composed for the annual October Festival, was rewarded with the Order of Lenin. Then, during the Second World War, he produced a *Second Symphony,* which took as its theme "the wrath of the Soviet people waging a struggle for humanity." For this effort, his name was inscribed on a marble tablet in the Moscow Conservatory, beside the names of its other distinguished alumni. His ballet, *Gayaneh,* at about the same time, won him the Stalin Prize of 100,000 rubles. This folk ballet about cotton pickers on a collective farm in Armenia is dominated by elements of the Russian Orient and Armenia, varying widely in mood. The bold, spirited *Sabre Dance* of the ballet is well known on American concert programs, for a concert suite of thirteen dances was made from the ballet score. His *Piano Concerto,* his *Violin Concerto,* and chamber music are also known to American audiences. One writer said of Khatchatourian: "He lives enmeshed in the harmonies and rhythms of his native Armenia. He is adding more songs to a lore already rich in material. And when he does become attracted to a four-bar melody of original music, he turns it inside out, making it a richer and more colorful song."

Khatchatourian's aim, as stated by Nicholas Slonimsky, was "the recreation of his native folk music within the bounds of new harmony." He said that he "is not and does not wish to be considered a 'national composer' in the narrow sense of the term." At the Second Congress of the Union of Soviet Composers in April 1957, when there was the usual criticism by politicians of the "formless and harmful modernism" of the new music, Khatchatourian defended the rising young artists of Soviet Russia, saying, "The seeking and daring artist is worth more than the well-trained craftsman who blindly copies . . . the great past masters." He himself, and his wife, Nina Makarova, also a composer, continued to seek and dare.

Born Tiflis, Georgia, Armenia, June 6, 1902
Living Moscow, Soviet Union

ZOLTAN

KODALY

EVEN BEFORE Béla Bartók and Zoltán Kodály made their historic trek together hunting folk songs with notebook and gramophone, some thousands of examples of native music had already found their way into young Kodály's rucksack. When the two men teamed up in 1906 for a joint folk-song excursion and afterward pooled their material, Kodály's contribution was between three and four thousand melodies. Some were published in the collection issued by Bartók, who gave full credit to his colleague. Some are still in manuscript.

With Bartók and Dohnányi, Kodály studied composition in the University of Budapest under Hans Koessler, a German who was passionately addicted to Hungarian music. Kodály's first field trips were undertaken to gather material for his Ph.D. thesis on *Strophic Construction in Hungarian Folk Song.* When he discovered in Bartók the conviction that the music being played under the guise of Hungarian gypsy folk song was nothing of the sort, and when he realized that Bartók's enthusiasm in pursuit of genuine, rooted-in-earth folk song was akin to his own, their collaboration was inevitable.

After their trips together, Kodály visited Berlin and Paris and returned to become, first, a professor, and then a deputy director in the university where he had been a student. He married an enormously wealthy wife of famous family some fifteen or twenty years older than he. Although she owned large estates, fancy cars, and other luxuries, Kodály retained his sturdy simplicity and abnegated luxury. He took the electric train to his work in the university, spurning the automobile at his disposal. When last heard from, after the Soviet Union had liquidated the Hungarian revolution of 1957, Kodály, an old man of seventy-five, was tenderly nursing his wife, who lay helpless with a broken leg in a village adjacent to the city.

His works have become well-known outside of Hungary. His chamber music was approved when the International Society for Contemporary Music presented it at annual festivals. The orchestral works which are most often played are the *Psalmus Hungaricus, Háry János,* and *Dances from Galanta. The Psalmus Hungaricus* was composed for the fiftieth anniversary of the merging of the twin cities of Buda and Pest into Budapest. Kodály used as his text a translation of a Psalm of David by the sixteenth-century Hungarian poet Michael Vég.

Háry János deals with a legendary Húngarian hero, a sort of Tyl Eulenspiegel, who brags and dreams and sees himself as a mighty conqueror who single-handed defeats the Grand Army and Napoleon with it. The orchestral suite he made from *Háry János* has become immensely popular.

Kodály created an individual musical idiom out of his material. Since the death of Bartók, and the departure of Dohnányi for permanent residence in the United States, there is no one to dispute his eminence as Hungary's leading twentieth-century composer.

Born Kecskemét, Hungary, December 16, 1882
Living outside Budapest, Hungary

ORLANDUS
LASSUS

WHEN Orlandus Lassus was a choir-boy in the church of St. Nicholas, where his golden voice drew hundreds to the place of worship, he was so good that other churches sent agents to try to entice him away, and in fact, he was three times kidnaped by rival churches. His boyhood was not happy, despite his musical talent, for he was desperately ashamed of a disreputable father, and left home very young.

He held various positions, sometimes as choirmaster and organist, sometimes as court as choirmaster and organist, sometimes as court musician to noblemen, prospered, and soon was hobnobbing as easily with kings and princes as with the dignitaries of the church, and composing prolifically for both. He spent some time at the court of Munich, where he was the life and soul of the court theatricals, a witty, learned, high-spirited man of magnetic charm.

In 1570, the Emperor Maximilian of Bavaria presented him with a patent of nobility, and a year later, Pope Gregory, in recognition of a volume of masses dedicated to him, bestowed on Lassus the Papal Order of the Golden Cross, later worn by Gluck and Mozart. His family life was happy. He was married in 1558, had four sons and two daughters, and took his family traveling with him luxuriously in Belgium, Italy, Germany and France.

One of his famous motets is *Gustate Videte* (Oh, taste and see how gracious is the Lord!). On the feast of Corpus Christi, a great pageant was preparing to parade through the streets of Rome, singing this motet. They gathered in St. Peter's, but when they were ready to start, a heavy storm blew up, the sky was covered with black clouds, and the reigning duke ordered the processional to remain indoors, in the church. They started to chant Lassus' motet. As they sang, the heavens cleared, the sun came out brilliantly, they paraded outdoors, as planned, and not a drop fell. When people wished to pray for fine weather after this, they sang *Gustate Videte.*

Lassus was the musical twin of Palestrina, whom he greatly resembled in appearance. They held choirmaster jobs successively in the same church, died in the same year, and greatly admired each other's works. Their writings represent the high point of sixteenth century polyphonic composition. But, whereas Palestrina was primarily a man of the church, majestic, dignified and serene, Lassus was adventurous, energetic, a man of the world, interested as much in earthly pleasures as in heavenly salvation. His religious and secular works combined add up to the amazing total of twelve hundred fifty, bound in a modern edition of sixty precious volumes. Four original volumes contain in Lassus' own handwriting his magnificent setting of the *Seven Penitential Psalms.* It was supposed for a time that these psalms, composed in Paris, were commissioned by the French King Charles as an expression of his remorse after the Massacre of St. Bartholomew. The date of composition has now been established as seven years before the massacre, but the Psalms have a somber beauty that would accord well with such a subject.

Lassus' last years were gloomy, despite the many honors heaped upon him. "Lassus" means "tired," and he had every reason to be so, after his years of industry and activity. He died in Munich, and was buried at the Franciscan Monastery there.

Born Mons, Belgium, about 1530
Died Munich, Germany, June 14, 1594

RUGGIERO

LEONCAVALLO

"LAUGH, CLOWN, LAUGH," sings Canio, the broken-hearted husband whose wife Nedda has betrayed him with a handsome ne'er-do-well. This is the great moment in Leoncavallo's famous two-act opera, *Pagliacci.* One great opera of the dozen he composed in his hardworking life is all that remains of his efforts. It is, however, an opera which was not only immediately successful when it was produced, but which caught on like wildfire in opera houses all over the world. Success came in the nick of time while the composer was having a run of bad luck.

He was attending lectures in Bologna when he composed his first opera, *Chatterton,* immediately after his graduation from the Conservatory of Naples and was immensely flattered when an impresario agreed to produce it. The impresario, however, changed his mind and decamped with all Leoncavallo's funds, leaving him stranded. He took to playing the piano in cafés, traveling to France, England, Germany, Holland, even Egypt. En route, he completed an opera, *The Medici,* which the house of Ricordi, Verdi's publishers in Italy, agreed to publish. They took their time about it, and Leoncavallo, annoyed by the delay, brought his next work, *Pagliacci,* to a rival publisher. The Ricordi nose must have been out of joint when *Pagliacci* brought solvency to both publisher and composer and created an artistic furore which endured.

There is an amusing story which has to do with Leoncavallo's habit of going incognito to hear his opera, so that he might enjoy the comments of the audience. On one such occasion, he sat beside a young woman who applauded with zest. Between the acts, she glared at the young man beside her, who applauded not at all. "Don't you like it?" she asked. "No, it's terrible, I'm sorry I came." "If that's your opinion, you know nothing about music," said the girl, rudely. "Just listen!" he replied. "There isn't an original idea in the whole opera. That last theme was stolen from Bizet, the one before taken from Beethoven." The young woman turned her back on him and said no more. But the next morning, the local newspaper reported the conversation with embellishments in an interview headlined "Leoncavallo on his opera *Pagliacci.*" The innocent young woman was a reporter! She had been the eavesdropper, he the victim.

Leoncavallo was a talented and well-trained musician and wrote libretti also. He wrote a libretto for his friend Puccini's opera *Manon* when both he and Puccini were poor young unknowns; *Manon* made Puccini's name famous. Leoncavallo composed an opera entitled *La Bohème,* which appeared at the same time as Puccini's on the same subject. In fact, while Leoncavallo's Mimi was coughing her last at the Teatro della Fenice in Venice on May 6, 1897, Puccini's heroine was simultaneously dying to deafening applause in another theater in Venice. Puccini's threw the lesser man's opera in the shade, and Leoncavallo's *La Bohème* is now forgotten. His fame rests on *Pagliacci.*

Born Naples, Italy, March 8, 1858
Died Montecatini, Italy, August 9, 1919

FRANZ LISZT

When he was a few weeks old, Franz Liszt was so puny that his father had him measured for a coffin, in full expectation of his dying in infancy. He lived to become a great pianist, a great composer, and a great lover. He must have been born under a lucky star, for success came to him without the usual struggle.

His father, who was employed as a steward on the estate of Count Esterhazy in Hungary, gave him his early training on the piano and, when he was nine, took him to a neighboring town to play a concert. Several noblemen who were present were so much impressed with his talent that they offered to stake him to his musical education for the next six years.

When the boy was eleven, Czerny, who was Franz's teacher in Vienna, asked his own teacher Beethoven to do him a favor and hear the boy play. Beethoven grumbled a bit, but appointed an hour for them to come to his rooms. He hardly looked up until Liszt played a Bach fugue, then he asked with sudden interest, "Can you transpose that fugue into another key?" "Yes, Sir," said the boy and transposed it into several other keys in succession. Beethoven stroked Liszt's blond hair and smiled approvingly. Liszt then played the first movement of Beethoven's C major piano concerto, and Beethoven, completely won over, kissed him, saying prophetically, "You are one of the fortunate ones, for you will give joy and happiness to many people."

Soon after this, Liszt went to Paris and applied for admittance to the Conservatoire. But Cherubini, the director, refused him because it was against the rules to admit foreign students to the French government's school. This made little difference to Franz, who took private lessons instead and progressed swimmingly. He was sixteen when his father died, and from then on he was on his own. He remained in Paris to study, teach, concertize, and Live with a capital L. The emotional climate of the Paris of Chopin, George Sand and Berlioz, of Balzac, Flaubert, Lamartine and Victor Hugo, was wholly agreeable to the temperamental young man, to whom the extravagant extremes of feeling indulged in by the so-called Romantic writers and composers were only to be expected.

By the time he was twenty-three he had had a number of love-affairs. In Chopin's salon, he met the great love of his life—for the time being. This was the Comtesse d'Agoult, who wrote novels under the pseudonym of Daniel Stern and fancied herself a second George Sand minus the cigar. Mme. d'Agoult was very beautiful, a volcano of passion seething under a glacial exterior. For Liszt she left her husband and lived openly "in sin." They had three children in the ten years of their romance, one of whom, Cosima, became the wife of Richard Wagner. During those ten years, Liszt departed frequently on concert tours which took him all over Europe. He sought publicity by every means in his power, going the showman Paganini, whom he greatly admired, one better. When he came on stage he wore gloves which he removed deliberately while the audience waited. He seated himself at the piano, not facing the audience, but with his handsome profile turned at the most favorable angle. He appeared on one occasion in full Magyar costume, complete with jeweled sword. He wore his hair longer than anyone else's. Rossini ran his fingers through Liszt's flowing locks, asking incredulously, "Is it real?"

He became visiting court artist in Weimar in 1843, and five years later was made director of the Weimar opera. By this time he had broken with Mme. d'Agoult, and he took with him to Weimar a new love, a cigar-smoking Polish princess whom he had met in Russia. She too left her husband for the fascinating Liszt. Their lavish household in Weimar became a Mecca for musicians. He raised enormous sums at benefit concerts for various causes—for the relief of flood sufferers, for the publication of Domenico Scarlatti's works, for the erection in Bonn of a statue of Beethoven. Composers flocked to lay their scores at his feet, and he constituted himself the champion of their music, the "music of the future." Wagner's operas, *The Flying Dutchman, Tannhäuser,* and *Lohengrin* were produced under his baton in Weimar in the teeth of strong opposition, as were Berlioz' *Benvenuto Cellini,* Weber's *Euryanthe* and others which have since made their mark. Liszt's encouragement of struggling composers was invaluable to them, and the adulation they gave him in return was invaluable to him.

From 1849 on, his working time was divided in three parts, one in Weimar, one in Budapest, one in Rome. He made his peace with the Church, which had refused permission for him to marry his divorced Polish princess, but permitted him to become an abbé. As Abbé Liszt he wore the picturesque flowing robes of his office and composed requiems for the salvation of his soul. He clung to his princess until she died, though this did not deter him from extracurricular amorous adventures. He was over sixty when a young student became so despairing over his cavalier termination of their love affair that she tried to kill herself and him. Fortunately she failed, and he continued to combine the religious life with the adventures of a Don Juan. No wonder that when he was asked to write the story of his life, he replied, "No thanks, it was hard enough to have lived it."

Liszt was visiting his daughter Cosima, Wagner's wife, in Bayreuth when he caught cold and died after a brief illness. His last word was a whispered "Tristan." During his life, Liszt the composer was overshadowed by Liszt the pianist and showman, but his compositions have an importance of their own. Although he did not invent the symphonic poem, as is sometimes claimed, he perfected it, and his one-movement program pieces, such as *Mazeppa* and *Les Préludes* pointed the way. The oft-performed *Hungarian Rhapsodies* are rousing show-pieces, superb of their kind, and when Liszt played them on the piano they brought down the house. Those who find his music banal or showy do not deny that it has an emotional appeal, is brilliantly conceived, and fills a need in the repertoire of piano and orchestra.

Born Raiding, Hungary, October 22, 1811
Died Bayreuth, Germany, July 13, 1886

JEAN BAPTISTE LULLY

BRILLIANT, unscrupulous, malicious, a master of intrigue, tireless in self-advancement, Lully the courtier of Louis XIV was hated and feared as much as Lully the musician was admired.

We see him first a monkey-faced little boy with a monkey's comic agility, helping his father to grind into flour the wheat the Italian peasants bring to his mill. Jean Baptiste is taught his letters by a priest, who also teaches him the guitar. Somehow, he teaches himself to play the violin quite well. When strolling players come by on their way to a carnival he follows them, and they give him a small part in their show. A French nobleman chances to see his act, and amused by his antics, picks him up and takes him to Paris.

Here his glorious career begins ingloriously. The Duc de Guise gives him to the wealthy Mlle. de Montpensier, thinking to amuse her. When she wearies of her new toy, she sends him to work as a scullery boy in her kitchen. He entertains the other help with the songs he makes up; *Au Clair de la Lune* is one of them. He plays the violin for them too, so well that Mlle. de Montpensier is told of it, relents, and has him take lessons. He becomes a violinist in her orchestra. When he is nineteen, he shows his gratitude by writing a comic song in which he maliciously lampoons her. She is furious, dismisses him from her service, and sends him to be tamed to her royal cousin King Louis XIV. But it is Louis who is tamed.

The "Roi Soleil" (Sun King) proves to be a

sun whose august beams quickly ripen Lully's talents. At first, Jean Baptiste is a violinist in the king's picked orchestra of twenty-four, Les Violons du Roi. But he connives and finagles until he is permitted to form an orchestra of his own, which he directs. He is a severe taskmaster. He insists that, to start with, every player must be able to read well at sight. He drills them until his sharp-tongued exactions have made of them a fine-sounding musical body. He gives them the pieces he composes for them, which are not solos with stereotyped and dull accompaniment, but in which there is a harmonious blending of tones of different groups and of the instruments within the groups. The king is charmed with Lully's orchestra, called Les Petits Violons. It is always at his service.

Lully studies composition, harpsichord and organ. He kisses the hands of the powerful at court, bestows an extra kick on those in disgrace, trims his sails to every wind that blows his way. At the same time he lives a life of dissipation that is notorious even at a court so indulgent as Louis'. But Louis winks at his vices, for Lully has become indispensable. For the gorgeous spectacles with which the court is regaled at Versailles, Lully works night and day. He writes ballets and dances in them too, often toe to toe with his royal master. He designs spectacular scenery, sings and acts, plays the violin and harpsichord, and directs the orchestra. It is Lully here, Lully there, Lully everywhere. He becomes a French Pooh-Bah, collecting jobs and the emoluments that go with them. He is made Instrumental Composer to the King, Composer to the King's Chamber Music, Music Master to the Royal Family. He marries a wife who brings him a large dowry and presents him with three sons and three daughters in six years. Louis and his queen sign the marriage contract as witnesses, an honor usually accorded only to those of royal blood.

A meeting with the playwright Molière in 1670 begins a collaboration. Lully's music for *Le Bourgeois Gentilhomme* and other Molière plays turns his thoughts to the opera. The King has granted a certain Abbé Perrin a patent to create an Académie de Musique for the performance of operas. Lully by hook and crook—chiefly crook—gets the patent for himself, while Perrin goes to prison for debt. Lully finds a librettist, the poet Quinault, who writes singable librettos. In a short time, Lully is the sole financial and artistic director of the opera in Paris. He proceeds to compose the series of operas which are his permanent contribution to French music. *Les Fêtes de l'Amour et de Bacchus* is not only the first truly noteworthy French opera, but the first of twenty composed by Lully while he is the arbiter of the Parisian stage.

He introduces many improvements into French opera. For the dry recitative which has always accompanied declamatory passages, he substitutes recitative with an artistic and harmonious accompaniment. Correct phrasing is his passion, both in words and in music. The words must come trippingly to the tongue and must be pronounced with beauty and clarity. In his ballets he replaces the stately court dances with lively allegros and engages artists who can dance to his piping however fast he pipes. He introduces female dancers into the corps de ballet. And he writes entertaining overtures to his operas in a form of his own known as the French overture to distinguish it from the Italian. His operas, *Thésée, Isis, Atys, Phaeton, Armide,* and *Roland,* written to please a king, delight the king's lesser subjects. Tradesmen, artisans, and humble working-men flock to the performances. The indefatigable Lully is stage-manager, scene designer, orchestra conductor, coach. His king once said, "L'état, c'est moi." (I am the State.) Lully might truthfully have replied, "Oui, mais l'opéra, c'est moi." (Yes, but I am the Opera.)

His complete writings fill twenty-nine large volumes. How many might there have been had he not met with a fatal accident at the height of his powers? He had composed a *Te Deum* to celebrate Louis' recovery from an illness. While conducting the performance, he struck his leg with the heavy baton. An abscess formed, blood poisoning set in, and within a few days he was dead. Not only Louis and his courtiers, but all of Paris mourned the loss of the "favorite son of the grand siècle;" as a musician, he was irreplaceable. Until Gluck appeared, Lully was the most daring innovator, the most original composer, the man to whom the most credit is due for locating opera permanently on the musical map of France.

Born Florence, Italy, November 29, 1632
Died Paris, France, March 22, 1687

EDWARD MACDOWELL

IN EDWARD MACDOWELL'S generation, there were perhaps only a dozen reasonably well-equipped American composers. He was one of the fortunate few whose parents lavished on his preparation for his chosen career loving solicitude, intelligence, and ample means. He repaid them by becoming the outstanding American composer of his generation. It is true that styles change in music, as they do in manners, and the romantic lyricism of the poetic MacDowell does not go over with audiences today as it formerly did. Nevertheless, his position as one of America's great talents is unassailable.

He began the study of the piano when he was eight years old. The fiery Teresa Carreño took an interest in the boy when she heard him play, gave him a few lessons, and advised his parents to send him to the Paris Conservatoire. Of his two years there his mother wrote enthusiastically, "They turned out a *musician* – whether he played the violin, piano or sang." She omitted to say that they almost turned out a painter instead of a musician. For MacDowell drew a caricature in class of a teacher whose nose resembled the celebrated beak of Cyrano de Bergerac. The teacher confiscated the drawing and MacDowell feared the worst. Instead, he was offered a scholarship to study painting, if he wished to switch. Backed by his parents, he refused.

After the Conservatoire he went to Germany and studied composition with Joachim Raff in

Frankfurt. One evening Raff paid him a surprise visit in his room and asked, "What have you been working at?" "A piano concerto," replied MacDowell, who had been doing nothing of the sort. "Bring it to the next lesson," ordered Raff. MacDowell did. He respected his teacher too much to do otherwise, though he had to work over-time to make good.

While studying he also taught. One of his pupils was pretty Marion Nevins, who objected to him as a teacher because he was too young, while he objected to taking her as a pupil because he considered most American students, especially girls, not serious. In the long run they accepted each other so completely that, when both had returned from their studies, they were married. They loved Germany and settled for a few happy years in Wiesbaden. But Raff's death before the publication and performance of Edward's *First Modern Suite* for piano and his *First Piano Concerto* was a heavy blow, and when Liszt, who had encouraged Edward, also died, the young couple decided to return to America.

In Boston, Edward's good looks and his charming young wife made friends in spite of his shyness. He had the poet's tendency to shrink from noisy crowds coupled with the musician's desire to be heard. The musician won, and he performed his *First* and *Second Piano Concertos,* the four big sonatas (which are compared with Beethoven's), and his smaller piano works to enthusiastic audiences. His forty songs, to many of which he wrote the text, were on living-room pianos everywhere. The "rotten melodies," as he called them, which his wife often fished from the scrap basket after he had crumpled them in disgust, are for the most part based on poetic images or on nature – for example *To a Wild Rose, Moonshine, The Robin Sings in the Apple Tree, Thy Beaming Eyes.* Of his orchestral works, the *Indian Suite* is the most successful, though on first being heard it was criticized on the one hand as "Indian but not beautiful," on the other as "beautiful but not Indian."

When MacDowell was invited to New York to head the newly created Department of Music at Columbia University in 1896, he was glad to share the gift of beauty with the younger generation. But the crowded classroom was not like his quiet study, and the bell which signaled the end of a period often interrupted his highest flights. Red tape and details harassed him. His students worshiped him, but the university authorities did not. When he handed in his enforced resignation in 1904, he was on the verge of a breakdown. A few months later he was run over by a cab, and the added shock brought about a complete mental collapse. He spent the last two years of his life reading fairy tales upside down or staring into space.

He had built a log cabin in the woods of Vermont where he composed many of his best works. After his death, young composers, writers and artists gathered there as members of a creative colony under the benign guidance of Marion MacDowell. The MacDowell Colony is a fitting monument to America's first great tone-poet.

Born New York, N. Y., December 18, 1861
Died New York, N. Y., January 23, 1908

GUSTAV MAHLER

MAHLER'S FRIEND Bruno Walter saw him as "invariably brisk, inspired, and charged with energy." And so he must have been to have completed ten enormous symphonies and the great song-cycles which culminated in *Das Lied von der Erde* (The Song of the World) while in the midst of an enormously busy life of conducting and organizing.

The son of a struggling Jewish tradesman, he astonished his father by playing on the accordion the marches of the soldiers in a nearby garrison when he was only four. At eight he gave piano lessons to a seven-year-old neighbor. He attended the University of Vienna, and by the time he was ready to study composition with Bruckner at the Vienna Conservatory he was already an excellent pianist. He and Bruckner are often compared, for both men admired Wagner, both composed large and lengthy works, and both were understood by the few musicians, and not by the many music-lovers.

Though Mahler wanted above all to compose, he became such a fine conductor that he went from one desirable post to another until he was engaged by the Vienna Opera. He brought the company to remarkable perfection but made so many enemies in the process that he was compelled to resign. Tendered the directorship of the Berlin Opera, which had previously been withheld on the ground that one of the directors did not like the shape of his nose, he refused in a telegram, "Cannot accept, nose still same shape." He had been baptized and had become a true believer in Christianity, but would never deny his Jewish origin.

His health was not good. He walked in his sleep and went into strange trances during his waking hours. After his resignation from the Vienna Opera, he was troubled by recurrent heart attacks. Nevertheless, in 1907 he accepted an invitation to New York to conduct the Metropolitan Opera. At the same time he reorganized and conducted the New York Philharmonic Symphony Orchestra. Only the need of money for his wife and child could have induced him to accept so staggering an assignment. It was too much for him in his weakened state. Furthermore, with all his ability he was not popular. The public and the critics of New York failed to understand what the sensitive, misanthropic little man was driving at. When he conducted his own symphonies audiences groaned, and one critic commented grumpily, "Mahler was convinced that no symphony could be too long, provided he was the composer." During a Philharmonic concert in 1910 Mahler collapsed on the platform. This was the end; he returned to Vienna to die.

Those who believe that the only great composer is a dead one may well point to Mahler. For there is a growing admiration for him, fed by frequent performances and beautiful recordings of his stupendous works. *Das Lied von der Erde* has been called one of his surest claims to immortality as a composer. The beautiful *Kindertotenlieder* (Songs for a Dead Child) are heart-rending in their simplicity and depth of feeling. Children and the beauties of nature were his solace when he was overwhelmed, as he often was, by the dread of death and annihilation. Though he loved life with fierce intensity, he was a somber man, and the music which vividly reflects his tortured soul is somber too. But in its own way it is powerful and at moments inexpressibly touching.

Born Kalischt, Bohemia, July 7, 1860
Died Vienna, Austria, May 18, 1911

PIETRO

MASCAGNI

LIKE HIS compatriot and contemporary, Ruggiero Leoncavallo, Pietro Mascagni composed operas industriously, and like Leoncavallo, he succeeded only once in hitting the bull's eye of success. Waking up one morning to find himself famous was evidently an upsetting experience, for he never produced another work of musical distinction after *Cavalleria Rusticana.*

His life began with that opposition to a musical career which many fathers feel duty bound to offer their ambitious sons. But Pietro escaped the study of the law by way of an indulgent uncle who offered to adopt the young composer, and invited him to live with him. When his uncle died, Mascagni returned perforce to his father's house. Then a wealthy amateur came forward to pay his tuition at the Conservatory of Milan. His student years there in the company of Puccini were happy ones, but he rebelled at the dry study of counterpoint and fugue and left of his own accord. For a time nothing was heard of him; then he reappeared with a wife and a half-completed opera score. He had been conducting a traveling opera company and learning about orchestration and stage technique at first hand.

He was twenty-seven, and teaching piano at a small school in an obscure Italian village when he heard of a competition for a one-act opera to be produced in Rome at the expense of the music publisher Sonzogno. Mascagni hurriedly prepared a score and rushed it to Rome at the eleventh hour. In May, 1890, *Cavalleria Rusticana* (Rustic Chivalry) was produced. It had won the prize! It became a nine days' wonder. Mascagni was hailed as Verdi's successor. The King decorated him as a Chevalier of the Order of Italy. He was fêted and wined and dined when he returned to his birthplace, Leghorn. All Italy honored him. Of course he resigned his small-town teaching position. Of course he himself and everyone else expected that he would go on to fresh triumphs. If he did not, it was not for lack of effort.

He composed fifteen operas. *Iris,* a three-act opera on a Japanese theme, was produced in various cities and at the Metropolitan Opera House in New York to lukewarm audiences. *L'Amico Fritz* and *Nerone* attracted mild attention. *La Pinotta,* the première of which he conducted fifty-three years after he had presented the score to his landlady in part payment of a board bill, is quite forgotten. They all lack *Cavalleria's* "Brutal strength and insidious charm . . . and the blood-red spontaneity that has given it a mighty impetus" and made it a model one-act opera. It is often teamed with *Pagliacci* to make a full evening of dramatic musical excitement.

Mascagni visited the United States; in fact, a too-long visit in 1903 cost him his position at the Conservatory in Pesaro. Until his death in Rome, when he was eighty-two, he dwelt in the aura of success of *Cavalleria Rusticana,* created when he was twenty-seven.

Born Leghorn, Italy, December 7 1863
Died Rome, Italy, August 2, 1945

JULES MASSENET

BECAUSE MASSENET's operas were singable and sentimental, because he wrote more than twenty-five in which he carefully avoided the "grand" in favor of the "light," and because he had an unerring eye and ear for the best in prima donnas, he became one of the most popular of French composers. Eventually his popularity extended beyond the borders of his own country, clear across the Atlantic Ocean. In New York there was deafening applause when Mary Garden sang the lead successively in *Manon, Thais,* and *Le Jongleur de Notre Dame,* applause that was shared with the smiling Massenet, who came to America for the performances. As usual Massenet had chosen his prima donna wisely, for her fame too had reached America.

He was twenty-five when his one-act comic opera *Don César de Bazan* was produced at the Opéra Comique in Paris. The experiences leading up to that moment were those common to most French composers: years of hard work at the Conservatoire, then graduation, the Prix de Rome, and the three years of study in Italy and other European countries that were a part of the grant. In Rome Massenet met Liszt without being unduly impressed—and vice versa. Before settling in Paris, he married one of his piano pupils with whom he lived happily ever after. She was practical and worldly wise, and apparently did not resent his pursuit of one prima donna after another. She realized that prima donnas provided the butter for the Massenet bread, and besides, as Carl Van Vechten said, "he dropped precious dots of ink on paper instead of sending them diamonds from the Rue de la Paix."

The opera *Hérodiade,* which appeared when he was thirty-nine, had made him known in France before *Manon,* three years later, sent his name skyrocketing. After Bizet's *Carmen* and Gounod's *Faust,* Massenet's *Manon* is the most popular of French operas. Massenet had the novel by Abbé Prévost about Manon Lescaut and her lover, de Grieux, very much on his mind when, on his daily stroll in Paris, he was attracted by a pretty young girl selling flowers in a shop. There was something about her wistful expression which made him say to himself: "There she is! That is Manon!" He never saw the girl again, but her image remained in his mind and inspired him all the while he was composing the opera. So he said in his memoirs.

Massenet's personal charm and the vogue for his light operas as opposed to Wagner's heavy ones carried to success his others—*Le Cid, Sapho, La Navarraise, Chérubin, Don Quichotte,* etc. He lived industriously, his days carefully organized. Once in the course of the thirty-four years that he taught at the Conservatoire an inquiring student, on being told that Massenet's first class was at seven in the morning, asked, "But when do you compose, Sir?" "When *you* sleep," replied Massenet. In his later years in his villa in Egreville he grew roses, tended grape-vines, and puttered happily, but still when he put on his red dressing-gown and settled down at his table Mme. Massenet knew that he was about to attack his stint of composing for the day. He was seventy years young when he died, and there were many besides his devoted wife and the prima donnas who mourned his loss.

Born Montaud, France, May 12, 1842
Died Egreville, near Paris, August 13, 1912

FELIX BARTHOLDY MENDELSSOHN

Felix is the Latin word for happy, and the good fairies showered upon Felix Mendelssohn gifts that would make anyone happy. He was handsome, intelligent, sensitive, affectionate, industrious, gay—and extraordinarily talented. He was born of cultured and wealthy parents, who nurtured without exploiting his talents. He had two sisters and a brother hardly less gifted than himself, and lived with them a close family life in which each lovingly appreciated the other.

His training was strict, to be sure. He once said that he and his brother Paul and sisters Fanny and Rebekah loved Sundays because on that day they did not have to get up to study at five in the morning. But there was another reason why they loved Sundays. Felix played his first piano concert at nine, composed prolifically from the age of ten, and by the time he was thirteen, he was ready to conduct the Sunday morning musicales that were the delight of his youth. In the garden of the rambling Mendelssohn house at No. 3 Leipzigerstrasse on the outskirts of Berlin, friends, neighbors and musicians gathered to hear the eager boy play the piano, the viola, or the organ, and conduct his youthful orchestra of brother, sisters and friends. He played his own compositions, too; the fairy strains of *The Midsummer Night's Dream Overture,* which he composed at seventeen, were first heard at one of these al fresco concerts.

As a twenty-first birthday present, given ahead of time, his grandmother bestowed upon him the unpublished score of Bach's *Passion According to St. Matthew.* She had had it copied for him by hand, because she indulgently thought that he might like to have it. Like it! He was swept away by it. He and his friend Devrient, a music-loving actor, made up their minds on the spot that the glorious work must be given a public performance. They went to Professor Zelter, Mendelssohn's teacher and director of the Berlin Singakademie, to enlist his help. He demurred. It was impossible, he said, to put on so complex a work with the resources at his disposal. Who would engage the soloists? Who would train the chorus? Who would play the organ? "I will," said Mendelssohn. Zelter relented.

Mendelssohn kept all his promises and raised money, sold tickets, and worked tirelessly besides. On March 11, 1829, almost eighty years after Bach's death, the *St. Matthew Passion* was performed to a sold-out, deeply impressed audience. Mendelssohn conducted. It was the first performance of the work since Bach had died. After the applause was finished and the lights had been extinguished in the hall, Mendelssohn said quietly to Devrient, "To think that it should have been reserved for an actor, you, and a Jew, myself, to restore this great Christian work to the people!"

Mendelssohn continued to work to bring Bach's music to people's attention. The formation of the Bach Gesellschaft (Bach Society) after Mendelssohn died was largely the result of his efforts during life to assure Bach of the recognition he had justly earned.

After conducting three sold-out performances of the *St. Matthew Passion,* Mendelssohn left Berlin on travels which were to last for three delightful years. A tour abroad was the last step in the thorough course of education prescribed for him. In pleasant, leisurely fashion, he went through Germany, Austria, Italy, Switzerland and France. Then back to London for a last fling, and so home. Among his souvenirs, he brought in his rucksack the beginnings of the *Scotch* and *Italian* Symphonies, the *Reformation* Symphony, a new piano concerto, and numerous other works and ideas for work. His father had no need to reproach him for wasting his time and neglecting his opportunities.

An appointment in 1835 to conduct the Gewandhaus Orchestra in Leipzig made him very happy. Leipzig was the city where Bach had spent his last years, and his disciple felt the master's spirit there, though the master was no more. Two years later Mendelssohn's marriage to Cecile Jeanrenaud—a love-match—and the subsequent birth of five children completed his happiness. During the twelve years that he directed the Gewandhaus Orchestra it became the finest in all Europe. He engaged an old friend, the distinguished Ferdinand David, as concertmaster. David played the first performance of the ineffable Mendelssohn *Violin Concerto,* which is dear to every violinist's repertoire, and particularly favored by young artists making a debut because of a kind of lyrical innocence which gives it a particular appeal. To the hospitable Mendelssohn home in Leipzig came Rossini, Chopin, Schumann, and every musician of note who lived in the city or passed through it. It was like earlier days under the paternal roof in Berlin.

Mendelssohn organized and became the director of the first German Conservatory of Music in Leipzig. He taught there himself and attracted to it a brilliant teaching staff. Besides teaching, he traveled frequently, at the king's command, to conduct the court orchestras in Berlin and Dresden. He made frequent tours as a pianist and was everywhere loved, praised, admired and applauded like a veritable Prince Charming. And withal, he never stopped composing.

The death of his father in 1835, of his mother a few years later, and of his youngest son Felix, dealt him a severe blow. The Mendelssohns were a short-lived family. He loved them all with rare intensity. He was quite unprepared for the death of his favorite sister Fanny in May 1847. She was his other self in music. Some charming songs which she had composed had appeared under his name, because in the middle nineteenth century a lady and a Mendelssohn did not publish music under her own name. She died suddenly in May 1847, shortly after his return from triumphantly conducting his oratorio *Elijah* in England. Weakened by overwork, prostrated by grief—he who had been accustomed all his life to happiness—he never recovered his health. In November of the same year he followed his sister Fanny to the grave.

In perpetuating the ideals of Bach and Mozart, in encouraging the composers of his day and performing their music, and in reviving neglected composers of the past, Mendelssohn did music a great service. The effortless flow, the glow and sparkle and delicacy and sweetness, the singing melodies, the fluency and polish of his own music are universally appealing. As Heifetz said, "If it is conceivable that the music of Mendelssohn can die, then all music can die."

Born Hamburg, Germany, February 3, 1809
Died Leipzig, Germany, November 4, 1847

GIAN-CARLO
MENOTTI

THE POSTMISTRESS of the little town of Cadegliano wobbled on her bicycle from the post office to the Menotti house, waving a cablegram in the air and crying aloud for all to hear, "Il Metropolitano, il Metropolitano!" Thus the whole town knew, even before his parents did, that Gian-Carlo's opera, *Amelia Goes to the Ball,* was to be given at the Metropolitan Opera House in New York. His mother was justly proud, for she had given him his first music lessons, had seen him compose his first piece at five, his first opera at eleven, and had sent him off to the Curtis School in Philadelphia, a gangling seventeen-year-old, to complete his education. Now here he was, twenty-six, a successful composer, a son any mother could rejoice in.

Amelia Goes to the Ball was melodious comedy in the tradition of Italian *opera buffa.* It was followed by a bubbling one-act opera, *The Old Maid and the Thief,* the first opera to be commissioned for radio performance. It turned out to be much too much fun to be restricted to the radio and was performed on the stage many times. *The Medium,* which was his first serious venture, was not only serious, it was so tragic that it touched all hearts. Menotti told of having been invited by his neighbors during a visit to Salzburg in 1936 to attend a spiritualist seance. He accepted the invitation very sceptically and was touched and amazed to find that his hosts, in their pathetic desire to believe, actually did see and hear their dead daughter. The evening made a lasting impression on Gian-Carlo, and nine years later, his opera *The Medium* resulted from it.

His genius for bringing together music, words and drama in a smooth and seamless union was uncanny. His sense of stagecraft aroused the envy of less gifted colleagues. He wrote all his own libretti, which dealt with the here and now, had believable plots, singable lines, and tremendous intensity. *The Consul,* his first full-length opera, is almost too poignant for those who went through experiences comparable to those of the heroine Magda in the Second World War. *The Saint of Bleecker Street* is a story of psychological conflict ending in violence, and its emotional pull too has a terrific impact on the audience. Between these two, Menotti composed a touching one-act opera *Amahl and the Night Visitors.* The first opera to be commissioned for the then new medium of television, it was performed on Christmas Eve, 1951, and became as staple a feature of Christmas Eve as Charles Dickens' *Christmas Carol.*

For the World's Fair in Brussels in 1958, he composed an opera *Maria Golovin,* dealing with a blind man and his ill-starred love. The same year, he instituted and directed an annual music festival in Spoleto, Italy. His opera *The Last Savage* was produced at the Met in 1964.

Menotti's output is not limited to operas; such other of his works as ballets, concerti, etc., were published and performed. But, far and away the most gifted opera composer sinçe Verdi, he modernized and vivified the music drama so that, in his hands, it created fresh excitement.

Born Cadegliano, Italy, July 7, 1911
Living Mt. Kisco, N. Y.

DARIUS
MILHAUD

After the death of Ravel, Milhaud was recognized as the most important composer in present-day France, and although he made the United States his home after 1940, his Frenchness remained alive and indestructible. Like most French musicians, he studied at the Paris Conservatoire, but his studies were interrupted by the First World War, and he never got as far as the Prix de Rome. For two of the war years he was attache to the French Legation in Rio de Janeiro, and there assimilated the rhythmic Brazilian songs and dances which he embodied in *Saudades de Brasil.* In Rio he became friends with the playwright, Paul Claudel, with whom he afterward collaborated in such important stage works as *Christopher Columbus* and *The Tidings Brought to Mary.*

His return to Paris in 1919 sent him off on a new tack. He met Erik Satie, a composer who believed that humor was a necessary element in music, especially in a war-torn world. Around a marble-topped table in a Paris café, Satie and a group of young followers, Honegger, Durey, Auric, Poulenc, and Tailleferre earnestly discussed and analyzed Satie's own satiric, witty pieces. Debussy sometimes joined the group. Milhaud was drawn in and presently found himself banded with the others in a group of six. For a time, the Six provided amusement and novelty for a postwar world badly in need of both. Milhaud's *Le Boeuf sur le Toit,* one of his popular works of this period, became the theme of a sort of circus comedy with that title which brought him a great deal of publicity. After the Six dissolved their association Milhaud's talent bloomed the brighter.

He was enormously prolific and composed in many styles and forms. He took on Debussy and impressionism, Brazil and exoticism, Stravinsky and modernism, jazz and Americanism, yet at the same time he remained Darius Milhaud. He related in his autobiography, *Notes without Music,* a trying moment when he played a *Ballade* at one of a series of concerts of modern music promoted by Dr. Walter Damrosch in New York under the title *Pleasant and Unpleasant Music.* The audience was asked to classify each piece as pleasant or unpleasant after hearing it. Said Milhaud, "I regarded this procedure as definitely unpleasant, whatever the verdict of the audience might prove to be."

After his marriage to his cousin Madeleine, an accomplished musician and actress and lifelong "best friend," Milhaud traveled widely, everywhere absorbing new ideas to be utilized in his art. He first visited the United States in 1922, where "le jazz hot" of Harlem took effect on him—no more so, however, than the music of Greece and Turkey, of Egypt and Russia and other little-traveled countries. His eventual arrival in the United States at the beginning of the Second World War gave him a new and fruitful field. He taught composition at Mills College in California while Madeleine held classes in diction and literature there and also produced French plays. They extended their activities to Tanglewood, Massachusetts, and Aspen, Colorado, where they gathered about them many devoted students. In his later years, Milhaud was crippled with arthritis and obliged to spend much time in a wheel chair, but his prodigious composing activity continued. The list of his works covers many pages of his biography; they reflect genuine creative gifts.

Born Aix-en-Provence, France, September 4, 1892
Living United States

CLAUDIO MONTEVERDI

"LET THE WORD be master of the melody, not its slave," was young Claudio Monteverdi's first commandment for the composition of opera. In this he anticipated Gluck and Wagner—and Gian-Carlo Menotti. It was the ambition of this medieval musician to fuse words, action and music into a complete whole, an ambition which his successors restated many times. He believed, too, that rules should be broken when it was necessary to do so in the interests of meaning and expressivity, and he did not hesitate to act upon his belief.

This led to "new wrinkles." He employed a fairly complete orchestra instead of a few tinkling instruments and gave the separate groups each a part to play. This produced a crude polyphony, unlike the guitar-like strumming in unison which was the general practice. He instructed the viols of the orchestra to play with bows instead of plucking the strings, and this brought new beauty to the string section. He composed recitatives to be chanted by a solo voice with instrumental accompaniment. And he introduced tremolo and pizzicato to the strings.

When he tried to explain to the violists how the tremolo should be played, they at first refused to do anything so ridiculous as repeat the same note sixteen times in rapid succession. Why, they wanted to know, wouldn't one long note do as well as sixteen short ones? "Because it doesn't convey fear, anxiety, suspense or anger in the same way," replied the composer patiently. They received his suggestion of plucking the strings "pizzicato" for certain effects with equal uneasiness, and he had fairly to bludgeon them into doing as he asked. Medieval orchestra men were not conditioned to such sound effects nor were medieval audiences, but they learned.

Monteverdi was a spirited lad in his teens when he started chafing at the restrictions imposed on music by tradition. While he was a student of Ingegneri in Cremona, from whom he received a thorough training, he questioned while dutifully memorizing the rigid rules of counterpoint. And in his first book of madrigals, issued when he was sixteen, he slyly took a few liberties, though for the most part these madrigals were modeled on his teacher's. Over the years, he composed altogether eight great collections of madrigals, which became more and more dramatic as he gained confidence and knowledge.

As court musician in the service of Vincenzo, Duke of Gonzago, the young man had many opportunities to broaden his mental horizon. To the duke's court in Mantua came Galileo, Tasso, and other great thinkers. Monteverdi accompanied his restless patron to the wars, too, and with two or three others sweetened the nights before battle with music. He accompanied Vincenzo on a more peaceful mission to Florence in 1600, to the wedding festivities of King Henry IV of France with the daughter of the Grand Duke of Tuscany. He reveled in the beauties of Florence and can hardly have missed hearing Jacopo Peri's opera *Euridice* performed at the wedding feast. Surely it awakened his desire to attempt that new and unusual form of music, the opera.

At any rate, Duke Vincenzo commissioned him to write one, and at the age of forty, he produced his first opera, *Orfeo*. He employed every device that occurred to him to make it dramatic and expressive. The orchestra became, not a grey duenna, but a lively participant in the mood and action. He gave the singers lovely melodies, and interpolated song-like passages into the accompaniment. Although this was his first attempt at opera, he already had rejected the past.

But the year that brought the birth of the first Monteverdi opera brought tragedy to its composer. His wife, Claudia, an accomplished harpist and his most congenial companion, fell ill and died. The taste of success became as ashes in his mouth. He was in the midst of composing his second opera, *Arianna*. Bereft though he was, he drove himself to its completion. Arianna's famous lament, "Lasciatemi morir," wrung from him in the year following his bereavement, is a cry of grief so profound that it moves hearers to tears. It was sung from one end of Italy to the other; so popular was it that Monteverdi later wrote it as a five-part madrigal. The success of *Arianna*, presented before a huge audience in the Duke's castle in Mantua, was overwhelming. It is deplorable that of the score only the Lament has been preserved. In fact, a great deal of Monteverdi's music has been lost to the world.

When his patron died the composer soon found another, better job. He went as choir master to the magnificent cathedral of St. Mark's. In Venice the arts were flourishing, and Monteverdi flourished with them. His masses, motets and other religious writings were heard to great advantage in the vast cathedral. He composed several volumes of madrigals in Venice, and operas now known only because he mentioned their titles in his letters. One, *Il Combattimento di Clorinda e Tancredi*, survives and is occasionally performed. Half ballet, half drama, it is an example of the skill with which Monteverdi made his music speak the language of emotion and action.

A plague ravaged Europe in 1630. When it reached Venice Monteverdi vowed that he would make a pilgrimage to the Madonna of Loreto if his life was spared. He escaped the plague and not only made the pilgrimage but took holy orders as well. This did not prevent his continuing to compose operas. *Il Ritorno d'Ulisse in Patria (Ulysses' Homecoming)* and *L'Incoronazione di Poppea* have been partially preserved. If the latter was actually written when Monteverdi was seventy-four, as the date of the manuscript suggests, its youth and vitality are phenomenal.

His ideas continued to flow until his death, at seventy-six. He was one of the wonderful older men, like Toscanini or Dr. Schweitzer, whose example inspires other men. His works are an outstanding landmark in the long history of music drama.

Born Cremona, Italy, Baptized May 1, 1567
Died Venice, Italy, November 19, 1643

WOLFGANG AMADEUS MOZART

A TINY BOY stands on a footstool at the harpsichord in the Mozart living-room in Salzburg. "Let me try Nannerl's piece," he begs his father. "You can't, you are too small. Wait till you are older," says Papa. But Wolfgang has his way. He plays by ear the minuet he has heard his sister practicing. And so, at four, begins the musical career of the greatest child prodigy the world has ever known.

During his childhood, he was probably the most kissed little boy in all Europe. His father taught him, traveled with him, wrote down the music he started composing at five, planned his every step, told him whose hand to kiss. With Nannerl, Papa took him on triumphant tours to the courts of Austria, Germany, France and England. It was at the court of Austria, when he was six, that he received the royal embrace of Marie Antoinette, a year older than he. He fell headlong over the long sword which was an unaccustomed part of his court costume, and she kissed away his tears of pain and chagrin. "When I am grown up, I will marry you," he promised her.

The royal kiss should have brought Mozart good luck, but that is the one gift the gods denied him. He was good-looking, intelligent, gay, lovable and loving, and the most precocious, prolific and many-sided musical genius the world has known. Yet his brief manhood was beset with disappointments.

In his teens he visited Italy and was elected a member of the Philharmonic Society of Bologna, an honor never accorded to one so young. The Pope made him a Cavaliere, a Knight of the Golden Cross as well. He lost his heart to Italy, especially Italian opera, and changed his middle name from Gottlieb to Amadeus, which means the same (Beloved by God). But after his return to Salzburg, where he and his father both played the violin in the archbishop's orchestra, fortune ceased to smile.

The easy-going Archbishop Hieronymus died and was succeeded by the parsimonious Colloredo who denied the Mozarts permission to make another tour. Mozart impulsively resigned from Colloredo's service, and with his mother as chaperone, went out into the world at twenty-one to seek his fortune.

In Mannheim he encountered the finest orchestra in Europe and composed many works for the Elector of Mannheim from whom he expected to receive a court appointment. He received flattering words but nothing tangible except a watch that didn't keep time. In Mannheim he made the acquaintance of the piano, which he much preferred to the harpsichord and clavichord and which he played to the amazement of all who heard him. In Mannheim, too, he fell in love with Aloysia Weber. Much alarmed by the budding romance as reported by Mama Mozart, Papa bade him in a thunderous letter to get to Paris at once and find himself a job.

The French nobles who had applauded the marvelous little boy were not amused by the worried lovesick young man nor by his music. His mother's death after a few months in Paris was a calamity. Bereft of her care and unable to earn his way, he was commanded by his father to return to Salzburg and the service of the detested archbishop. But when Colloredo ordered his court to Vienna in the spring of 1781, the young man found himself in the city he loved best of all. He resolved to stay there and again to leave the archbishop's service which had become increasingly distasteful in the beckoning distractions of the lovely city. He went to tender his resignation. In a historic scene he was bodily kicked out of the archbishop's antechamber. But at least and at last he was free!

He married Constanze Weber, the younger sister of his first love, Aloysia, and named the heroine of his opera, *The Escape from the Seraglio,* after her. Though the opera swept Vienna off its feet when it was produced in 1782, Mozart's patron, Emperor Joseph, said patronizingly, "It has too many notes for my ears, my dear Mozart." Bad luck again! Joseph gave the finest composer in his empire such unworthy commissions that Mozart scrawled on an accounting of his annual income, "Too much for what I produce, too little for what I could produce."

Yet he and Constanze had many moments of happiness during the nine years of their marriage. All musical Vienna came to the Mozart Sunday mornings, when Haydn, Mozart, and two friends played string quartets. "From Papa Haydn, I learned to write string quartets," said Mozart, and dedicated a set of six to him. Upon hearing them, Haydn said to Mozart's father, "I declare to you upon my honor that I consider your son the greatest composer that I have ever heard."

But there was never enough money to pay the bills for his growing family. Constanze had six babies in nine years. Besides, she loved to spend money. So, for that matter, did her husband.

From Lorenzo Da Ponte, he obtained excellent Italian libretti for his best-loved operas—*The Marriage of Figaro* (1786), *Don Giovanni* (1787), and *Cosi Fan Tutte* (1790). He composed incessantly and with the utmost spontaneity. The result is an incredible number of works in every known form, more works in more different forms than any composer produced.

His last opera, *The Magic Flute,* was created when he was ill and depressed, yet it sparkles with wit and gaiety. A *Requiem Mass* was commissioned in the same year by a stranger, whose mysterious appearance and demand for absolute secrecy convinced Mozart that he came from the world beyond the grave. The Mass was only half done when, weakened by work and worry, Mozart became fatally ill. More than ever, in his weakness, he was convinced that the *Requiem* was for his own funeral. So, in fact, it proved to be.

He died, at the age of thirty-five, on December 5, 1791. His mortal remains lie in an unmarked grave, for there were no funds for a decent burial. But his immortal works have an enduring place in the hearts of all who are attuned to the language of music which he spoke in accents of sublime perfection.

Born Salzburg, Austria, January 27, 1756
Died Vienna, Austria, December 5, 1791

MODEST MUSSORGSKY

THE RUSSIAN giant, Mussorgsky, had a rugged strength and individuality which set him apart from the other four of "The Five" composers who were his pals. One writer calls him "a cuckoo in a nest of singing birds," for his rough, untaught song grated on the ear when compared with their chirpings. He refused to submit to conventional musical training, and went straight to the mark in direct, uncompromising fashion. As a result, his songs, piano pieces, dramatic and orchestral works (a long list) bear the stamp of his crude but unique genius.

Had he composed nothing but the opera, *Boris Godunoff*, he would have earned his place among the immortals. As *Carmen* is the perfect French opera, so *Boris* is the perfect Russian opera. The composer minced no musical words in this powerful tonal blast against tyranny. In crashing chords and ringing arias he cried out for justice for the masses, charity for the poor, and punishment for evildoers. The lesser subjects of the Czar did not dare to express approval of such subversive utterances, the aristocrats feared them, and so, after twenty performances, *Boris* was withdrawn. When Mussorgsky died, his executors found the score, forgotten, in a mass of dusty manuscripts. Its rugged strength leapt out at them, and they decided that the opera must and should be presented. To Rimsky-Korsakoff was entrusted the task of polishing it. The composer Liadoff, invited to collaborate in the task, refused. "It seems easy enough to correct Mussorgsky's defects, but when this is done, it is impossible not to feel that the result is no longer Mussorgsky," he said. The result of Rimsky's editing proved the truth of Liadoff's statement, yet even in its touched-up form, *Boris* grips and holds audiences in a hypnotic spell, and is today one of the glories of the operatic repertoire.

Twenty performances of *Boris* took place in 1874, five years after its completion. Mussorgsky patiently revised it in 1871, but even so, like other operas, it encountered many obstacles before production. Tchaikowsky wrote his brother Modest from Moscow: "I have been thoroughly studying *Boris Godunoff*. With all my soul, I send Mussorgsky's music to the devil; this is the most vulgar and vile parody on music!"

But shortly before this, the maligned composer had written to a friend, "I am living *Khovantschina* as I lived *Boris*, and I am eager to do a people's drama—I am so eager!" This opera tells of the conflict between the Old Order and the New under Peter the Great. The composer exulted over his second act, "The opera is boiling." The whole opera boils with national feeling, aided and abetted by native folksongs, typical of the Russia of its time and after. It arouses enthusiasm whenever it is presented.

As a song writer, Mussorgsky achieved great distinction. His children's cycle, *The Nursery*, so touched Franz Liszt that he declared he would dedicate a composition to Mussorgsky. Exclaimed the flattered composer, "Fool or not in music I may be, but in *The Nursery* it seems I am no fool, because an understanding for children, and a view of them as people in their own little world, and not as amusing dolls, prevents the composer from having a foolish attitude." The Songs in *The Nursery* are entitled: (1) With Nanny, (2) Go into the Corner, (3) The Cockchafer, (4) Dolly's Cradle Song, (5) The Evening Prayer, (6) The Hobby Horse, and (7) The Cat and the Bird-Cage. In his songs about peasants, and in the mature cycles *No Sunlight* and *Songs and Dances of Death*, we note the same overwhelming tenderness and strength, the militant sympathy for suffering and for the downtrodden, the same humanity as in *The Nursery*. "There are days when cats scratch at the heart," he said. Fortunately, there were days when he could laugh too, as his lighter works testify. The whole psychology of Russian life can be reconstructed from Mussorgsky's songs, written in the simple, everyday language of the people.

The son of a land-owner, Modest spent his first ten years on his father's estate. He picked up folksongs and stories from the moujiks, and listened with childish sympathy to their grievances. After being sent to the School for Cadets to be made into an officer and a gentleman, he went through the period of dissipation considered normal, and became a uniformed dandy in a crack Russian regiment, where his chief military duty consisted in drinking his brother officers under the table. This duty he performed with such zest that drinking became his besetting sin.

All this time, he knew music only as an amateur. His manicured fingers improvised pretty pieces on the piano for the ladies, but he didn't really care. Then he met Dargomijsky, who introduced him to Balakireff, César Cui, and Rimsky-Korsakoff. He turned to music like a flower to the sun. Balakireff taught him the rudiments of composition, but he was instinctively unwilling to discipline his wild talent to the conventional pattern, and after a time he drifted away from Balakireff and the others, to go on his own way.

At nineteen, he resigned his commission and went to work as a government clerk. The salary was so small that he lived on the ragged edge of starvation. Since his father had lost his fortune when the serfs were liberated in 1861, Modest could look for no help from his family. For a time, he shared an apartment with Rimsky-Korsakoff, who did his gentlemanly best to subdue his friend's tonal violence. When they separated, Mussorgsky lived alone, and it was not good for him. He took to vodka and narcotics to relieve the black depression and sense of failure that dogged him. He shuffled around in a slovenly dressing-gown, big, bearded and unwashed, sinking lower all the time, pitiable in his degradation. His friends turned away from him, his money gave out, and when fatal illness attacked him, he became a charity patient in the St. Nicholas Military Hospital, where he died, at the age of forty-two, a pathetic figure.

He was the first musical realist in Russia. He raised his voice against Tsarist iniquities, he composed music that stirred masses and classes, he sought not only beauty, but the greater beauty that is truth.

Born Karevo, Russia, March 21, 1839
Died St. Petersburg, Russia, March 25, 1881

JACQUES
OFFENBACH

This composer might have stepped from the pages of one of his own operettas, for his ascent from rags to riches was as sensational as that of any hero of musical comedy. He was born in the town of Offenbach, near Cologne, the son of the cantor of the Hebrew Synagogue in Cologne. His early years were lived in the ghetto; his early recollections were the sight and smell of the secondhand clothing stores on his street. His name in those days was Jakob Levy.

Jakob Levy became Jacques Offenbach, debonair dandy of the boulevards of Paris, more French than the French themselves (though he never quite lost his German accent). He became the favorite composer of the Second Empire in France. The steps which led him up the ladder to this eminence were some ninety elegant, satirical light operas, composed in a span of twenty-five years beginning in 1853.

As a boy he played the cello in the cafés of Cologne and did so well that his father sent him to Paris to study in the Conservatoire. At the same time, he played in the orchestra of the Opéra Comique and learned all the tricks of the opera trade. His first outstanding success was *Orphée aux Enfers (Orpheus in Hades)*, produced in 1858. *La Vie Parisienne, La Belle Hélène, Barbe Bleue, La Perichole,* and *La Grande Duchesse de Gérolstein* are other favorites. At his own theater, Les Bouffes Parisiens, Offenbach conducted his operettas; the gay little corner of Paris which he made his own became a favorite resort of the tired businessman, who found the relaxation and recreation he craved in the impudent topical texts and the melodious, witty music of these operettas. They were sung and whistled in the streets of all Paris. One afternoon the prima donna who took the part of the Grande Duchesse de Gérolstein wished to drive through a part of the Tuileries gardens reserved for royalty. A guard barred her entrance. "But I am the Grande Duchesse de Gérolstein," she protested haughtily. "Pardon, Madame." The guard bowed low at the familiar name, and let the carriage through.

Offenbach toured the United States in 1876 and wrote a book about his experiences, *Notes d'un musicien en voyage*. To his mind there was no place in the world that could compare with Paris, and he took a dig at the barbarity of the new country, the musical ignorance he found there, the quaint custom of non-alcoholic Sundays. He never cared to go far away from his beloved Paris except to make unfavorable comparisons.

Several of his light operas are still sung, notably *La Perichole,* which had a riotous run at the Metropolitan Opera in New York in 1957. But strangely, it is by his one serious opera, *Les Contes d'Hofmann (Tales of Hofmann)*, that he is best remembered. He worked very hard at it while seriously ill and prayed that he might live to see the first production. He did see a private preview, with piano accompaniment, but he did not live long enough to revise it, as he intended, nor to complete the orchestration. Its enthusiastic reception would have cheered him had he been there to see it. It was performed over a hundred times in Paris in its first season and found its way into opera houses all over the world.

Born Offenbach-on-Rhine, Germany, June 20, 1819
Died Paris, France, October 5, 1880

GIOVANNI PIERLUIGI DA PALESTRINA

THE TOWN OF Palestrina is today a wretched maze of dark alleys and broken-down wooden hovels inhabited by bandits and outcasts. But when little Giovanni Pierluigi roamed its streets, it was a place of stately palaces and beautiful gardens, the ancient Praeneste which vied in beauty and wealth with Rome. From its church issued music which the boy loved passionately. He had a sweet voice and soon was able to sing what he heard coming from the church, and from ballad-singers in the streets, too. When he was fourteen a family council was held to determine how and by whom he should be educated. A musical career was chosen. His father owned a house and a vineyard but was not wealthy. His mother volunteered to sell a plot of land of her own to pay for his education. She did well, for her son became the greatest composer of church music of his era.

He was the organist and choirmaster in Palestrina until Pope Julius invited him to sing in the choir of the Sistine Chapel in Rome. In the meantime Giovanni had married the girl of his heart and at twenty-four was the father of three children. He moved his family to Rome, prepared to bask in the Pope's patronage for the rest of his life. But he had been there only a short while when Pope Julius died. His successor, Pope Paul, decided to cut down expenses and to start with the choir-singers. Some of those in the Sistine Chapel were jealous because Giovanni had been admitted without the usual examination. They complained to the Pope that his voice was no good and that furthermore he was married and had no right, as a married man, to sing in the choir. Pope Paul dismissed Giovanni and two other married men and salved his conscience by allowing them six scudi (ten dollars) a month as pension. Giovanni took to his bed with the sixteenth century equivalent of a nervous breakdown.

He arose a sadder and a wiser man, and was appointed to St. John's Lateran Church as choirmaster. Giovanni and his growing family spent five tranquil years in a little house on the Cœelian Hill, happy years untouched by the jealousies and intrigues of Rome. He went daily to the church and had leisure for contemplation and composition. From this peaceful retreat he was summoned by the accession of still another Pope, Pius IV, who called him back to Rome and the Sistine Chapel. Fortune smiled once more and so did Giovanni. On the title-page of his *First Book of Masses* is a woodcut which portrays the composer, kneeling, offering an open book to the seated Pope, who takes the book with one hand, raises the other in blessing. From his twentieth year until his death, Giovanni's whole life was passed in figuratively kneeling positions; only the face under the papal crown changed. He served eleven popes altogether. His fortunes rose and fell with theirs.

In the dedication of his *First Book of Motets* in 1563, he wrote: "The function of music in the church is the seasoning of devotion by the added delight of sweetness of song and variety of harmony. The sharper blame therefore do those deserve who misemploy so splendid and great a gift of God in light or unworthy things, and thereby excite men, who of themselves are inclined to all evil, to sin and misdoing."

So well did his music embody this pious belief that a commission appointed by the Council of Trent in 1564 to purify the music of the church left Palestrina's compositions unchanged as being beyond reproach. One of the cardinals had described the singing in the Sistine Chapel: "Methought I heard a herd of pigs grunting and squealing, for I could not understand a single word." Others complained that words and music of bawdy street songs were being interpolated into the church service. But no adverse criticism was brought against the religious chants of Palestrina. (By now he called himself by the name of his town, which he took for his own.) The purity of Palestrina's glorious *Mass of Marcellus,* which he had composed some time before the Council of Trent, moved the then reigning pope to tears when he heard it after a committee of eight cardinals had pronounced it fit for papal ears.

Against the gorgeous background of sixteenth century Rome, Palestrina moves, a serene figure going from home to chapel, loved and honored by all. When, in 1575, his townspeople made a pilgrimage from Palestrina to Rome on his fiftieth birthday, he led the procession over the hills. As they entered the capital city, maidens dressed in white and youths carrying olive-branches met them, singing Palestrina's songs. It was a happy moment in his life.

Fate struck him a cruel blow when he lost, within four years, his beloved wife, two sons and two grandchildren. In his grief he thought he would become a monk and went so far as to have his head shaven in a tonsure. He reconsidered before it was too late, let his hair grow in, and took a second wife. In directing her thriving fur business he profited greatly and employed his profits to have copies made of his collected compositions. Never was money more wisely spent than on the sixteen large volumes of Palestrina's works, a treasury of religious music. The combination of piety and business ability in Palestrina was remarkable. He was an idealist, but not a dreamy, impractical one. He saw no inconsistency in directing the choir in the Julian Chapel of St. Peter's, pouring out masses and madrigals of purest ray serene, and at the same time driving a good bargain in the business world.

In all the long list of his compositions there was not one that was unworthy. The sacred words could be clearly heard throughout. The polyphonic music with which they were joined could be understood by all. These were the requirements of the Council of Trent. "Enlighten Thou my eyes," prayed Palestrina while he composed. His prayer must have been heard, for purity, clarity, brevity and simplicity, combined with the banishing of all secular elements in his music, won for him the title "Prince of Music," engraved on the simple leaden plate that marks his tomb.

Born Palestrina, Italy, about 1525
Died Rome, Italy, February 2, 1594

GIOVANNI PERGOLESI

Since Pergolesi died before he was thirty, there is more of promise than performance in his output. Still, he left twelve operas, three oratorios, and a number of masses, cantatas, and other music for the church, including the famous *Stabat Mater*. One of his operas, *La Serva Padrona (The Maid Mistress),* is so far ahead of its time in the unusual life and color of its music and its dialogue that it exercised an appreciable influence on succeeding composers.

La Serva Padrona was composed as an intermezzo between the acts of a heavy tragic opera *Il Prigionero Superbo (The Haughty Prisoner).* Audiences openly walked out on the featured opera, returning long enough to enjoy Pergolesi's intermezzo and then going to a café to laugh reminiscently at the witticisms they had been listening to.

Romance colors his story. He was the only son of a poor couple in an obscure country town, and received his musical training at the Conservatory for the Poor in Naples. He was very handsome, resembling the painter Raphael in appearance and was the protégé of the Director of the Conservatory. After his graduation he found patrons and patronesses, especially the latter, and a teaching job. Pergolesi loved life and lived it to the hilt. His first serious opera, *Guglielmo d'Aquitania,* was a great success, which he celebrated by plunging into dissipations that were remarkable even in those tolerant days. If he had not done so he might never have composed the *Stabat Mater,* written from the depths of his remorseful soul when he knew himself to be dying. A repentant sinner must have something to repent; Pergolesi saw to it that he had plenty.

At one time—perhaps after the performance of *Guglielmo d'Aquitania*—a high-born lady, Maria Spinelli, fell deeply in love with him. One story says that at the performance of his last opera, *L'Olimpiade,* when the fickle Italian audience was booing the music and throwing rotten oranges at stage and composer, Maria came to the rescue. She quieted the crowd and whispered words of love to Pergolesi. Her three big brothers marched in on the love scene which ensued and gave Maria her choice of death or marriage with a wealthy suitor of their choice. She entered a nunnery, and Pergolesi found other fair ladies to conquer.

But the tuberculosis which racked him he could not conquer. Weak and wasting away, he retired to the monastery of Pozzuoli. There, cared for by the monks, he composed much religious music, including the *Stabat Mater*. Passionate and dramatic, operatic rather than religious in style, it was described by Bellini as a divine poem of suffering. Pergolesi's short life came to an end soon after the completion of his masterpiece.

La Serva Padrona came into its own long after the composer was dead and buried. It was brought to Paris by a traveling Italian opera company in 1753 in time to throw its weight on the side of Italian opera as against French in the famous controversy in which Rameau's supremacy was in question. Its vivacity and sparkle were a blessed relief from the stilted formal writing then in vogue and set a new fashion in opera.

Born Jesi, Italy, January 4, 1710
Died Pozzuoli, Italy, March 16, 1736

SERGEI

PROKOFIEFF

SERGEI PROKOFIEFF was the original "laughing boy." In his youth, he was always in mischief, always playing tricks. His mother caught him between laughs long enough to teach him to play the piano effortlessly and well. He completed his first composition at the age of five, and after that nobody suggested that he become anything but a musician. He had composed three operas by the time he was thirteen. He studied composition with Glière, then went on to St. Petersburg Conservatory. During his student years there he poured his youthful inspiration into more than a hundred pieces.

When his *Scythian Suite* was performed in 1914, its driving dynamic power, masculinity, grotesque and barbaric harmony and rhythm so outraged the composer Glazounoff that he stamped noisily out of the hall in protest, but Prokofieff was undisturbed. He composed the totally different *Classical Symphony* with tongue in cheek to demonstrate that he could write like Mozart if he had a mind to.

Exempted from military service by a heart murmur, the blond six-footer left Russia to travel. He arrived in America in 1918 and tasted triumph here when his jolly fairy-tale opera, *The Love for Three Oranges,* was put on by the Chicago Opera Company.

From the United States he went to Paris, to the Russian ballet impresario Diaghileff. *Chout (Clown),* a comic pantomime which Prokofieff had composed in 1915, was so successful that Diaghileff commissioned others—*Le Pas d'Acier (The Age of Steel)* and *L'Enfant Prodigue (The Prodigal Son).* In Paris Prokofieff composed three symphonies, a *Fourth* and *Fifth Piano Concerto,* and a *Symphonic Song for Orchestra.*

At forty-three, Prokofieff settled with his wife in Moscow and made annual concert tours of Europe and America for some years afterward. As he grew older, he guided his inspiration with a canny hand and an eye on Soviet ideology. His later works are less fantastic, less humorous, but more lyrical. He composed outstanding scores for three films directed by Serge Eisenstein: *Lieutenant Kije, Alexander Nevsky,* and *Ivan the Terrible.* His whimsical musical fairytale, *Peter and the Wolf,* in 1936, demonstrates the instruments of the orchestra while it relates the delightful tale of Peter and his animal friends. It is a classic of its kind, a favorite with young people from six to sixty. His *Grand Cantata* for the twentieth anniversary of the October Revolution, completed the following year, is an all-out Soviet work, scored for symphony orchestra, military band plus accordions and percussion,, and two choruses, with a text composed of the sayings of Lenin, Stalin and Karl Marx. The supreme effort of his last years was the opera *War and Peace* from Tolstoi's novel, performed on American television in 1956 in a cut version.

By this time the composer had died from a cerebral hemorrhage. He was buried in the Russian equivalent of Westminster Abbey, near Scriabin and other famous compatriots, one of the few composers of the twentieth century whose name was well on the way to immortality during his lifetime. "He belonged to the ages before he belonged to the Kremlin," said an obituary notice.

Born Ekaterinoslav, Russia, April 23, 1891
Died Moscow, Soviet Union, March 4, 1953

GIACOMO PUCCINI

PUCCINI looked like the hero of one of his own operas. He was a big, broad-shouldered, bushy-haired man, who dressed picturesquely in blouse, scarf and beret to match, who wore yellow boots and drove a fast car. With childish satisfaction, he remarked, after his spectacular rise from peasant to plutocrat, "Just think of it, if I hadn't hit on music, I should never have been able to do anything in the world."

He was twenty-two when a grant from the Queen of Italy enabled him to study at the Conservatory of Milan. Here he fell in with three jolly boon companions, with whom he enjoyed the Bohemian life he was to depict so charmingly in *La Bohème.* All four shared the prize of 1000 lire won by Puccini's *Capriccio Sinfonico* in a prize contest. When Ricordi, the music-publisher who had discovered Verdi, commissioned an opera from young Puccini, the four went in a body to discuss terms with him.

It took Puccini five years to compose *Edgar* for Ricordi, and the opera failed. Ricordi continued to back him, however, and cleaned up on *Manon Lescaut.* This opera overtook in popularity even Massenet's on the same subject, and a steady rise up the ladder to fame ensued for Puccini.

The première of *La Bohème,* conducted by Toscanini in Milan, was sensational. Puccini identified himself so closely with its hero Rodolfo that he is said to have burst into tears as he set down the nine simple chords that accompany Mimi's gasping farewell to life.

Seeking "a libretto that can move the world," he read thousands before he composed *Tosca.* The story is melodramatic enough, and when it is underlined by Puccini's music, suspense and emotional tension grip the audience. The composer himself preferred the gentle, though equally tragic, *Madame Butterfly.*

La Bohème, Tosca, and *Madame Butterfly* have all been performed on television, a sure indication of their proven public appeal. Puccini came to New York in 1910 to attend the performance of *La Fanciulla del West (The Girl of the Golden West).* Italian-singing cowboys on the stage were not convincing to American audiences, despite the Puccini music they sang, despite the presence of Caruso on the stage and Toscanini in the pit. The visit was a disappointment.

La Rondine (The Swallow), a tuneful but trifling opera; *Il Trittico (The Triptych);* and *Turandot,* an oriental tragedy, complete the list of the well-known. *Turandot* was unfinished when Puccini was taken ill. He died in Brussels, aged sixty-six.

Puccini's biographer Francis Toye wrote of him, "He had a sense of the theater unsurpassed even by Verdi, and no man has ever known how to translate theatrical situations into music with so few rapid, vivid strokes; he used his orchestra with consummate skill and he wrote for the human voice with a care and a knowledge that cannot be overpraised."

Born Lucca, Italy, December 23, 1858
Died Brussels, Belgium, November 29, 1924

HENRY PURCELL

About Henry Purcell, composer in chief to court, church, stage and chamber, there hovers a quaint aura of the legendary, due partly to the incomplete accounts of his life and death, partly to the old English in which these accounts are cloaked. There is doubt on the name of his father, not for the ordinary reason, but because, in most accounts, the name of Henry, instead of Thomas, is given. But a letter from Thomas to the Reverend John Gostling, containing the sentence, "My sonne Henry is composing, wherein you will be deeply concerned" seems to resolve that question. The Reverend John had a deep bass voice, which made light of the difficult anthems young Henry composed for it. He would naturally be interested in "my sonne Henry's" compositions, according to the musicologist, Harvey Grace.

Henry was unusually young to be a choirboy of the Chapel Royal when he was admitted. He was only six. But it may have been just as well, for he died at thirty-six, which gave him only thirty active years. In the Chapel Royal, the boy earned a tidy annual income, and was given, besides, food, clothing, medical care, and an education in Latin, writing, organ, lute, and violin. When Henry's voice broke, at fourteen, he received a smaller stipend, but became "keeper, maker, mender, repayrer and tuner of the regalls, organs, virginals, flutes and recorders and all other kind of wind instruments, in ordinary, without fee, to His Majesty." At fifteen, he was allowed to tune the organ in Westminster Abbey at an annual salary of two pounds ($10); at twenty, he succeeded John Blow as organist of the Abbey, with all the honors thereto appertaining. He had the added duties of Composer to the King's Violins, a post which provided him with a captive audience for the songs, organ works, and instrumental compositions he now began to produce in profusion.

He was married at twenty, and the first of his official odes appeared that year. A *Song to Welcome Home His Majesty from Windsor,* an expression of the joy of the king's subjects at his return from a brief absence was the subject of Purcell's song. All his life long, he was destined to produce pieces for royal birthdays, weddings, victories, absences and returns. He was to write music for the theater, too, of which many appealing airs have been preserved. At twenty-three, he brought out a volume of sonatas for two violins and bass with organ or harpsichord. It carried a preface, in which he expressed "his hearty wishes that his Book may fall into no other hands but theirs who carry Musical Souls about them, for he is willing to flatter himself into a belief that with such his labors will seem neither unpleasant nor unprofitable." A wish that might be echoed by every composer!

His notable anthem, *They That Go Down to the Sea in Ships* was the result of a near shipwreck. The King's barge was bound on a pleasure trip to the Kentish coast. They ran into a storm so severe that King and courtiers fell to their knees on the deck to pray for deliverance. The low D in the anthem with which Purcell celebrated their safe return to London signifies the point to which their spirits sank during the hours of terror. The average bass singer can go as low as F. Only the Reverend Gostling could make the low D. It was he who suggested the now famous text to Purcell, and who sang the anthem in the Chapel Royal, in a service attended by all the members of the sailing party, except Charles II, the monarch responsible for the sailing.

Purcell's only surviving opera, *Dido and Aeneas,* was commissioned by a young ladies' seminary in Chelsea, and was performed by the young ladies, yet it is a powerful piece of music. We cannot help wondering how the amateur Dido sang the wondrous *Lament,* and the aria *When I Am Laid in Earth,* in which "technique and passion are miraculously fused in one." Three centuries after its composition, *Dido and Aeneas* remains a perennial delight.

Purcell was a master of English declamation. A number of his songs are marred by obscene or unduly frivolous words, but his instrumental writings are pure delight. If he had lived in the reign of good Queen Bess instead of under the frivolous Charles II, her encouragement might have made him the very greatest Master of Musicke. He and his music were popular with men of high and low degree. There is an apocryphal story that he met his death because of his popularity with the fellows in the tavern. He stayed out too late one night, having just one more with the boys, and his wife resentfully locked him out. It was raining and he developed pneumonia.

He had written an anthem, *Thou Knowest, Lord, the Secrets of our Hearts,* "so Heavenly in Operation that it drew tears from us all," when it was sung at the burial of Queen Mary. Six months later it was sung for Purcell's own burial, beside the organ in Westminster Abbey. His tombstone in that honored spot is inscribed: "Here lies Henry Purcell, who left this life and is gone to the Blessed Place where, only, his harmony can be exceeded."

Born London, England, about 1659
Died London, England, November 21, 1695

SERGEI RACHMANINOFF

When Sergei Rachmaninoff walked on to the stage of Carnegie Hall to play a piano recital, his tall, spare figure appearing taller and sparer because of the frock coat he wore, his lined face set in a somber yellow mask, he was the very image of the melancholy Russian of literature. All that was needed to complete the picture was a samovar, presided over by an unfaithful wife. He seated himself at his instrument, introspective, detached from the audience. But the minute his hands touched the keys, he became a part of the piano, and his remarkable playing, his dignified authority, and a strange and indefinable magnetism drew the audience to him.

There was not very much for him to smile about, after all. The son of a wealthy army officer, he spent a luxurious childhood on his father's vast estate. But the family fortune dwindled, and when he was ten, his mother took him to Moscow, and entered him in the College of Music, with no thought of his making music his profession. Talented but indolent, he loafed through his studies, and did not really work in earnest until he became a student of Zveroff at the Moscow Conservatory. He and Tchaikowsky met there, and formed a mutual admiration society; the latter's death when Sergei was only twenty removed a sorely-needed prop.

When Rachmaninoff's one-act opera, *Aleko,* won a graduation medal, his hopes were high. But it was the *Prelude in C sharp minor,* which he composed the following year, that carried his name around the world. No matter how many better pieces he produced, this was "It." It brought him an invitation to conduct in London and was the clinching argument in favor of an engagement as pianist-conductor in the United States in 1909.

Meanwhile, he had troubles. His *First Symphony* pleased neither him nor the public. "If there were a Conservatory in Hell, Rachmaninoff would gain the first prize there for that symphony," growled a fellow-composer. Sergei brooded over its failure until he fell into a genuine depression. He had a commission for a piano concerto, but he could do no work. To Dr. Dahl, who restored him to mental health, he dedicated the *Second Piano Concerto* which he finally roused himself to write. It won the Glinka prize of five hundred rubles. He married his cousin, Natalie Satin, and settled down to a few peaceful years of composing and conducting. His symphonic poem, *The Isle of the Dead,* and a *Second Symphony* appeared, the latter as emphatic a success as the *First Symphony* had been a failure.

But the Bolshevik Revolution again plunged the composer into gloom. This aristocrat no longer felt at home in his homeland. He and his family emigrated. When they arrived in the United States in 1917, an inquiring reporter wanted to know what he thought of the political developments in Russia. "There is no Russia," he growled. The United States became his home. In fur-collared overcoat and tall sealskin cap, he was a familiar sight on New York's Fifty-Seventh Street. An old-world figure in the newest of worlds, irreconcilably bound to the past, an aristocrat in a democracy, he must have felt tragically homesick. He never actually "belonged" here, though he made many friends. When he died of pneumonia while on a concert tour, he was deeply mourned.

His colorful Slavic music is a valuable link between the romantic tradition of the past and the hard reality of the present. He believed that "a composer's music should express the country of his birth, his romantic life, his religion, the books that influence him, the pictures he loves—in short, the sum total of his experience." He said, "I compose because I must give expression to my feelings just as I talk because I must give utterance to my thoughts."

Born Oneg, Novgorod, Russia, April 1, 1873
Died Beverly Hills, Cal., March 28, 1943

JEAN PHILIPPE
RAMEAU

WITH HIS last breath Rameau corrected the priest at his death-bed for chanting off-key. This is an indication of what a stickler for correctness he was, a pedagogue to the end, with a passion for accuracy which triumphed over the pangs of death.

In his childhood he was remarkable for the ease with which he mastered music and the difficulty with which he learned his school subjects. At seven he could read at sight on the harpsichord any piece that was placed before him, and he learned to play the organ and violin also. Nevertheless, his father, who was the organist of the Dijon Cathedral, cautiously decided that Jean had better study law. But the boy persisted in writing music in the margins of his law papers and singing aloud in the classroom. His career in the law was brief.

An abortive love-affair at seventeen caused him to be packed off to Italy. When he returned, whole in heart, he became organist successively at Avignon, Clermont, Paris, Lyons, and again at Clermont. In the leisure these posts afforded him, he studied philosophy and the science of sound, came up with some original discoveries, and embodied them in a volume, *Traité de l'Harmonie (Treatise on Harmony).* It clarified and amplified the existing rules, added new ones, and established the basic system on which the science of harmony has rested since. His motto was "Soyez raisonable." (Be reasonable.) The book reveals him as an original thinker and musical analyst of positive genius.

Having gone to Paris to have his book published, Rameau now admitted to a secret passion for the stage. Finally he found a patron, M. de la Pouplinière and a librettist, the Abbé Pellegrin. The Abbé wrote the text for the opera, *Hippolyte et Aricie* and was so charmed with Rameau's music that after the first performance he publicly destroyed the contract in which Rameau had agreed to pay the librettist, whether or not the opera was a success. The composer was then fifty. From then until his death at eighty-one, he composed twenty-four operas and ballets. Voltaire was librettist for *La Princesse de Navarre,* which won Rameau an appointment as Composer of Chamber Music to Louis XV. *Castor et Pòllux, Les Fêtes d'Hébé,* and *Les Indes Galantes* are representative examples of his stately style.

When, in 1752, an Italian company brought Pergolesi's *La Serva Padrona* to Paris, the bubbling gaiety of this opera buffa won so many friends that Rameau's unsmiling operas were quite put in the shade. He himself said wistfully that he wished he were twenty years younger and could write like Pergolesi. But his operas, as they are, are important in the history of French music. They carried on the tradition of Lully, whom Rameau had supplanted.

Although married to a singer twenty-two years younger than himself, Rameau never learned to write well for the voice; the declamation and songs are the weakest features of his operas. But in the instrumentation he practiced what his treatises preached and produced rich chords, piquant rhythms, novel harmonies, and fresh, pleasing melodies. The overtures to his operas are often played, as are his charming compositions for the harpsichord.

Born Dijon, France, October 23, 1683
Died Paris, France, September 12, 1764

MAURICE RAVEL

When the name of Maurice Ravel is mentioned, the first response is often, "composer of *Bolero,*" the Spanish dance introduced to New York by Toscanini in 1929. This is hardly fair, for Ravel composed many far finer works, though none which created so immediate a sensation.

The invigorating dash of Spanish verve which impelled him to the *Bolero* was very much a part of him, for he was born in the Basque region, in a sea-coast town close to the Pyrenees. He was lulled to sleep with the regional folksongs, and recalled that he found music too in the rhythmic click and roar of machinery when his father took him, as a small boy, to visit a factory. He was educated in Paris, entered the Conservatoire, and won the second Prix de Rome. While still in his twenties, he composed the glittering *Jeux d'Eaux (Fountains)* and *Pavane pour une Infante Défunte (Pavane for a Dead Infanta).* For these works, he should have received his musical spurs, but not a single spur was his until other characteristic compositions had appeared. He combined his delicate French perfectionism with Spanish vigor and intensity in such works as *Miroirs* and *Gaspard de la Nuit* for piano; *Histoires Naturelles* for voice and orchestra; *L'Heure Espagnol,* a gay one-act opera; and *Rhapsodie Espagnole* for orchestra.

The most rewarding of his pre-War works was the ballet *Daphnis and Chloe.* He later made of it an orchestral suite which is much played. But the ballet itself was composed for the Ballet Russe of Diaghileff. In order to complete it without interruption, Ravel went to stay alone at the country house of some friends who were away. The house was on the bank of a river, which was flooded by heavy spring rains. Ravel was at the piano when neighbors came to warn him to leave at once. Water was already seeping through the floor of the room where he was working, but, completely absorbed, he had noticed nothing. He escaped in the nick of time.

He was thirty-nine when the First World War rocked France, and he patriotically volunteered to drive an ambulance. He went in, a high-spirited, gay young man. He emerged, shocked and saddened by the suffering he had witnessed, his hair prematurely gray, his nerves shattered. When he had sufficiently recovered, he composed *Le Tombeau de Couperin,* which he dedicated to six of his comrades who had died on the battlefield. Like some of his other works, this was orchestrated by him after first appearing as a piano piece. It is interesting to note that when he orchestrated the piano suite by Mussorgsky, *Pictures at an Exhibition,* he seems to have absorbed the totally different spirit of that craggy Russian as completely as he had done with the elegant and courtly Couperin. He was a perfectionist, and though there are some who maintain that there was too much artifice in his art, that it is too well-ordered, too formal, they usually admit that, within the pattern, he achieves original, graceful and intense beauty.

After the war, he lived quietly in a villa in Montfort l'Aury, near Paris. He crammed his "doll's house" with a collection of bibelots and paintings, plus six Siamese cats. He never married, but an affectionately bullying housekeeper cared for him, and kept open house for the fellow-musicians who came from Paris to talk and make music until the small hours. After the success of *Bolero,* he was compelled to accept engagements to conduct here and there, and appeared in Vienna, London and Paris, a small bird-like man, a witty conversationalist, a composer of growing stature.

An automobile accident in 1932 brought on a mental breakdown, and though Ravel lived for another five years, his creative power was destroyed, his memory gone. He died after a brain operation.

Born Ciboure, France, March 7, 1875
Died Paris, France, December 28, 1937

OTTORINO RESPIGHI

Many composers have imitated the songs of birds in their music. Recent contemporaries have employed actual machinery in a few pieces. Ottorino Respighi did both when he introduced a gramophone record of a nightingale's song into his orchestral work, *The Pines of Rome,* and by so doing created a minor sensation. When, at one performance, the man entrusted with the delicate task of placing the needle on the record missed his cue, despite careful rehearsal, there was consternation indeed. This was the moment the audience waited for—will he make it or not, they wondered.

The gentle Respighi was a serious composer, who generally avoided sensational experiments and was regarded as a conservative by the more daring of the young Italians. He attended the Liceo Musicale in Bologna. Then, as first viola of the Opera Theater in St. Petersburg, he worked for some months with Rimsky-Korsakoff, and finally he took courses in composition with Max Bruch in Berlin. He was about twenty-six, and playing the viola in the Mugellini Quartet, when his *Notturno* for orchestra was performed in New York, but he himself did not come to the United States until twenty years later. Meanwhile, thanks to the conductors Stransky, Molinari, Mengelberg and Toscanini, his name had become well-known here through performances of his works.

In 1925, he came to New York to appear as soloist with the N. Y. Philharmonic in his *Concerto in the Mixolydian Mode.* This, and the later *Concerto Gregoriano* for violin reflect his preoccupation with the Greek modes, which he employed freely. However, he reveled in jazz, too, which he discovered while here, and in which, he said delightedly, "the rhythm came first and the music second." Paul Whiteman was his hero at that time. He had a discriminating but catholic taste, and produced a greater number and more different kinds of works than any twentieth century Italian composer. They range from a band piece, *Huntingtower Ballad,* in memory of John Philip Sousa to arrangements of Monteverdi, Vitali and Bach.

His operas, *Re Enzo, Semirama, Maria Vittoria, The Sunken Bell, Belfagor, La Fiamma;* the puppet play, *The Sleeping Princess;* ballets, like *Venetian Scherzo, La Boutique Fantasque,* etc., are his better-known stage works. When his miracle play and opera in concert form, *Maria Egiziaca,* was performed in New York in 1932, the beaming composer, who resembled Beethoven except for the beam, conducted it in Carnegie Hall. His wife and ex-pupil, Elsa Olivieri, acknowledged with him the enthusiastic applause. His symphonic poems, especially *Pines of Rome, Fountains of Rome,* and *Festivals of Rome,* evoked interest even in opera-conscious Italy, and were particularly well liked in the United States. In colorful and poetical sonorities, they hymn the city he loved.

His students of the St. Cecilia Academy in Rome adored him. His private life, in his villa on a hill above the city, was peaceful, removed from the bustle of the Appian Way beneath his study window. When he died, he had had the gratification, granted to few composers, of conducting, playing, or at least hearing performances of many of his works, and of knowing that they had made their mark.

Born Bologna, Italy, July 9, 1879
Died Rome, Italy, April 18, 1936

NIKOLAI RIMSKY-KORSAKOFF

NIKOLAI RIMSKY-KORSAKOFF was born to the purple, the son of aristocratic and wealthy parents, and was educated as befitted his station. He fitted neatly into the uniform and the duties of a naval officer, and edified his brother officers with his performances on the cello and the violin. During his early years, his interest in music was wholly amateur. The operas of his countryman, Michael Glinka, *Life for the Tsar* and *Russlan and Ludmilla,* enchanted him, and he was further awakened to the importance of Russian music for Russians by Balakireff, the guiding spirit of "The Five." From Balakireff he learned the rules of composition. To Balakireff, he brought his *First Symphony,* composed to relieve the tedium of a long tour of sea duty. Although Rimsky-Korsakoff, then twenty-one, did not realize it, his was the first symphony of any importance by a Russian composer. Tchaikowsky had not yet been heard from.

In 1871, still a lieutenant in the navy, he was appointed Professor of Practical Composition and Instrumentation at the Conservatory of St. Petersburg. He had composed a symphonic poem, *Sadko,* and an opera, *The Maid of Pskov,* but he knew little of the technique of "practical composition and instrumentation." He kept one jump ahead of his class in the text-book, and so became, as he laughingly pointed out, one of the Conservatory's best pupils. His marriage with Nadejda Purgold, a concert pianist, brought still more music into his life, and he resigned from the navy.

He drifted away from Balakireff's circle, and became the center of a group of talented pupils of his own, including Glazunoff, Liadoff, and Gretchaninoff. A publishing house was founded to publish their works, a symphony orchestra directed by Rimsky-Korsakoff to play them, and his appointment as inspector of naval bands completed the pattern of success. His folk-tale operas, *The Maid of Pskov, The Snow Maiden, Mlada, Sadko, The Tsar's Bride, Tsar Saltan,* and *Kastchei the Immortal* derive from the inexhaustible storehouse of Russian legend. The orchestral suites *Antar* and *Russian Easter,* and the ever popular *Scheherazade* are a kaleidoscope of gay peasant shawls, Oriental silks, colored Easter eggs and Arabian Nights' dreams. He dwelt on the colorful aspects of his beloved country, which he revealed to the public in music of restraint and refinement. His capacity to learn while he earned is evidenced in a *Textbook of Harmony* and a book on *Principles of Orchestration,* a study of which was regarded as a minimum essential for Russian music students. He edited works by his colleagues, Dargomijsky, Borodin and Mussorgsky, and generously took the poverty-stricken Mussorgsky to live with him for a time.

When his students at the Conservatory revolted against authority, Rimsky-Korsakoff took their side. Police were sent to break up a crowd of students trying to enter the Conservatory, whose doors had been barred against them, and some violence ensued. When the doors were opened, with no promise of the self-government demanded, the students in their turn went on strike. Rimsky-Korsakoff was more than ever on their side. In a carefully worded letter to the directors, he presented the students' grievances. For his pains, he was dismissed from the Conservatory and again it was closed. He wrote a letter to the leading newspaper of the city and he found himself a hero to the students and a large section of the public.

In his honor, the students gave a gala concert, at which his opera *Kastchei* was to be presented. But impassioned speeches were made after the first act, there were shouts of "Down with the autocracy," and the demonstrations were so noisy that the rest of the performance had to be canceled. After this, Rimsky's name could be spoken in the city only in whispers, and his works were banned. In fact, *Le Coq d'Or (The Golden Cock),* a satire on the stupidity of rulers, could not be shown until two years after the composer's death. But private pupils flocked to him, and as the political excitement subsided, he found himself honored, not only as a leading Russian composer, but as an honored revolutionary. Three years after the "revolution," he died suddenly, on his country estate, of a heart attack.

Born St. Petersburg, Russia, March 18, 1844
Died St. Petersburg, Russia, June 21, 1908

GIOACCHINO ROSSINI

UNLIKE THE real swan, the Swan of Pesaro, as Rossini is called, sang his sweetest in the early years of his life. There is no record of his having uttered the dying bird's traditional song of unearthly beauty. He wrote forty operas before his thirty-eighth birthday, not one thereafter, though he lived to be seventy-six. Was he lazy? Discouraged? Dismayed by competition? Written out? Who knows? He was in reality no devil-may-care young man but high-strung, nervous and easily upset. When, in a spirit of adventure, he took a ride in the then brand new steam train he fainted with excitement and was ill for several days afterward. He never again consented to ride in a train; coach and horses were fast enough for him.

When he was young he was so handsome that the townspeople called him "the angel," and he looked every inch the part in the choirboy's vestments he wore as he sang in the church of Pesaro. At twelve he was engaged to play the piano in an opera house in Bologna, where his father, nicknamed Vivazza because of his gaiety, played the trumpet in the orchestra, and his mother sang. Rossini composed his first opera, a comedy in one act, when he was eighteen. *La Cambiale di Matrimonio (The Marriage Contract)* contains an extraordinary stage American, a Mr. Slook, who puts his feet on the table, keeps his hat on his head, and gives away millions of dollars.

When Rossini's first serious opera, *Tancredi*

di Siracusa (Tancred of Syracuse), was given in Venice three years later its tunes caught on immediately, first in Venice, then in all Italy. "I expected that after hearing my opera, they would put me in a mad-house," he said. "On the contrary they were madder than I."

He probably expected that after the *Barber of Seville,* which he tossed off in two weeks' time, he would be cheered from the housetops. Nothing of the sort. The first performance was so badly received that the young man went home after the second act. The prima donna hurried to his house after the performance to console him and found him in bed, sleeping peacefully. Everything had gone wrong. The hapless tenor had broken the string of his guitar while tuning it for a serenade. The booing of the claque sent by a rival composer had made things worse. A black cat had seized that moment to walk across the stage, bad luck in any country. Rossini had applauded at the end of the second act to encourage the singers, and the claque, thinking he was applauding himself, had hissed louder. But Rossini felt sure that the mockery and hissing were fleeting, that his music would endure. And sure enough, after two more performances, *The Barber of Seville* caught on and the twenty-four-year-old Rossini found himself a successful composer.

During his years of glory, he traveled with his wife, Isabella Colbran, a handsome contralto seven years older than he, from one opera house to another. He sold, faster than he could write them, opera scores on which the ink was barely dry. Admirers harnessed themselves to his carriage and drew it through cheering crowds. A series of "amiable protectresses" brought the additional glamor of a reputation as a Don Juan. In England, France, Austria and Germany, he was honored above those countries' own composers. He visited Beethoven in Vienna and is said to have wept on seeing the poverty and discomfort in which the great man lived. Humble in his attitude toward Beethoven and other famous composers, Rossini said: "Mozart is the angel of music; who would dare touch him without committing sacrilege?" and "If Beethoven is a prodigy among men, Bach is a miracle of God." He studied the scores of the Beethoven symphonies assiduously in preparation for the writing of *William Tell.*

At thirty-two, he became director of the Théâtre des Italiens in Paris and composed one or more operas a year for the next six years. At first the Parisians teasingly called him "Mr. Crescendo," because of the many dramatic crescendo passages in his music, but he was their darling, to be loved, honored and obeyed above all others in their musical world.

With *William Tell* his luck took a turn for the worse. He spent six months laboring over the opera and strained his eyes. He developed insomnia. Never had he slaved so long and so devotedly on a single composition. When it was given, the five acts were cut to three. "Too long," said the impresario. Even worse, after a few performances the impresario told him, "I hope you won't be annoyed, but tonight we play only the second act of Tell." "What, the whole of it?" was Rossini's barbed retort.

A severe nervous breakdown followed. Rossini went to Bologna for a rest-cure. After this, he composed no more operas. "La commedia e finita," he might have said, in the words of Leoncavallo's Pagliacci.

In 1839 he became honorary president of the Liceo Musicale, the Conservatory of Music in Bologna. He concentrated on the vocal department, himself taught classes, and built up a strong department. "A singer needs only three things—voice, voice and voice," he said, but he saw to it that the voices which came to the Liceo were well-trained.

When Isabella died Rossini married again, and in 1852 he went to live in Paris with his second wife, Olympe. Their salon at No. 2 Rue Chaussée d'Antin was soon famous for good food (Rossini's salad dressing was as much discussed as his operas), witty conversation, and the charming little piano pieces with which he entertained his guests. A *Stabat Mater* was the only big work he composed after *William Tell.*

When he died, in 1868, he was given a great funeral. An ensemble of saxophones, new instruments which had just been introduced by the Belgian Adolphe Saxe, played the funeral march from Beethoven's *Eroica Symphony.* Rossini's enormous fortune went to found a Conservatory of Music in his birthplace, Pesaro, and a home for aged and infirm singers in Auteuil, France.

Born Pesaro, Italy, February 29, 1792
Died Paris, France, November 13, 1868

CHARLES CAMILLE SAINT-SAENS

CAMILLE SAINT-SAENS was a cultured, witty gentleman, endowed with a keen and precise intelligence, great power of enjoyment, a facile talent, and enormous versatility. He has been called a French Mendelssohn. In personal charm and conversational ability, in the breadth of his travels and his reading, in the influence he exerted on César Franck and other French composers, and in a certain happy facility of invention, this completely French monsieur did indeed resemble the darling of the gods, Mendelssohn.

In order to escape the admirers who thought to flatter him by whistling snatches of his music as they passed him on the boulevards in Paris, he sometimes traveled incognito to out-of-the-way places. On one of these excursions he disguised himself in a long black cloak and with an assumed name and went to the Canary Islands. He had not been there long when word got around about a mysterious stranger who spent the day seated at a table, making suspicious marks on large sheets of paper. Could he be a spy? The police made it their business to find out. When Saint-Saens realized that he was being followed, he changed lodgings. The police decided to await him on his new doorstep. As he approached the house, a Parisian tourist happened to pass, looked closely at him, and raised his hat, saying, "Pardon me, you are M. Camille Saint-Saens, are you not?" Even in the Canary Isles, his name was known, and of course the police withdrew. Now admirers started to follow him in the streets of the little town, as they had in Paris, and, his privacy gone, he returned home.

He composed prodigiously—piano and organ music, symphonic and chamber music, cantatas, oratorios, songs and choral works, operas and operettas, transcriptions and arrangements. His best-known works are the opera *Samson and Delilah;* the symphonic poems *Rouet d'Omphale* (Omphale's Spinning-wheel), *Danse Macabre* (Dance of Death) and *La Jeunesse d'Hercule* (The Youth of Hercules); the musical joke, *Carneval des Animaux* (Carnival of Animals); four symphonies, five piano concertos, three violin concertos, two cello concertos, and the popular orchestral *Suite Algérienne.* From the age of six to eighty-six, he produced music "as an apple tree produces apples."

He recalled that when he was about two and a half, the sounds of a clock striking the hour, of a hissing steam-kettle, and of a piano were equally music to his ears. He made his debut as a pianist when he was ten, then went back to school like a normal boy. After graduating from the Conservatoire, he held various posts as teacher and organist, and in 1867, his setting of a cantata won a prize, in competition with over one hundred contestants. The following year he was decorated with the Legion of Honor, only one of many honors and degrees bestowed upon him in the course of years.

He plunged into work, into travel, into varied pursuits. It was while on a final visit to Algeria that he was taken ill and died, far from home.

Born Paris, France, October 9, 1835
Died Algiers, December 6, 1921

DOMENICO SCARLATTI

LIGHT-HEARTED, free-wheeling Domenico Scarlatti is a lovable Italian composer of the seventeenth-eighteenth century who "stepped out with a kind of diabolic masterfulness on the harpsichord," to quote Sir Hubert Parry. His freedom on his instrument may have been his way of revolting against the rigidity of his father and mentor, Alessandro. Alessandro composed some one hundred and fifteen operas, and was highly respected. He conducted the King's orchestra in Naples, and conscientiously developed his son's talent.

When Domenico was twenty, his father sent him to Venice to complete his studies, and in a letter commending him to the kindness of Ferdinand de Medici, he wrote, "This son of mine is an eagle whose wings are grown." Erelong Domenico was audibly flapping those wings. A few dutiful attempts to add his own operas to his father's long list proved to him that the harpsichord was more congenial to his talents, and he brought to it a relish and gusto that gave it new life, both in composition and performance. His meeting with Handel in 1708 was important to both young men. At a masquerade ball in Venice, Handel, improvising at the harpsichord, suddenly found himself clasped in the embrace of a tall figure in a domino. " 'Tis the famous Saxon or the devil!" cried a voice from behind the mask. The two men literally fell into each other's arms, and presently traveled together to Rome. Cardinal Ottoboni, patron of the arts, invited them to a party at his palace where they were pitted against each other on organ and harpsichord. Handel carried off the organ honors, but Scarlatti tied with him on the harpsichord. In later years, when Scarlatti's playing was praised, he would say, "If you think I'm good, you ought to hear Handel." He always crossed himself piously when he mentioned his friend's name.

At thirty-two, he declared his independence of his father's control and started rolling jovially around Europe, gambling recklessly, but composing, playing and teaching wherever he went. He was the first man to introduce big skips and wide arpeggios in playing, the rapid repetition of a single tone to simulate one long legato tone, and the crossing of hands on the keyboard. The crossing of hands added greatly to the brilliancy of his performance, even after he grew so stout that it was difficult for him to get his hands between his stomach and the instrument. His compositions, many of them based on Italian and Spanish folksongs, are as lovely when played on the modern piano as on the eighteenth century harpsichord on which he performed in Rome, London, Paris, Lisbon, Dublin and Madrid. The manuscripts of his six hundred compositions were scattered everywhere, like calling cards, and not until his sonatas were collected by Alessandro Longo, and published by Ricordi one hundred and fifty years after his death, was the extent of his contribution realized.

One of his best loved pieces, *The Cat's Fugue*, gave rise to an amusing anecdote. A student came to Scarlatti's villa early one morning, accompanied by a pet dog. While waiting for his teacher, he watched Scarlatti's cat, a privileged character, frisking around the room. When the cat jumped up on the harpsichord, the student picked up his dog and placed him on the cat's back, saying, "Here, Pussy, give your guest a ride." The mewing cat raced up and down until she had shaken off her unwelcome burden, then executed a dance of triumph on the keys. Scarlatti came in during the rumpus. "That is the theme I have been waiting for!" he exclaimed dramatically. "Pussy, you have found it!" To the student he said, "I must write this music at once while it is fresh in my mind. No lesson today. Please come tomorrow." The next day, he played for the student his now famous *Cat's Fugue.*

The place of Domenico's death is uncertain. He may have returned to Naples; he may have died while in Madrid. He left his wife and children in dire straits, having gambled away all that he had amassed through the years. They had not even the satisfaction of knowing that their gifted husband and father was, in a sense, the father of modern piano playing, his influence discernible in the technique of Chopin, Liszt and Mendelssohn, his sparkling compositions the mainstay and infinite delight of all who play or enjoy keyboard music.

Born Naples, Italy, October 26, 1685
Died probably Madrid, Spain, 1757

ARNOLD SCHONBERG

When Arnold Schönberg arrived in the United States in 1933, he appeared at a reception in his honor, a soft-spoken, mild-mannered little man, unable to converse in English, but with a prepared speech which he had memorized. The guests fairly engulfed him in their hearty American welcome, and he blinked in bewilderment behind his thick spectacles. When it was time for his speech, he was so excited that he broke down in the middle of it. Had he been permitted to make his acknowledgment in music, there would have been no such embarrassment for him, but perhaps for them, for it would have been their turn to blink at what they heard. One of the great controversies of the twentieth century raged about the dissonances of this determined revolutionary.

He arrived at his original style of writing in fairly conventional fashion. Mostly self-taught, except for lessons in violin and composition with Alexander Zemlinsky in Vienna, he accepted Bach, Mozart, Beethoven, and Wagner as models, and at first composed accordingly. A sextet, *Die Verklärte Nacht,* "a sort of *Tristan und Isolde* on strings," was generally well liked. But he was the slave of an internal power which drove him toward new means of tonal expression. He married Zemlinsky's sister, became professor of harmony at conservatories in Berlin and Vienna, and industriously composed, experimented, analyzed and synthesized.

In 1907, he boldly came out with the new ideas that had been simmering. The *Second String Quartet, Pierrot Lunaire, Gurrelieder, Die Glückliche Hand,* many piano works and other pieces demonstrate in practice the theories in his carefully written *Treatise on Harmony.* This textbook explains the Schönberg twelve-tone system. Schönberg earnestly stated that the particular things he had to say could be best expressed in the twelve-tone scale. "I write what I feel in my heart," he said, "and what finally comes on paper is what first coursed through every fiber of my body. For this reason I cannot tell anyone what the style of my next composition will be. For its style will be whatever I feel when I develop and elaborate my ideas."

The demonstrations against his music when it was first publicly performed in Austria and Germany were so hostile that often police had to be called in. Schönberg founded in Berlin in 1920 the Society for Private Musical Performances, to which only invited guests were admitted. The concerts featured piano performances of modern works of all kinds, but naturally included many pieces by the founder and his followers. The same year, Gustav Mahler conducted some of Schönberg's works at the festival in Amsterdam, and there the audience gave them favorable attention. On the composer's fiftieth birthday, a celebration at Vienna's town hall assured him that he had won serious recognition. He taught at the Prussian Academy of Arts in Berlin until 1933, when he was dismissed because his music represented "degenerate art." It was then that he came to the United States. He taught at the University of Southern California from 1936 until his death in 1951.

He left controversy behind him; he aroused controversy here. But what sounded ugly on first hearing, had power and expressiveness which was later recognized, and even his detractors now admit that his ideas are challenging, progressive, and worthy of close study.

Born Vienna, Austria, September 13, 1874
Died Los Angeles, Cal., July 13, 1951

FRANZ SCHUBERT

A FLABBY, bespectacled little man, unprepossessing yet strangely magnetic—such was Franz Schubert, "Franzl" to his friends. His mother, a cook, his father, a village schoolmaster, had thirteen children beside Franzl. Franz's father taught him to play the violin, his brother Ignatz taught him piano, and the choirmaster of the local church trained his voice. He was sent at eleven to the Konviktschule in Vienna, a school for choristers of the Imperial Chapel. The school offered free board, lodging and tuition to boys with promising voices. The board was meager, but of music there was plenty.

Franzl sang a clear soprano in the choir and played second violin in the school orchestra, where he learned to know and love the works of Haydn, Mozart, Cherubini and Beethoven. He remarked that Mozart's G minor Symphony "shook me to the depths without my knowing why" and that the Overture to *The Marriage of Figaro* was "the most beautiful in the whole world." Without formal instruction in composition, he began to "put his thoughts into notes." Too poor to buy music-paper on which to write them down, he accepted it by the ream from an older student Joseph von Spaun, almost as poor as he. Von Spaun was the first of the Schubertians who were to form a guardian circle for the care and feeding of Schubert.

The boy's voice broke at fifteen and he knew that his days in the "prison," as he called the Konviktschule, were numbered. Before he left the following year, he had completed his first symphony. He unwillingly became a teacher in his father's school, that career having been inexorably fixed for him in advance. For three years he stuck it out, but when he scribbled music instead of corrections once too often in a student's notebook, there was a stormy scene with his father and the student's parent, and Franz quit. He went to Vienna and lived there for the rest of his life, always on the edge of starvation but always creating.

From time to time he stayed with friends. At first young von Schober gave him a home. The poet Mayrhofer, whose verses he set to music, invited him for a visit. Count Esterhazy engaged him for a season as musician on his estate in Hungary. The circle of Schubertians grew. When a new applicant presented himself, Schubert would peer though his spectacles asking, "Kan er was?" (Can he do anything?) They nicknamed him "Kanevas."

Most of his days Franzl spent in a shabby dressing-gown in a dingy little bedroom, writing from six in the morning until well into the afternoon. Then the fun began. With songs or chamber music under his arm, he would issue forth to a friend's house or to a convenient café to play what he had written. The sessions often lasted far into the night.

He was eighteen when he composed *Der Erlkönig (The Erlking)* perhaps the greatest song ever written. He set Goethe's poem to music in one afternoon and sang it for his cronies when the ink was hardly dry upon the paper. They were critical. They had never heard a song like it. Moreover, they objected to the dissonances in the accompaniment. But Professor Ruzicka, one of the teachers in the Konviktschule, quieted them, saying, "If Franzl wrote it, it must be right. His ideas come straight from Heaven."

That same year, 1815, saw the composition of one hundred and forty-four of the six hundred songs he wrote in his life. He brought the art-song to ultimate perfection. Instead of verse and chorus, the song followed the line of the poetry, while the accompaniment, which followed both, helped to create the proper mood. For a man possessed by melody, as Schubert was, the "composed-through" song was an ideal vehicle.

"I complete one song only to begin another," he said. Sometimes he composed seven or eight in an afternoon, and "whelmed" them down on paper (his own expression).

Sitting in a café with a friend one afternoon, he picked up a copy of Shakespeare lying on the table and opened it to "Hark, hark, the lark." "I wish I had some music-paper," he said. "The loveliest melody has just come into my head." His friend took the menu-card, ruled a few staves and pushed it across the table. In a few moments, Schubert had jotted down on the back of the menu-card his immortal song.

Another time, on a walking trip with the singer Vogl, he met a local music lover in the little town of Steyr. "Why not compose a piece of chamber music to your song *Die Forelle (The Trout),*" asked the new acquaintance. "Why not?" replied Schubert. That afternoon he wrote four string parts of a quintet, and that evening, without writing out the piano part, he played it with four local musicians. This was the flashing, sparkling, incomparable *Forellenquintet.* Schubert was twenty-two. He composed other chamber music. He wrote several operas, eight symphonies, piano pieces, etc. All were pure song, whatever the form they took.

Until his death, he composed continuously. But his compositions brought him no money. And although they became well known, he was blackballed when he applied for admission to Vienna's select music club. The nearby town of Graz invited him to become a member of their Musikgesellschaft, and he wrote a symphony to express his gratitude. His friend Anselm Huttenbrenner, a Schubertian, accepted it for the town of Graz, but it was not played. It was laid away in a desk with other Schubert manuscripts. Forty-three years later, the conductor Herbeck came to Graz in search of a "new" work by Schubert. "I have many of his manuscripts," the old Schubertian told him. And Herbeck carried away a treasure, the *Unfinished Symphony.* Schumann was to "discover" Schubert's *C major Symphony* in much the same way, and to give it to Mendelssohn to present to the world years after its composition.

Schubert lived to be only thirty-one. Almost the last act of his life was to visit the dying Beethoven, whom he had timidly worshiped from afar. He was a pallbearer at Beethoven's funeral and Beethoven's was the name he called most often in his delirium, when he lay dying. His grave in Währing Cemetery was close to Beethoven's, its tombstone inscribed, "Music hath here entombed a rich treasure but a still fairer hope."

Born Lichtenthal, Austria, January 31, 1797
Died Vienna, Austria, November 19, 1828

ROBERT SCHUMANN

One night, when Robert Schumann was a very little boy, he had a bad dream and woke up crying in the middle of the night. Nobody heard him. He crept downstairs in his bare feet, found his way to the piano in the dark, and as he sobbed out his terror, he played somber chords suggested by the nightmare. Many years later, while reading Byron's poem *Manfred* aloud to some friends, his voice faltered, his eyes filled with tears, and he was obliged to stop reading because he was so deeply affected. The emotional susceptibility of his childhood persisted into his manhood.

The books he read while he was growing up were not a steadying influence. His father, a publisher, placed in his willing hands the novels of Sir Walter Scott, the poems of Byron, and the writings of the extreme German romanticists, E. T. A. Hoffman and Jean Paul Richter. Robert so worshiped Jean Paul that when a girl friend criticized his idol, he indignantly refused to have anything more to do with her.

The older Schumann was proud that his son could play the piano at six and compose at seven. But when Robert was in his teens his father died, and his practical, bourgeoise mother, disregarding his obvious musical talent, condemned him to the study of law. "I have not been to a single lecture," he boasted to a friend, after some months at the University of Leipzig. He was working at music and wrote to his mother, "I discover that I have some imagination and perhaps a turn for creating things myself." But she did not respond, and during his student years at Leipzig and Heidelberg, the repression of his musical ambitions strained his nerves to the breaking point.

When he decided, in spite of opposition, to

become a concert pianist, he went to study with Herr Wieck in Leipzig, who strengthened his resolution. Herr Wieck had a daughter, Clara, who was to become one of the most renowned pianists in Europe. She was nine, Robert was twenty-one, when he first met the pretty, serious child seated at her square piano, which even then she played better than he did. He waited patiently for her to grow up, with only a brief romantic interlude when he became engaged to another girl. When Clara was eighteen, Robert asked Herr Wieck's permission to marry her. But her father frowned upon her union with his penniless student and whisked her away to Dresden. *Warum?* (Why) asked Robert in a hurt little plaint for piano.

For the next three years, he translated to the piano his alternating hope and despair as he secretly wooed his beloved. Clara played the F sharp minor piano sonata he dedicated to her right under her father's nose at her concert in Leipzig. Robert, listening, knew that she had understood his "unique cry of passion," and that she returned his love. The ensuing months of separation inspired the *Noveletten*, the *Fantasie in C*, the *Piano Concerto without Orchestra*, the *Fantasiestücke*, *Kreisleriana*, *Kinderszenen*, *Arabeske*, *Blumenstück*. Robert's musical lovemaking, as played on her European tour by Clara, made both their names famous.

He had ruined his chances of becoming a concert pianist by practicing long and hard with a contraption of his own invention. It was designed to strengthen the fourth finger, but instead it deprived him of its use. However, once married to Clara, he had a full-time collaborator to publicize his compositions. On Clara's twenty-first birthday, despite paternal opposition that dragged Robert into the law-court as a drunkard, the lovers were married.

For the first time in all his life, Robert was happy, and his happiness went into his music. During that ineffable first year he composed more than one hundred and thirty songs, including *Myrthen*, *Frauenliebe*, *Dichterliebe*, and *Liebesfrühling*. He worked on a piano concerto (A minor). And then, since neither voice nor piano was big enough to give utterance to the surge of joy when his first child was born, he produced three symphonies in rapid succession. The next year, 1842, he turned to chamber music, the year following to choral music. "Schumann loved to dream with the pedal down," said Sir Hubert Parry. His dreams during those years were happy ones which resulted in great music.

When Clara had to leave Robert for a tour, he composed very little, but each time she returned provoked a burst of musical eloquence. He was eloquent in other ways, too. When he was twenty-three, he and a group of other musicians had got in the habit of meeting at a café in the evenings to discuss music. Robert was disgusted with what he called the honey-daubing which passed for musical criticism. He founded a magazine, *Die Neue Zeitschrift für Musik*, of which he was the editor and chief contributor. It was dedicated to the truth. There was no preferred treatment for flatterers or advertisers, yet Robert's honest approval encouraged and won public recognition for Mendelssohn, Berlioz, Liszt, Chopin, Schubert, Brahms, Weber, and many more. He paid tribute too to the honored dead, to Bach, Haydn, Mozart, and Beethoven.

Yet he was subject to recurrent fits of depression, which nothing could dispel—neither hard work, Clara's wifely devotion, his own musical and literary success, or public acclaim. In 1850, he was invited to Düsseldorf to direct the orchestra and chorus. He accepted with hesitation. He did not care for Düsseldorf, and besides there was a mental hospital in the town the mere sight of which sent a prophetic shiver through him. But he accepted, and tried to lose himself in his work. He composed the *Rhenish Symphony*, the *Manfred Overture* and various pieces of chamber music. They lacked the luster of happier days.

Even the frequent visits of his friend Johannes Brahms, who had become the closest friend he and Clara knew, could not lighten the gloom that enveloped him. In 1854, he made a despairing attempt to commit suicide by throwing himself into the Rhine. He was rescued and a short time later was placed, at his own request, in the very mental hospital he had so dreaded. Two years later, aged forty-six, he died there in Clara's loving arms. In the light of history, he stands as the leader of the romantic movement in German music, a highly expressive composer, a penetrating and discerning critic.

Born Zwickau, Germany, June 8, 1810
Died Endenich, Germany, July 29, 1856

DMITRI SHOSTAKOVITCH

As UNOFFICIAL composer-laureate to the Soviet Union, Dmitri Shostakovitch carried himself safely through revolutions and counter-revolutions, through the slings and arrows of criticism, to renown. There are those to whom his identification with politics was so distasteful that they refused to accept his music as music and dismissed his symphonies as prolonged rabble-rousers unworthy of serious consideration. On the other hand after the electric shock of his first symphony galvanized audiences in every land to attention, there was a growing belief in him and his music.

"I am a Soviet composer," he wrote, "and I see our epoch as something heroic, spirited and joyous. Music cannot help having a political basis. . . . Lenin himself said 'Music is a means of organizing broad masses of people.' " And further, "I consider that every artist who isolates himself from the world is doomed. . . . I always try to make myself as widely understood as possible, and if I don't succeed I consider it my own fault."

Until his twentieth year this Soviet composer lived in a state of poverty, in fact, near-starvation. In a dingy movie house the frail youth played the piano for three shows daily. After the evening performance he staggered home at midnight from the ill-lit, poorly ventilated theater, only to repeat the dreary round the next day. How he managed to study music at the Leningrad Conservatory is a mystery. For a time he was without the rented piano on which he practiced, because he could not meet the payments. And yet, somehow, he composed his first symphony.

Humbly he showed it to his teacher at the conservatory. Nicolaev was impressed and showed it to the Conservatory authorities. They thought so highly of it that they paid to have the parts copied so that it could be performed. Dmitri was encouraged. He was chosen to represent Leningrad's young composers at a conference in Moscow, and this boosted his self-confidence. On May 12, 1926, after his return to Leningrad, the symphony was performed with great success. Dmitri was then twenty years old, a shy, owlish youth with horn-rimmed spectacles. He had his diploma, had taken a post-graduate course in composition, and was ready to go to work.

The following year he was commissioned by the government to write a *Second Symphony*, in commemoration of the tenth anniversary of the Bolshevik Revolution. This *October Symphony* was repeated every year at the October celebrations. The third, *The May Day Symphony*, stirred the masses at the May Day celebrations. Now he composed a small opera, *The Nose*, and found himself in disgrace. A powerful grand opera, *Lady Macbeth of Mzensk*, plunged him deeper into the sea of "bourgeois decadence." Stalin walked out on *Lady Macbeth*, Soviet critics pronounced it "unSoviet, unwholesome, cheap, eccentric, tuneless and leftist." But Shostakovitch rode out the storm. He taught quietly at the Leningrad Conservatory, composed for piano, films, and chamber music, and waited without resentment.

His *Fifth Symphony* spelled vindication for him. "Glory be to our people which procreates such talents," exulted one Soviet reviewer. Two symphonies later we find the composer continuing to create but in a country at war. During the Second World War he served as a volunteer fire fighter and also as a member of the Theater Section of the People's Volunteer Army.

In July, 1941, he started work on the *Seventh Symphony*, parts of which were written in a bomb shelter during a German attack. He conceived this symphony as a "musical embodiment of the supreme ideal of a patriotic war." He said, "I wrote with a superhuman intensity. I continued to compose marches, songs, and film music, and attended to my organizational duties as chairman of the Leningrad Composers' Union, and then would return to my symphony, as though I had never left it." He dedicated the *Seventh* to "the ordinary Soviet people, the heroes of the patriotic war." At the Moscow premiere, on March 19, 1942, the audience sat through an air-raid alarm, too intent on the music to heed the sirens.

The *Eighth Symphony* celebrated the twenty-fifth anniversary of the birth of the Soviet Union, the *Ninth* marked the end of the Second World War, a time of rejoicing and the hope that "all which is ugly and evil will disappear, and only the good will triumph," in the composer's words.

In the quiet of his home in Leningrad with his wife and two children, the composer went on to create his *Tenth*, *Eleventh*, and *Twelfth Symphonies*.

Born Petrograd, Russia, September 25, 1906
Living Leningrad, Russia

JEAN
SIBELIUS

"I LOVE the mysterious sounds of the fields and forests, water and mountains. It pleases me greatly to be called an artist of nature, for nature has truly been the book of books for me," said Sibelius. A student once described to him his joy on returning to Finland after an absence, and expatiated on the "low, reddish granite rocks emerging from a pale blue sea . . . the solitary island of a hard archaic beauty . . . It's the cradle of the Vikings," he said proudly. "Yes, and when we see those granite rocks, we know why we are able to handle the orchestra as we do," assented Sibelius.

The Grand Old Man of Finland, honored by his countrymen in his twenties, by the whole world in his nineties, came of a family which had been Finnish for many generations, with a mild touch of Swedish intermarriage. His father was a surgeon, who directed him to the study of law. Nevertheless, he received piano lessons at nine, violin lessons at fifteen, and an excellent general education. He loved to roam the rugged woods near his home, his violin under his arm. Perched on a tall rock, he gave concerts for the birds, an appreciative audience. It can have been no surprise to his family when, in his second year of law at Helsinki University, he announced his intention of switching from the law to music.

When he returned to Finland after several years of study in Berlin and Vienna, his country was in revolt against Russian attempts to suppress independence, free speech and the right of assembly. Sibelius composed a symphonic poem, *Kullervo,* in the folksong idiom of the people, a patriotic outcry which stirred them deeply. The following year was an important one. He married Aino Järnefeldt, a woman of culture and distinction. He composed the tone poem, *En Saga,* which revealed him, says Olin Downes, as "the creator of a new kind of orchestral music." Soon after this, there followed the *Spring Song for Orchestra,* and the four *Lemminkainen Legends.* These include *The Swan of Tuonela,* a touchingly beautiful work.

Finland treated her favorite son with generosity. In 1897, the government voted him an annual salary, which was later increased. Free to compose without financial worry, he produced songs, pieces for solo violin and piano, the tone poem *Finlandia,* "hot with the spirit of revolt," a string quartet, and, most important, seven symphonies. His admirers consider them second only to those of Beethoven, and, in fact, call him the Finnish Beethoven.

For more than fifty years he lived in a simple cabin at Jarvenpäa, near Helsingfors. If anyone in the house sang or whistled a tune without his express permission he was upset. However, when he relaxed with a good cigar, music and talk were in order. The two World Wars interrupted his peaceful way of life and, during the Russian invasion of Finland in 1940, he was forced to leave home with his family and seek safety. But he returned to live peacefully and quietly until his death in 1957.

Born Tavastehus, Finland, December 8, 1865
Died Jarvenpäa, Finland, September 20, 1957

BEDRICH SMETANA

SMETANA'S COMPATRIOT Paul Stefan says of him, "His music sings to us today of the Bohemia of old—its woods and cultivated plains, its villages, its romantic hills and old legends, its great past and even its future. It is all one great pageant of song and dance—dancing to native rhythms of astounding variety, singing to melodies of a unique beauty."

Smetana was the first Bohemian composer to sing so eloquently of his fatherland. His country was under the iron heel of Austria while he was growing up. When it was liberated he joyously dipped his pen in ink of the national colors before he composed the music which made him famous. It seemed that his whole life had been a preparation for that moment.

He was a child prodigy. When he was only five he played the first violin part in a Haydn quartet, in which his father, a brewer, played second. At six he made his first public appearance as a pianist. At eight he wrote modestly in his diary, "I wish to become a Mozart in composition and a Liszt in technique." As he grew older, his father did not favor these ambitions and could only with difficulty be persuaded to allow his son to desert the law for music. The boy went to Prague to study music with little encouragement and less money. He had a hard time to make ends meet until the director of the Conservatory recommended him as music master to the family of Count Thun. Assured of shelter and three meals, he taught the young Thuns five hours a day and had the rest of the time to himself for composition. He fell in love with another pianist, Katerina Kolàr, who later became his wife and assistant teacher.

The revolution of 1848, which ended in defeat and heavier oppression for the Czechs, left

Smetana under a cloud. He had composed patriotic songs for the revolutionists, which endeared him to them but not to their Austrian rulers. However, he married his Katerina and settled in Prague as director of a conservatory financed by his idol, Franz Liszt. Robert and Clara Schumann visited him in Prague; they loved and admired him greatly.

In 1856 he went to Gothenburg, Sweden, where he conducted the new Philharmonic Orchestra, gave piano recitals, and composed many works, among them three symphonic poems—*Richard III, Wallenstein's Lager,* and *Haakon Jarl.* He breathed deep of the free air of Sweden and enjoyed his association with the enthusiastic music lovers he found in Gothenburg. However, Katerina became ill and begged him to return to Prague. They set out for home, but she died before they could reach there. A year later he remarried and went on a tour of Germany, Holland and Sweden.

While visiting Liszt in Weimar, Smetana was stung by a remark of the Austrian conductor Johann Herbeck to the effect that Czechs were simply reproductive artists. Added to the criticisms of his first opera as "imitation Wagner," this spurred his determination to create a representative, characteristic Czech music.

When he returned to Prague, he found the Austrian rule somewhat relaxed and the national spirit coming to the fore. This was his opportunity. He led the way in founding a Czech National Theater and a permanent orchestra, the Czech Philharmonic Society. He directed the orchestra and the Choral Society. He helped found the Society of Artists which championed modern music. He was made director of the new National Opera House. He became Bohemia's Number One Man of Music. He had enemies and detractors, as everyone does, yet these were happy years. He composed and produced eight operas, national in spirit. The *Brandenburgers in Bohemia, Dalibor,* and *Libusa* were stories of Czech heroes who fought for freedom. *The Bartered Bride,* a comedy, is the embodiment in folk style of hearty peasant merrymaking, a most ingratiating work. The *Bride* wound her fluttering colored ribbons around the hearts of music lovers in every land. *The Kiss* was another well-loved comedy.

Smetana was busy, happy and famous, but he was not fated to remain so. One evening in 1874, he returned from a performance at the opera much elated, seated himself at the piano and improvised far into the night. The opening theme of his cycle, *My Fatherland,* came to him while he played, and he went to bed in a state of pleasurable contentment. He awoke to find himself stone deaf. Without previous warning, he suffered the most crushing affliction that can befall a musician. He could not hear a sound. The doctors could not help him, and he was compelled to withdraw into a world of unbroken silence.

Like Beethoven he composed his maturest works from the depths of despair. His autobiographical string quartet, *Aus Meinem Leben,* after singing of his happy boyhood, youthful romance and productive manhood, goes tragically into a long, shrill, high note representative of the distracting sounds he heard in his mind after becoming deaf. Of the heroic cycle for orchestra, *My Fatherland,* which he completed from 1874 to 1879, he never heard a note. When it was performed in Prague, in 1882, the audience stood up after each of the six sections, cheering for Smetana and for Bohemia, waving hats and handkerchiefs. At the end they crowded around the composer, embraced him, covered his hands with kisses, showered him with flowers. Smetana, broken in body and spirit, could only stand mutely before them, "happy," as he said later, "in the knowledge that he had made others happy."

His mind could not endure the strain of constant pain, coupled with the isolation of total deafness. In 1883, he suffered a complete mental breakdown and had to be placed in a mental hospital, where he died two months after his sixtieth birthday.

Born Litomysl, Bohemia, March 2, 1824
Died Prague, Bohemia, May 12, 1884

JOHN PHILIP SOUSA

Heroism to the beat of a Sousa march is in the best American tradition. The Civil War was before his time, but in the Spanish-American and the two great World Wars men were inspired to victory by the stirring marches of the American composer and bandmaster, John Philip Sousa.

His father was a Spanish musician, of whom John Philip smilingly remarked that, "he knew everything except how to make a living." He knew about brass bands, for he played in one, and he taught his son a great deal about the band instruments, so that, when John Philip became director of the U. S. Marine Band at twenty-six, he knew how to produce unusually beautiful sounds from brasses.

After twelve years directing the Marine Band, which under his baton became the best in the country, he organized a group of his own. He cut down the brasses and percussion, increased the number of soft-voiced woodwinds, added a harp, and carefully instructed his men that tone-quality was all-important.

With the famous Sousa band he toured the world. Dressed always in immaculate white, with decorations bespangling his chest, his black goatee wiggling in time with the beat of his baton, he became a familiar figure on the stages of many countries. His best-known march, *Stars and Stripes Forever,* was composed on board ship, on the way home from Europe. He had received a disturbing telegram. His manager had died, and it seemed that his band's tour of the states might be cancelled. He paced the deck, pondering his reply, looked up and saw the flag fluttering against a gray sky. The sight cheered him. The music of *Stars and Stripes Forever* which flashed into his mind, further cheered him. He hastened to write it down, and the march was prominently featured a few months later, when the band did go on tour. Foreigners, hearing it for the first time, have been known to spring to their feet, believing it to be the American national anthem.

Sousa had the distinction of introducing European royalty to ragtime, as well as march-time. The brisk two-four rhythm of ragtime and march contrasted pleasantly with the waltzes which had swept Europe. Their Majesties enjoyed *Smoky Mokes* as well as *Hands Across the Sea, Semper Fidelis, Washington Post, El Capitan, The Thunderer, Manhattan Beach,* and other marches—especially when they were played by Sousa's incomparable band.

Sometimes he programmed a tune from one of his dozen or so light operas, or symphonic music for band. But his marches, youthful in spirit, optimistic, patriotic, all-American, were his distinctive contribution. He once said that, "a march should make a man with a wooden leg step out." His marches did.

In his instruction books for band instrument players, and his autobiography *Marching Along,* he reveals that he enjoyed not only teaching, but trapshooting, riding, long walks, good food and cigars, and most of all, friendships. When he died suddenly, after a banquet in his honor, the mourning was international. The President and four ex-Presidents attended his funeral, as did all the Pullman porters he had democratically fraternized with on his travels.

Born Washington, D. C., November 6, 1854
Died Reading, Pa., March 6, 1932

JOHANN STRAUSS

JOHANN STRAUSS, known as the Waltz King, lived and died in the city whose spirit was incarnated in his incomparable waltzes. So completely Viennese was he that when he was obliged to go away, even for a short trip, he pulled down the blinds in the train so that the landscape speeding by would not remind him that Vienna was being left behind. When he paid his one and only visit to America in 1872, the seasickness he suffered on the voyage was undoubtedly a form of homesickness. Though he conducted monster concerts for the American Jubilee in Boston and New York for which he received a startling fee, though audiences stood on their chairs to applaud and he was fêted like a king, he was unhappy until he was homeward bound.

Johann's father was no less a waltz king than his son. A whole generation danced to his melodies and applauded his band when he toured Europe. His three sons were all musical. The developing talent and initiative of the eldest, Johann, who composed his first waltz—not bad—at six, aroused his particular jealousy. In 1844, when young Johann was nineteen, matters came to a head. The young man had quit his father's dance-band, and had been engaged at Dommayer's Café, to play for its fashionable patrons. Papa Strauss, having done everything in his power to prevent his son from getting the job, sent a faithful friend to Dommayer's on Johann's opening night, with instructions to hiss. But when the handsome, graceful young man appeared, when he led the band not only in his own waltzes, but in his father's also, when the cheering crowd hoisted him on their shoulders and carried him in triumph around the room, what could faithful friend do but join in the applause? Father and son later kissed and made up.

Johann Junior formed his own band, "worth walking to Vienna to hear." He played the violin, facing the audience, while the band played his dreamy waltzes for the court balls. *The Beautiful Blue Danube, Artist's Life, Vienna Woods, Wine, Women and Song,* were written to be danced to, but they made delectable listening. Those few who had not been swept to their feet by the waltz craze found themselves waltzing internally to the lilting rhythm and vivacious melody of these Strauss pieces, which retain their appeal, and are heard today on radio, recording, and television.

Johann composed fifteen operettas, of which *Die Fledermaus (The Bat)* is a shining example. It was first performed in Vienna on New Year's Eve, 1874; since then, the Viennese insisted on *Fledermaus* with their New Year's champagne. *Der Zigeunerbaron (The Gypsy Baron)* is only a step behind *Fledermaus* in popularity.

Johann, who was married twice, both times to singers, lived to be seventy-four years young, his heart beating in three-quarter time until the very end. His golden jubilee was celebrated in Vienna with tributes from all over the world. "When he died," says Louis Biancolli, "something of Vienna died with him. Actually in all his music he hymned the enchantments of his immortal city for all time."

Born Vienna, Austria, October 25, 1825
Died Vienna, Austria, June 3, 1899

RICHARD STRAUSS

A SCHNEIDERPOLKA for the piano, composed when he was six, was the earliest indication of Strauss' talent. His father, the first horn player of the Munich State Opera, saw to it that he received one of those thorough German educations which used to be the envy of educators in other countries. Papa Strauss, who disliked Wagner's music, tried to keep his son clear of its contaminating influence and to expose him only to the classical composers. But when Strauss at twenty came under the spell of Alexander Ritter, German literary romanticist, he turned his back on the classics, and, to his father's disgust, went all out for those musical romanticists, Wagner, Liszt and Berlioz. At that time, he was assistant conductor to Hans von Bülow, who had characterized his piano pieces as "immature and precocious," adding, "not a genius, I am convinced, but at most a talent."

Von Bülow revised his judgment when Strauss's symphonic fantasy, *Aus Italien,* appeared. The young man had translated his impressions of his rambles through Italy into music of Wagnerian proportions, which foreshadowed the massive tone poems to follow. *Don Juan, Macbeth,* and *Tod und Verklärung (Death and Transfiguration)* then appeared in rapid succession. Strauss followed the form of the symphonic poem as set by Liszt, but he enlarged it, working at the same time toward a descriptive musical language that everyone could understand. He supplied a program which explained in words the humor, satire, or irony, the rage, hysteria or perversity in the music depicted. He had every right to call his symphonic poems "program" pieces.

At thirty, he was comfortably successful. He married a singer, Pauline de Ahna, and embarked upon a pleasant career of composing pieces and guest-conducting them. Deaf to what the critics said—and they fulminated—he turned out more tone poems: *Til Eulenspiegel, Also Sprach Zarathustra, Don Quixote, Ein Heldenleben (A Hero's Life),* and *Sinfonia Domestica.* "Vulgar, shocking, indefensible!" cried some. *Ein Heldenleben* was criticized because of its upsetting dissonances and elaborate orchestration, but also because it was said to be autobiographical. "Strauss a hero! Who says so? What conceit!" cried his detractors. Yet today *Ein Heldenleben* is acclaimed for its magnificent writing.

Strauss visited Bayreuth in 1891, and on the principle that "anything Wagner can do, I can do better," he then composed operas. *Salome* and *Elektra,* and *Die Aegyptische Helena (Egyptian Helen),* and *Der Rosenkavalier* appear likely to remain in the repertoire. There is a story that when he was conducting *Rosenkavalier* for the first time, he leaned over to the concert master, and asked in a stage whisper, "I say, isn't this awfully long?" "Well, Maestro, you composed it," replied the man. "Yes, I know, but I never thought I'd have to conduct it," sighed the composer, mopping his brow.

It was too bad that Strauss continued to write after the well of inspiration had run dry. His later works are sterile, and unworthy of him. He liked to play cards and drink beer, he liked to collect the paintings of Renoir, Tintoretto and Utrillo, and best of all, he liked to make money and hang on to it. Perhaps in materialism lies the explanation of the spiritual dry rot that marked his last years. His reputation, which is considerable, rests on his operas, his art songs and on the ear-filling, vital, realistic tone poems, composed before he was forty, of which he is the first, perhaps the only worthy exponent in Germany.

To express reality in music was Richard Strauss's ambition, and he succeeded. To face reality in life is another story, especially when that reality contains an Adolf Hitler. Easy success and comfortable living had not prepared Strauss to defy the Nazis when they came to power and invited him to head their Kulturkammer (Chamber of Culture) in 1933. His acceptance discredited him with the anti-Nazi world. It is only fair to his memory to say that, after a brief tenure of office, he found he could not stomach the Nazi doctrines and resigned. In 1948 he was cleared by a de-Nazification Board of all taint of collaboration and died the following year, his reputation restored.

Born Munich, Germany, June 11, 1864
Died Garmisch-Partenkirchen, Germany, September 8, 1949

IGOR STRAVINSKY

ON THE seventy-fifth anniversary of his birth in 1957, Igor Stravinsky could look back with pride on a career in which one man in his day played many parts. Born on St. Igor's Day, and named for his patron saint, he was a dedicated Russian during his early years. Rimsky-Korsakoff the composer and Diaghileff the ballet impresario were the stars by which he steered his course, Russian folk song, his rod and his staff.

Stravinsky was twenty, and trying to decide between music and law when Rimsky-Korsakoff made up his mind for him. The great man sternly indicated the errors in his youthful compositions but, at the same time, admitted that they were original, and advised further study. In time, he accepted Stravinsky as his student, and the young man became his favorite disciple. In 1908, when his daughter was to be married, his student's wedding gift was a new composition, a dazzling symphonic work, *Feu d'Artifice (Fireworks).* Stravinsky mailed the score to Rimsky-Korsakoff's country estate in time to be rehearsed for the wedding feast. A few days later, it was returned to him, unopened, marked "not delivered on account of death of addressee." This was how he learned of the death of his beloved teacher! He expressed his grief in a "chant funèbre," a funeral song, and for months composed nothing.

But the brilliance of *Fireworks* dazzled Diaghileff when he heard it, and he attached the young man to his staff in Paris, having tested him with an assignment to orchestrate pieces by Chopin for the ballet, *Les Sylphides.* The years with the ballet in Paris were busy, happy and successful. Scores for *Le Rossignol (The Nightingale), L'Oiseau de Feu (The Fire-Bird), Petrouchka,* and *Le Sacre du Printemps (The Rite of Spring),* masterpieces all, enriched the

Diaghileff repertoire. For the first time in the history of the ballet, the music was more talked of than the gorgeous choreography. The "Petrouchka chord," a combination of the tonalities of C major and F sharp major, introduced into the *Petrouchka* score, is said to have sparked other composers' interest in polytonality, as represented in the electrifying music of *Petrouchka.* The first performance of *Le Sacre du Printemps (The Rite of Spring),* which carried polytonality even farther, was given in Paris on May 29, 1913. This made history. Half of the audience stood up and cheered, the other half stood up and booed or shouted insults. "I went to hear Stravinsky's *Sacre du Printemps,*" said Puccini. "The choreography is ridiculous, the music sheer cacophony . . . taken altogether it might be the creation of a madman." But this madman knew what he was about: *Le Sacre* brought Stravinsky to the fore as a fearless new creative force.

He had composed extravagant, sumptuous, overwhelming large-scale works in the Russian manner. There occurred now one of those lightning changes which have kept his admirers guessing. After the First World War, the Russian Revolution of 1917, and the post-War depression, he decided that economy was necessary in music, and promptly pared down his ideas to a smaller scale. The witty *Histoire du Soldat (Story of the Soldier)* of 1918 is sparsely written for a narrator and seven instruments. *Mavra* is an opera in one act. Hand in hand with economy went a classic detachment, and the ensuing period is known as his neo-classic phase. A *Serenade for Piano* and an *Octet for Strings* illustrate this neo-classicism.

In 1925, he came to the United States for his first visit, and conducted the New York Philharmonic. Returning to Paris, he became a French citizen. He, his wife and their four children became so completely French that they and everyone else forgot that he had ever been Russian. However, his works became immensely popular in this country, and in 1941, when France fell, he applied for American citizenship. He settled in Los Angeles, California, to teach, conduct, compose, and concertize. In his later phase, he turned back to the past, reconstructed Tchaikowsky's melodies in *Baiser de la Fée (The Fairy's Kiss),* Lully's in *Duo Concertant,* Pergolesi's in the *Pulcinella Suite.*

To celebrate his eightieth birthday, he composed a dance-drama, *Noah and the Ark,* which was premièred on television, and also recorded. Despite his love of experimentation, he showed no interest in electronic music. He was content to reap the rewards of his many achievements, to compose, and to influence the young men of America.

Born Oranienbaum, Russia, June 17, 1882
Living Los Angeles, Cal.

SIR ARTHUR

SULLIVAN

GILBERT AND SULLIVAN were to London and England as Offenbach was to Paris and France. In a remarkable series of light operas, they courted, adored, mocked and castigated their country because they loved her so much. Gilbert's text and Sullivan's music are equally brilliant, and the artistic marriage of their congenial souls endured for almost twenty-five years. Only when Gilbert became jealous of his mate, and querulous at his periods of non-productivity, did the pair separate.

The final separation occurred over a silly quarrel about who should pay for a new carpet for the Savoy Theater, which had been built especially to house their triumphs. After this, they wrote no more together, and what they wrote separately has been forgotten. But the divorce did not become final before fourteen "operettic" infants had been born of the union. In order of appearance, they were: *Thespis, Trial by Jury, The Sorcerer, Pinafore, The Pirates of Penzance, Patience, Iolanthe, The Princess Ida, The Mikado, Ruddigore, The Yeomen of the Guard. The Gondoliers, Utopia Limited,* and *The Grand Duke.* They continue to be produced on stage, screen, radio and television, their satire as pointed, their melody as infectious, as when they first appeared.

From the time he could blow up a toy balloon, Arthur played with and on the instruments of the band, his father being a band master. A period as a red-robed chorister in the Chapel Royal, a course at the Royal Academy of Music in London, and finishing studies at the Conservatory of Leipzig, trained him for his profession. When he returned from Leipzig, a handsome young man of twenty, his music to Shakespeare's *The Tempest* was performed at the Crystal Palace, and made his name. He earned a living as organist in various churches, composed *Onward, Christian Soldiers, The Lost Chord, Orpheus and His Lute,* and other serious works, until opportunity knocked at his door in the person of W. S. Gilbert.

It was 1875 when D'Oyly Carte, the manager who was to become famous by producing the works of Gilbert and Sullivan, suggested to Gilbert that he show Sullivan the text of a one-act play he had written, *Trial by Jury.* Carte wished to use it as a curtain raiser before Offenbach's *La Perichole.* Gilbert chose to visit Sullivan on a day when a heavy snowstorm was raging, he had an equally heavy cold, and was in a vile temper. Without removing his hat, coat or muffler, he took the chair Sullivan offered and hoarsely read his play aloud. Sullivan listened without comment, and at the end, the grouchy Gilbert, offended by his silence, rose to take his departure. "Hold on!" spluttered Sullivan. He had been laughing silently, so hard that he could not speak. He took Gilbert's text, and in a fortnight composed the music. *Trial by Jury* is not merely a mock trial; it is a mockery of all trials, and of the process of the law in England. In the same way, Gilbert and Sullivan were indirectly to criticize, all in the spirit of good clean fun, the Army, the Navy, The House of Lords, and other sacred English institutions. Queen Victoria never missed an opening night, and although she encouraged him to compose the grand opera *Ivanhoe,* the cantata *The Golden Legend,* and other weighty works, she unbent to his light music with unqualified approval. Because of it, he was knighted, made Doctor of Music at Oxford and Cambridge, and finally buried in Westminster Abbey.

Born London, England, May 13, 1842
Died London, England, Nov. 22, 1900

PETER ILITCH TCHAIKOWSKY

His first governess described Tchaikowsky as "a porcelain child," exquisite, sensitive, extraordinarily charming, but fragile. That he broke under the stresses and strains that go along with an artist's career is not surprising. Two events of his childhood left a deep impression, which intensified his morbid tendencies.

When he was ten his mother took him to boarding-school in St. Petersburg. When her carriage rolled away from the door without him, he ran frantically after it and tried to seize the wheels to keep them from turning. He had to be forcibly held back, and it seems that he never forgot the pain of that parting, big boy though he was. For months he brooded over their separation. When, four years later, his mother died of cholera, his grief was almost insupportable. Perhaps his inability to care for another woman can be traced to this extreme devotion to his mother.

Otherwise his youth was in no way remarkable. He studied law, and at nineteen he became a clerk in the Ministry of Justice in St. Petersburg, elegant, superficial and incompetent. He was a popular young man, for he played the piano nicely, danced well, and was always ready to attend an opera or a ballet performance. When he was twenty-one, a cousin showed him how to modulate from one key to another on the piano, and he became fiercely interested in this new indoor sport. He persuaded his father to allow him to take courses at the Conservatory of St. Petersburg. After a couple of years, he resigned his boring job in the ministry and gave himself completely to the study of music. In Anton Rubinstein's class in orchestration, the foppish young man was transformed into a hot-eyed, threadbare, hard-working student. After his graduation in June, 1866, he accepted an ill-paid job with Nikolai Rubinstein, Anton's brother, in the newly-formed Conservatory of Moscow. He suffered the first of many nervous breakdowns when the performance in Moscow of his *First Symphony,* over which he had labored with passionate intensity, was denied. For this, he cherished a grudge against Nikolai Rubinstein.

The grudge was deepened by Rubinstein's reception of the *B flat Minor Piano Concerto,* known to everyone today. Tchaikowsky wished to dedicate it to his teacher and rushed to play it for him the minute it was finished. It was received in hostile silence, followed by a flood of criticism. A far less sensitive man than Tchaikowsky would have shrunk from the unexpected deluge of cold water; Tchaikowsky was shocked into bitter resentment. "I'll not change a note of it," he shouted as he rushed from the room. He erased the dedication, left Rubinstein's house in which he had been living, and inscribed the work to von Bülow, who praised it. Yet, many years later, his resentment softened by time, he made a number of the proposed changes. And Rubinstein, on second thought, took the piece into his repertoire.

During Tchaikowsky's first ten years in Moscow, he made the acquaintance of the writers Turgeniev and Tolstoi, the composers Liszt, Wagner, and Saint-Saens. He mingled with "the Five," Russian composers whom he described as amateurs, and who flung the accusation back at him. He became engaged pro tem to Desirée Artot, an opera singer five years his senior, who considerately married someone else, leaving him still free. The yearning Juliet theme of the *Romeo and Juliet Overture,* composed at this time, may have been inspired by this passing affair.

When he was thirty-four, a tragedy interrupted and threatened to end his life. A psychopathic young woman, Antonia Milyukova, a casual acquaintance, proposed that he marry her. She went so far as to threaten suicide if he refused; to save her life he gallantly assented. After two weeks of marriage it was he who tried to commit suicide by standing immersed to his neck in the icy waters of the Neva river, hoping to catch pneumonia. He failed, and returned to Antonia for another brief period, at the end of which he hysterically fled, never to return.

After the inevitable breakdown, his brother Modest nursed him back to health. Living quietly in Switzerland, he finished the works interrupted by his marriage, the opera *Eugen Onegin* and the *Fourth Symphony.* He composed the luscious *Violin Concerto,* a long piano sonata, and other smaller works. In his relief at his escape, he produced masterpieces.

Fortunately, he was not obliged to compose with one eye on the almighty ruble, for a "beloved friend and patroness," Mme. von Meck, was making him an annual allowance which supported him comfortably. He never met Mme. von Meck, a wealthy widow who, though she admired his music, preferred to remain at a distance. But his letters to her and hers to him reveal a touching congeniality and devotion, a true marriage of minds. When, without explanation, she abruptly withdrew her support after fourteen years, her act precipitated another nervous breakdown. Tchaikowsky missed her companionship more than her money, for by this time (1890) he was so famous that he could support himself.

In 1891 he was invited to New York to conduct the gala concert at the opening of Carnegie Hall. He was homesick before he ever started. But his music was received with enthusiasm, and so was he, and there were happy moments before he returned to Russia. Nevertheless, black depression settled on him after his return, and in that mood he finished his sixth and last symphony, aptly titled the *Pathetic.* Its Adagio lamentoso seems, says Philip Hale, "to set the seal of finality on all human hopes." The first performance in Moscow in 1893 was coolly received.

Nine days after the concert he complained of feeling ill. Saying he was thirsty, he gulped a drink of water from a tap. A cholera epidemic was raging in Moscow at the time. Tchaikowsk's reckless disregard of the simple sanitary precaution of boiling the water he drank brought death.

He was possibly the greatest symphonist after Beethoven, certainly the most popular. And he was by far the most expressive Romantic composer that Russia produced.

Born Votkinsk, Russia, May 7, 1840
Died Moscow, Russia, November 6, 1893

RALPH VAUGHAN WILLIAMS

RALPH VAUGHAN WILLIAMS studied music at the Royal Academy in London, took his degree of Doctor of Music in Cambridge, and polished off his musical style with Max Bruch in Germany and Maurice Ravel in Paris. No wolf howled at his door, nor creditors at his bank, so he could enjoy the rare luxury of composing with inspiration as his incentive. Of this, there was no lack, for he found music, he said, in everything, in "the lilt of the chorus at the music hall . . . children dancing to a barrel organ, the rousing fervor of a Salvation Army hymn, St. Paul's and a great choir singing in one of its festivals . . . the Welshmen striking up one of their own hymns . . . the cries of street pedlars, the factory girls singing their sentimental songs."

Always interested in folk song, too, he considered the sounds he heard in the streets of London and the byways of villages as truly folksong as any ballad from Elizabethan days. He inclined to Tudor madrigals and modal counterpoint, which agree well with folksong. He became a member of the English Folksong Society in 1904, and undertook leisurely research in Norfolk before embodying the folksongs he found there in *Three Norfolk Rhapsodies* for orchestra. *Hugh the Drover,* a ballad opera composed at about the same time, bristles with folk melodies. "If the roots of your art are firmly planted in your own soil," he said, "and that soil has anything to give you, you may gain the whole world and not lose your own soul." His roots are firmly planted in England.

In appearance, he was the typical Britisher—a big, genial man in baggy clothes, heavy walking stick in hand, briar pipe between his teeth, a tweedy, tobacco-scented country squire. "He flounders about in the sea of his ideas like a vast and ungainly porpoise, with great puffing and blowing. . . . His personality is wholly and without admixture English, and this is at once his virtue and his defect," says his fellow-Englishman, Cecil Gray.

One of his best known works is *A London Symphony,* which pictures the quiet Thames, the bustling Strand, the Embankment with its mingled comedy and tragedy, and the chimes of Westminster Abbey. The British Music Society pronounced the *London Symphony* the most significant work produced by an Englishman.

After the First World War, in which he saw active service, he accepted a position as a professor at the Royal College of Music, became President of the English Folksong Society, and basked in the satisfaction of writing music in varying forms and styles. He composed five symphonies, some chamber music, large choral works, and carols, part-songs, and folksong arrangements. His was an individual style, compounded of tenderness, wit, and respect for tradition, with an occasional touch of impressionism, and an individual turn of expression that was his own. He lived quietly with his family in Dorking, a suburb of London, enjoying a creative leisure, until his death at eighty-five.

Born Down Ampney, England, October 12, 1872
Died London, England, August 26, 1958

GIUSEPPE VERDI

GIUSEPPE VERDI was twenty-eight when he completed his first opera to be produced, *Oberto.* It was successful, and he settled down contentedly in Milan with his beautiful wife, Margherita, and their two babies. He loved Margherita devotedly; theirs was a romance based on shared piano duets, and on the kindness of Margherita's father. Signor Barezzi had first given Giuseppe a job, then raised money for his musical education in Milan, and finally given him Margherita to wife. After his early days of poverty, it was good to be able to devote himself to his family and to the writing of operas. He had a contract with the impresario Merelli to compose three operas for immediate production. He was a happy man.

But it was tragedy that prepared Verdi for the creation of the magnificent operas which have stirred the world. With devastating suddenness, his domestic life was cut short. First one child, then the other, and finally Margherita died within a few months of one another of a violent fever. Verdi was inconsolable. He could not work. He was ill for some months. By a supreme effort, he completed his partly-written comic opera—a comic opera at such a time! It was called *King for a Day,* and ran for just about that length of time. The audience, heedless of the composer's private tragedy, hooted and jeered. Verdi vowed to write no more, and asked Merelli to cancel his contract.

One evening he met the impresario on the street and walked along to the theater with him. "Please read this libretto and tell me what you think of it," said Merelli, handing him a book. Verdi indifferently stuck the book in his pocket, and when he got home threw it on a table. As it fell open, one line caught his eye—"Go, my thought, on golden wings." "Hm, not bad," thought Verdi. He read a little more and went to bed. He could not put the poetic lines out of his mind. After tossing, sleepless, from side to side, he arose, took up the book again, and before morning he had read it through three times and had committed most of it to memory.

As he read, music filled his mind like sensation returning to a numb limb.

"Write me a score," ordered Merelli. This was what he had wanted of Verdi. In three months, the young man had completed the score of *Nabuco.* Merelli produced it during the Carnival season, to such roars of approval that Verdi, in the pit, was frightened and mistook the noise for booing. He was reassured by the tributes showered upon him, and by the admiration of the prima donna, Strepponi. In due time, he married her and again found some measure of happiness.

In 1848, when Italy was struggling to free herself from Austrian tyranny, Verdi allied himself with the revolutionists. Choruses from his operas, *I Lombardi, Ernani, Attila,* even *Macbeth* were selected for their patriotic appeal to further the national cause. Verdi bought a large tract of land outside of the little town of Busseto, where he was born, and made it into a model farm. It was an experiment in democracy which worked well. When times were hard and many peasants emigrated to America, Verdi could boast, "*My* workers do not have to go to America; they make money here." He took a more than passive interest in politics, and when the war with Austria was finally over, he became a deputy in the first national parliament.

But politics did not long detain him from his true vocation. With *Rigoletto,* produced in Venice in 1851, began the series of magnificent operas that made his name famous. *Il Trovatore, La Traviata, I Vespri Siciliani, Simone Boccanegra, Un Ballo in Maschera* were produced before the sober political interlude of 1866. *La Forza del Destino* and *Don Carlos* came afterward.

Then the Khedive of Egypt asked Verdi for an opera, to be sung at the opening of the Suez Canal in 1869. Verdi demurred; twice he refused. Then he came by chance on a scenario by the French Egyptologist, Mariette Bey, which fired his imagination as *Nabuco* had done. This was *Aida.*

The opera took two years to write, but it was worth waiting for, as even the impatient Khedive admitted. It was produced in Cairo with royal magnificence on Christmas Eve 1871. Authentic costumes and instruments, copied from ancient inscriptions on the Egyptian tombs, gave the staging genuine conviction. Live elephants in Rhadames' triumphal procession gave it realism. Verdi, floating down the Nile in an Egyptian barge to attend the performance, could be assured that every detail was in order. His music swept that first audience as it has swept audiences ever since. It is lyrical, virile, expressive, enormously skillful, enormously touching. The song, *Celeste Aida,* is a rapturous musical sigh, the high point of an opera steeped in beauty.

After *Aida,* Verdi might have rested on his laurels. But he was not one to rest. A *Requiem* for the writer Manzoni was the largest of his works in the fifteen years between *Aida* and *Otello.* Arturo Toscanini conducted it at Verdi's funeral, with tears running down his cheeks for the dear friend he deeply mourned. And in February 1957, Toscanini in his turn was laid to rest in Italy to its noble and touching strains.

In strong contrast is Verdi's last opera, *Falstaff,* the comedy which immortalizes in music Shakespeare's roistering hero. The composer was eighty when he wrote it, yet it is a marvel of clarity, wit and brilliance, a rare blending of words and music. Old age brought no slackening of his powers, but an added subtle wisdom that is sometimes the fruit of experience.

Verdi was a natural-born opera composer. Save for the *Requiem,* the little else that he wrote is negligible. Naturally he was compared with that other giant of the opera, Wagner, and was accused of trying to imitate him, as almost every other composer did. His genius is of so different an order that the accusation seems absurd. Verdi never bullied music, he wooed it. His music had great refinement. He was interested in Wagner's magnificent orchestral effects but adapted them in his own individual, ingratiating, yet powerful fashion.

As a small child, he smashed a spinet in a rage because he could not draw from it the sounds he sought. As a man, he directed that rage into creative channels. All his life, he gave of himself, freely and lovingly. After his death, and his wife's, his fortune went to found a home for musicians. A Verdi Concert Hall, and a Verdi Museum in Milan, are further monuments to this beloved Italian composer.

Born Le Roncole, Italy, October 10, 1813
Died Milan, Italy, January 27, 1901

HEITOR
VILLA-LOBOS

The compact, dynamic figure of Heitor Villa-Lobos was known in the United States before his arrival to attend the Lobos performances which celebrated his seventieth birthday. Such characteristic works as *Bachianas Brasileiros* and *Rude Poêma* for piano and orchestra, his symphonies and *Choros* had been presented by leading orchestras, and the League of Composers had done its part in presenting his chamber music. Since he had composed to date well over a thousand works, there was no lack of material to choose from. His tonal audacity and freedom of expression, the originality and starkness of his musical language, won him admiration in every country.

The son of a lawyer who played the cello, he too took up the cello. But his father died when he was only eleven, and he was obliged to play in cafés and theater orchestras to support himself. Except for harmony lessons, he had to teach himself the rules of composition. Presently he went on a concert tour, in the course of which he joined a scientific expedition to collect folk music. He accumulated so much that once, when asked, "What is meant by folklore?" he replied, "*I* am folklore." Having literally cut his way through the jungle into the heart of Brazil to find indigenous songs, he could claim that authority.

At twenty-four, he married a concert pianist, Lucille Guiomares, and made his home in Buenos Aires. He was playing the cello in a hotel lobby, in one of his own compositions, when the pianist, Artur Rubinstein, came into the lobby. Rubinstein stopped short to listen, and much excited, asked to meet the composer, and invited the whole orchestra to play for him later in his hotel suite. He requested more music by Villa-Lobos, the orchestra played all night long, and as a result, the composer was later subsidized on a trip to Paris for stimulation and study. He had met Milhaud in Brazil and had become interested in modern French compositions. To Rubinstein he dedicated a long piano work, *Rude Poêma (Primitive Piece)* which the pianist played at many of his concerts before Villa-Lobos made it into a work for orchestra and piano.

Villa-Lobos founded and conducted his own orchestra in Rio de Janeiro, and as Supervisor and Director of Musical Education, he made important changes in public-school music, which included providing a much-needed training school for teachers. On one of his supervisory trips, he took a train which ran on a single-gauge track, winding round and round a mountain. The rhythm of the wheels, the gasping of the overworked engine, and the frequent tooting of the whistle fascinated him, and on the train he composed *The Little Train of the Caipira*, for piano and cello. He orchestrated it, and it became an extremely popular concert piece. He could, in fact, write music about practically anything. For the World's Fair in 1940, he orchestrated the skyline of New York, producing music that followed the shape of the skyline. His music was Latin in its force, vehemence and sensuousness, yet exquisite and completely civilized when he wished it to be so.

Born Rio de Janeiro, Brazil, March 5, 1886
Died Rio de Janeiro, Brazil, November 17, 1959

ANTONIO VIVALDI

THERE is a newly awakened and growing interest in Antonio Vivaldi, the contemporary of Johann Sebastian Bach, who not only influenced the great Bach, but himself composed notable concertos for stringed instruments.

Antonio's father, Giovanni, was a violinist in the Cathedral of St. Mark's in Venice, and took Antonio there with him when the child could barely toddle. The boy fell in love equally with the music and with the church in which he heard it played. Not much is known of his early years. He studied the violin with his father, and possibly with other teachers also, and became an outstanding virtuoso on that instrument. When he was thirty-two, he entered the service of the Landgraf Philipp of Hesse-Darmstadt, a German prince who was then living in Italy. He remained in the Prince's employ from 1707 until 1713, then returned to Venice, and the following year, became first violinist at St. Mark's. He was director, at the same time, of a foundling home, the Ospedale della Pietà (Hospital of Pity), where he organized and conducted an all-girl choir and orchestra, a pioneering effort which bore excellent results. He was known as "il prete rosso" (the red priest)—no reflection on his politics—because his hair was red, and he often wore a semi-clerical suit of that color.

In addition to priestly and directorial obligations, he composed constantly and voluminously. He was, in fact, better known as a composer than Bach in his own day. His forty operas are never sung, his hundred or more religious works are seldom played, but some of the hundreds of concertos and sonatas for stringed instruments have received fine performances and an appreciative hearing. Many are still in manuscript in the Library of Turin, placed there by one of his descendants, but gradually they are being brought to notice.

He fell from grace with the church in characteristic fashion. While officiating at the Mass one day, he was seized with an irresistible desire to write down some music that occurred to him. So unbearably did his fingers itch to exchange the rosary for the pen, just for a moment, that he succumbed to the temptation. In the middle of the service, he slipped into the sacristy, wrote as fast and as much as he could, and returned to his duties, hoping that his absence had gone unnoticed. But he was dismissed from the church, went into retirement, and died a few years later.

Of his compositions for strings and voices, the twentieth century Italian composer Casella wrote: "The prodigious wealth of musical invention; the dramatic force, which recalls so imperatively the brilliance and fire of the great Venetian painters; the mastery of choral polyphony; the marvelous dynamism of the instrumental part, the incessant movement of which, independent of the voices and chorus, plainly forecasts the Wagnerian style (of opera), and finally, the high quality of the emotion which animates his works, all these put Vivaldi in a wholly new light."

Born Venice, Italy, about 1675
Died Vienna, Austria, July 1741

RICHARD WAGNER

"YOU ARE a man of genius, but you write such eccentric stuff it is impossible to sing it," was the complaint of the Venus in the first production of Wagner's opera *Tannhäuser*. The complaint, uttered in 1845, has since been heard in opera houses all over the world. For Richard Wagner, utterly possessed by his grandiose conceptions, forgot that there are limits to human endurance and pushed his singers to outrageous lengths. In his mind singers existed only as tools for the working out of his ideas. When he damaged or broke a tool, he threw it away and took another.

In his other relationships, he was no different. With friends, family, colleagues, even royalty, he was probably the most self-absorbed egotist on record. Like some other egotists, he became a dictator whose influence on nineteenth century opera was overriding and irresistible.

He erupted into his career spontaneously, with no systematic early training to guide him. He knew the stage, back and front, for his stepfather, an actor, introduced him to the fascinating world behind the footlights when he was a very small boy. When he was eleven he heard Weber's opera *Der Freischütz,* and its extreme romanticism, on the same lines as the literature he was devouring, struck a responsive chord. Beethoven's *Fidelio,* with which he fell in love at sixteen, set him well on his way to becoming an opera composer.

His days as a student in Leipzig University were brief but wild, enlivened by passionate gambling and more passionate love affairs. But he read Shakespeare and Schiller and studied composition seriously with Theodore Weinlig. When he was twenty he completed his first opera, *Die Feen,* a trial effort which he did not succeed in having produced.

At twenty-three he married Minna Planer, an actress whom he pursued madly until she consented, with many misgivings, to marry him. She should have been called Minna Com-planer, for she heaped so many reproaches on him for his conduct that he might well have developed a guilt complex. Certainly he gave her plenty to complain about—a penniless composer, heavily in debt, who could not hold the conducting job she found for him and who soon was openly unfaithful.

Together they went to Russia, she to sing, he to conduct in the opera house in Riga. But there, too, he quarreled with the management, and they decided to leave Russia and try Paris. Their trip to Paris is noteworthy for two reasons. It was made by boat instead of coach for the sake of their St. Bernard dog, Robber, who was too big and unmanageable to be taken on the coach. And it was so stormy that the sea-voyage, which should have taken a week, took a month. Minna was sure they would be drowned. Richard stayed on deck listening to the sailors' yarns. One of them, the story of a Dutchman condemned for a crime to sail the seas until redeemed by the love of a pure young girl, so interested Richard that he took it as the plot of *The Flying Dutchman.* He completed that opera in Paris. He also composed *Rienzi* in Paris. But he could not have them performed there and was hard put to make his living.

Performances in Dresden of *The Flying Dutchman* and *Rienzi* in 1843 led to a well-paid appointment at the court of Saxony. That too was terminated when he threw in his lot with the revolutionaries of 1848. "It is forbidden to discuss politics or Wagner," read a sign in a German café—both being equally controversial topics. He was outlawed, and with the long-suffering Minna, he fled to Switzerland.

New friends, Mathilde and Otto Wesendonck, offered him a "charming refuge on a green hill." He appreciatively made love to Mathilde, an affair which lasted on and off until Minna made so many scenes that the situation became unendurable. Minna might as well have saved her breath, for Mathilde was replaced concurrently by Cosima, the daughter of Liszt, and the wife of the conductor Hans von Bülow. She bore Wagner three children before they were legally wed in 1870. As a birthday surprise for her he composed the *Siegfried Idyll,* one of the most agreeable of his compositions.

His compositions had as many ups and downs as his private life. *Tannhäuser* was hissed off the stage in Paris because Wagner had not seen fit to introduce a ballet into the second act as was customary. The influential Jockey Club raised such a row over the omission that Wagner hastily wrote one, but the damage had been done, and the opera was withdrawn after three performances. Even *Tristan und Isolde,* which many music lovers consider his greatest opera, had hard sledding. It was to be given in Vienna, but was shelved as "unperformable" after fifty-seven rehearsals and a great expenditure of time and money.

In the *Ring* cycle, Wagner's personality is most triumphantly assertive. The text, written by himself, deals with supermen and superwomen, gods and goddesses. The music weaves themes for each of the characters into a continuous thread of narrative melody. The orchestra gives plangant expression to the conflicting loves and hates of the characters. It took Wagner twenty years to complete the four operas, and though overlong, repetitious, and romantic to the point of absurdity, they remain the high point of nineteenth century opera. Wagner introduced bass clarinets and English horns into the orchestra, brought the brasses to prominence, divided the string choirs and combined tones in harmonies of unusual sensuousness. Later composers, who adopted many of his mannerisms, could not match his concepts. He was a great innovator.

On his fifty-ninth birthday the cornerstone of the Festival Theater in Bayreuth was laid and a home, Wahnfried, was presented to him. The world had accepted him at his own high valuation. Festivals of Wagner, and only Wagner, operas were held in Bayreuth every year after the triumphant première of *Parsifal* in 1882 until the Second World War put an end to such celebrations. Wagner witnessed the *Parsifal* première, though he was ill. After the performance he went with his family to Venice to rest, and there a final heart attack brought his turbulent life to a peaceful end.

Born Leipzig, Germany, May 22, 1813
Died Venice, Italy, February 13, 1883

CARL MARIA VON WEBER

"CARL, YOU MAY become anything you like, but a musician you never will be," was the exasperated comment of the older brother who tried to guide Carl Maria's baby fingers on the piano. His father, like most ambitious parents of the day, saw no reason why the child could not become a second Mozart and compelled the delicate, sensitive boy to work for hours on end at the piano and the violin. When this treatment failed to reveal a prodigy, the father turned him to drawing and painting, but he proved no prodigy at that either.

A gypsy life as a strolling player in his father's troupe worked out more satisfactorily. Carl not only became thoroughly at home in the world of the stage, more than any other composer, even Wagner, but in the course of his roving life he encountered teachers who awakened him to the magic of music as his brother and father had been unable to do. To Herr Heuschkel, a pianist-organist-composer with whom he studied when he was only nine, he expressed undying gratitude. Michael Haydn and later Michael's distinguished brother Joseph, Vogler, and Hummel, "the most elegant pianoforte player in Vienna," contributed at different times to his musical education.

At eighteen, he became conductor of a theater in Breslau, where the brilliance and originality of his piano improvisations and the songs he composed and sang to his own guitar accompaniment made him immensely popular. But in Breslau, he lost his voice, and almost his life. One evening he had promised to play the overture of his new opera *Rübezahl* for a visiting friend. The friend arrived to find Carl unconscious on the floor beside the piano. He had drunk what he believed to be a glass of water, but what was in reality poisonous nitric acid, which his father had carelessly left on the table after making some etchings. Carl was very ill and his life was despaired of. He recovered, but his vocal cords were damaged and his speaking voice was permanently affected.

When he left Breslau to become secretary to the Duke of Württemberg in Stuttgart, he found himself plunged into a life of dissipation which he thoroughly enjoyed. A passionate affair with a singer at the opera in Stuttgart took his mind off his music and cost him almost every cent he owned. The dissolute doings at the Duke's profligate court prevented his paying attention to his duties as music-master to the Duke's children. Then, to make matters worse, he was accused of misappropriating funds entrusted to him, and though his innocence was established, the Duke, in order to be on the safe side, banished him and his father.

He went first to Mannheim, Mecca of musicians. He went to Darmstadt, where he and the composer Meyerbeer formed the Harmonia Society which gave him the opportunity to write timely musical criticism. He became director of the opera in Prague, and when that engagement was terminated he accepted another in Dresden. But his days of wandering and dissipation were over. In Dresden he married Caroline Brandt, a prima donna, the first woman who really understood and loved him. In Dresden, he composed an opera in which he deliberately turned his back on the popular Italian style. A German, he composed an opera which was one hundred per cent German.

Der Freischütz (The Sharpshooter) was performed at the opening of a new theater in Berlin in 1821. After the performance Weber wrote in his diary, "Greater enthusiasm than this there cannot be, and I tremble to think of the future, for it is scarcely possible to rise higher than this." His second opera *Euryanthe* was more ambitious than *Der Freischütz,* but it failed to stir the audience in the same way, and as elated as Weber had been by his first success, so was he cast down by the comparative chill of the reception accorded *Euryanthe.* For some time after, weakened by tuberculosis, he was a prey to melancholy and when asked, "What are you writing now?" he replied, "I cough and am lazy." But he composed songs and piano pieces, including the well-known *Concertstück.*

An invitation to conduct *Der Freischütz* in London and to prepare a new opera for performance there roused him to a spurt of energy. He was convinced that he had not long to live and was determined to leave his family provided for. He feverishly studied English, since the text was to be in English, and within a few months, he had mastered the language sufficiently to compose his fairy opera *Oberon* to an English text. Once in London, he coughed his way through the season, and lived up to his contract to conduct the first twelve performances at Covent Garden. The reviews were lukewarm, and he was ill. He yearned to go home to die, but weakness overcame him, and he drew his last breath far from the country he loved.

Germany honors him as one of her favorite sons, and with every reason. Weber originated the leitmotif before Wagner thought of using it. He practically revolutionized the orchestra, blending strings and woodwinds as they never had been blended, creating effects which Berlioz and Wagner did not hesitate to adopt. In his showmanship and restless originality, his posing and elocutionizing, and his exaggerations, he expressed in music the romantic spirit which swept German life and literature of his day. His operas epitomize nineteenth century romanticism.

Born Eutin, Germany, December 18, 1786
Died London, England, June 5, 1826

HUGO
WOLF

If ever a man displayed the eccentricities of genius, that man was Hugo Wolf. But he had the genius, which is more than can be said of most eccentrics, and in evidence thereof he left songs which compare with, some say surpass, those of Schubert.

From early childhood he seemed to be possessed by a demon, a force beyond his control. It destroyed him eventually, but not until it had driven him to tortured, ecstatic creation. When in its grip, he was compelled to write music or go mad. When it left him, as it did for long periods, he could only write to a friend, "I have given up all idea of composing. Pray for my poor soul."

Because he resented discipline and defied authority, he was expelled from one school after another. His long-suffering father taught him to play the violin and piano, and he composed surreptitiously during these school years. When he was fifteen, he met Wagner and loved him on sight. Though the meeting was casual and of short duration, and though Wagner barely glanced at the boy's piano compositions, Wagner was the hero he worshiped from that day on. He wore down his father's opposition to a musical career and attended the Conservatory of Vienna, but even here he was too impatient of the 3 R's, restraint, rules, and regulations, to complete the course. On the park benches of the Prater, or in the library, he feverishly studied borrowed scores. A few pupils, a few odd jobs in music, none of which he could hold, barely provided one meal a day. His fiery temper and impatient spirit were no assets to him as a teacher.

His refuge was poetry. To him, "a song was poetry absorbed and recreated in terms of something which was neither melody by itself nor mere declamation, but a fusion of the two." He would read aloud chosen verses, to himself, or to a friend, until the words sang to him, then he would lock himself in his room for days, to emerge red-eyed, ravenously hungry, unshaven and unwashed, but with a pile of manuscript. In this way he wrote almost three hundred transcendent songs. Between 1888 and 1890, he composed songs to poems by Mörike, by Goethe, by Eichendorff, also forty-four Spanish and a few Italian songs. Then, for five whole years, he could think of nothing to write. "Why hast thou deserted me?" he asked his demon as he tossed, sleepless, on his pillow. Suddenly, without explanation or preparation, in 1895, he was again inspired to compose twenty-two more Italian songs, and within a few weeks' time, the piano score of his only opera, *Corregidor.* Then again, frustration and emptiness. But now he was recognized as a composer, and was no longer obliged to starve to prove his claim.

A furnished house and an annuity, and the formation of a Wolf Society to perform his works, provided a pleasant lull before the storm of mental illness burst upon him. In the clairvoyant mood of creation he attempted a new opera, *Manuel Venegas,* but he never finished it. At thirty-seven he became violently disturbed and was placed in a sanitarium. After a brief rest he was discharged as cured, only to be confined again. After five wretched years, he was released from suffering at forty-three, by death.

Born Windischgratz, Lower Styria, March 13, 1860
Died Vienna, Austria, February 22, 1903

SOME BOOKS ABOUT COMPOSERS

IF IT IS FASCINATING to write about composers, it is also fascinating to read about them. In order to clothe the bare bones of biography with the flesh and blood of life, one must be on a friendly footing with each man as a human being. This involves going to sources which deal not only with the composer and his work, but with his friends, his times and his social, political, family, economic and musical background, and often the search leads far afield.

For example, revealing details about Frédéric Chopin appear in a biography of his mistress, George Sand, by André Maurois. Johann Sebastian Bach becomes a lovable husband and father as seen in an imaginary diary of his second wife, *The Little Book of Anna Maddalena Bach* by Esther Meynell. Mozart in all his miraculous precocity and charm is recreated in *A Mozart Handbook* by Louis Biancolli. The composers who lived in Paris during the nineteenth century appear in the vivid biography *Hector Berlioz* by Jacques Barzun.

A complete list of all sources, from the dusty memoirs of four centuries ago to the sprightly magazine articles of the present, the biographies, autobiographies and collections of biographies that have been consulted in compiling *History's 100 Greatest Composers* would cover several pages, and has no place here. Facts have been checked for accuracy against such well-known encyclopedias as *The Dictionary of Music and Musicians,* edited by George Groves; *The International Cyclopedia of Music and Musicians* edited by Oscar Thompson and re-edited by Nicolas Slonimsky; and *The Oxford Companion to Music,* edited by Percy Scholes. Two previously published collections of our own have been consulted:—*Minute Sketches of Great Composers* (in collaboration with E.vB. Hansl) and *The Story of One Hundred Great Composers.* From the living great we have received letters, lists of publications and helpful comment.

In addition to these, some recent books have been so enjoyable that we name them for the benefit of readers thirsting for more details than could be compressed into these pages.

Men, Women and Pianos	by Arthur Loesser
The Concert Companion	by Bagar and Biancolli
Men of Music	by Herbert Weinstock
The Treasury of Opera	by Henry Simon
Great Orchestral Music	edited by Julian Seaman
Olin Downes on Music	by Olin Downes